Don't Be Denied

Don't Be Denied
MY STORY

M.L. CARR
With **Bob Schron**

With an Introduction by **RED AUERBACH**

Quinlan Press
Boston

Library of Congress
Catalog Card Number 87-42861

ISBN 1-55770-019-2

Printed in the United States of America
September 1987

To my wife Sylvia, for being my replacement while I, a long-distance father, traveled all over the world.

M.L.C.

To the memory of my dad, Donald Schron, who always wanted to be a sportswriter, and to the memory of my Uncle Dan Daniel, who was one. And to my wife, Edna Talbott-Schron, and our daughter, Laura Ruth, whose love and inspiration give life to Dad and Dan's memory every day.

B.H.S

I would like to thank my parents for providing me with a home full of love; my brother John and sisters Mary, Lavoice and Linda for caring through the years; my wife Sylvia for being a true friend. Sylvia—you often took the pain of being overlooked while others made their way to get a handshake, an autograph or a hug, and you never complained. You never wanted the fame; you are a special lady and I love you dearly.

Thanks to George Keith, my very best friend from day one. You taught me to be proud of who I am. To all my teammates and coaches, thanks for helping me learn to be competitive and work with others. To Davis Lee, Norman Blass, Phil McLaughlin, Jim Davis, Barry Allen and Red Auerbach, thanks for trusting and believing in me.

To all the fans around the country who cheered or booed me—you gave me the challenge, the need to concentrate, and a burning desire to succeed; and to my many fans from Wallace Rose Hill High School, Guilford College, the Spirits of St. Louis, the Detroit Pistons and my favorite, the Boston Celtics.

And most of all, my greatest thanks to God for blessing me in so many ways.

M.L.C.

I would like to acknowledge the Carr family's help and giving attitude, and their sacrifice of much-needed vacation time to answer my persistent questions, especially M. L., who has helped show me how to live life energetically and productively. I would like to thank the Boston Celtics' front office, coaching staff and players. Their unparalleled unity, pride and sense of accomplishment are constantly instructive and enlightening. I owe a debt to the professional and collegiate sports media, whose search for the truth is as important to our culture as the sports they report on. For the support of the Steven and Barbara Schron and Dr. William and Marilyn Likosky families; to Henry Quinlan, publisher, and Kevin Stevens, editor—thanks.

B.H.S

Contents

Introduction

It is a great feeling to be associated with an athlete or former athlete who has been and is a credit to sports. Such a man is M. L. Carr. M. L. is really special as he is a "giver" not a "taker." He is always looking to help people in addition to showing tremendous appreciation to the community. His enthusiasm is contagious, not only to fans but to everyone in all walks of life.

M. L. likes people and people like M. L. because of his friendliness, humility and genuine attitude towards them.

They talk of Celtics pride, mystique, loyalty, and so on; well, he happens to have all these wonderful characteristics. Therefore, if M. L. has something to say, we should all pay heed to it. His book *Don't Be Denied* gives a great insight to the man, his philosophies, his ideals, thoughts and attitude. It shows his preparation for life after sports and, believe me, he is very successful at it.

May I recommend the book as it is: "M. L., man of the people."

Red Auerbach

Credo

Call me silly. Call me unrealistic. Call me sick. But I cannot sit idly by when I see all the problems eating away at our young people. Many of them are just babies when it comes to life's experiences. Problems like alcohol, drug abuse, illiteracy and teen pregnancy cannot be ignored. Dr. Martin Luther King, Patrick Henry, Harriet Tubman and many others found special causes that were bigger than their own personal lives and spent their whole lives trying to create a more unified existence.

I have found my cause: helping young people create a more powerful feeling of self-worth. I work to help kids develop some basics to deal with peer pressures.

The problem? Kids need love and are not getting it. *The symptoms*? Dropouts, pregnancy, drugs, runaways, suicides. The time, money, educational programs and private- and government-sponsored research are wisely invested. The kids are representations of ourselves, projected into the future. Our investment in them is our investment in a sound structure. Together we will build a happier culture.

Too many people are floating through life without a sense of purpose. They are totally confused because they are operating without established goals. They lack a game plan. Floating can be eliminated by taking an introspective view of oneself.

My life has taught me the importance of understanding exactly who you are and what your potential is. It is very easy to become overwhelmed when you look around and see all the accomplishments of people around you. But we must stop subjecting our young people to the pressures that say they must be as advanced as the next person in all competitive situations. Sports, the classroom, creative skills, the competition for employment are examples; young people need to know that their individual measurement is not and should not be anyone other than themselves and their individual potential.

Show me a team, a family, a department, a church, a corporation, a country without a game plan, and I'll show you a game that probably will not be won.

PART ONE
DON'T BE DENIED

Chapter 1

High and Low

"M. L.! M. L.! M. L.!" The cheers of the crowd roared as thousands of fans spilled onto the court, nearly suffocating me. Only seconds before I had been out on the parquet floor of the Boston Garden, my arms thrust straight up toward the championship banners hanging from the rafters. Larry Bird had the ball, dribbling, pivoting away from Byron Scott. Cedric Maxwell was out near midcourt with me, and we watched the clock wind down. We were within seconds of the 1984 National Basketball Association championship, the second of my career. The fans, who were also winners that night, were celebrating frantically on the sidelines. Gerald Henderson was calling me, embracing me, as we both realized that our season of hard work and personal sacrifice as a team had resulted in this, the sweet, gratifying feeling of a team championship. Another banner for the rafters. Finally the clock ran out and the crowd shook the very foundation of the building. Now the fans of the Boston Celtics were touching me and asking me to share that experience with them. *Happy to do it.*

Winning the 1984 NBA championship was the greatest feeling I ever had in sports. I had helped the Boston Celtics accomplish the impossible. I had helped my team overcome a worthy opponent, the Los Angeles Lakers, in a classic series. This series had it all: Magic Johnson against Larry Bird; Kareem Abdul-Jabbar versus Robert Parish; James Worthy against Cedric Maxwell; the tradition of the Celtics against the showtime of the Lakers. Two great teams, teams that blended the highest talent with a relentless work ethic, had battled to the limit of a seven-game series. Many teams in professional sports market themselves with symbols of grace and efficiency, but rarely has a sports confrontation been as true to those symbols as this championship was. I was proud to be part of it.

Three years later, those tumultuous shouts of joy still ring in my ears. On the wall of my office I have a picture of myself standing in that crowd, my arm raised in the air. The picture freezes that significant moment. For me it is a symbol of rising to the occasion, of achieving the impossible no matter what the goal might be. In 1984 the Celtics were a group of people who came together to win the title. Not too many people had confidence in us, but we did it. We were not denied.

I remember that day frequently, not only for the game itself but also for the memories that seemed to dominate me all during the day of the game. After our shootaround, I was interviewed by a Boston television station outside our locker room. I told the reporter that all of the successes of my basketball past were coming back to me: my high school days, my championship at Guilford College, my individual accomplishments in the American Basketball Association and the NBA. Naturally I set thoughts such as these aside during the game; games in the NBA finals demand supreme concentration. But when the game was clinched and the Garden about to erupt, I somehow became removed from my physical self and had my most intense flashback of memory. At the highest moment of my sports career, I suddenly remembered my lowest. My mind drifted back to another night when emotions were rampant, but emotions of a totally contrasting nature. I was twenty-two years old, and my world was crumbling down. I was lost. I feared I had no way out...

It was 1973, the fall after I had graduated from Guilford, where I had been First Team All-American, co-captain of the team as a senior and a key player on the school's first national championship team. I eagerly awaited the pro drafts; I knew that, given the chance, I could make a living as a professional ballplayer. My life was centered around basketball; after a knee operation before my senior year I had rededicated that season to making it back and leading my team to the championship. I had to make personal, emotionally gripping sacrifices: most significantly, I had broken my engagement to Sylvia Harris, whom I would later marry. My knee surgery had made many pro teams apprehensive, and for the first time in my life I was feeling insecure.

The founding of the ABA in 1967 had created a different scene in professional basketball at that time. Players of at least two levels of ability had an additional choice: outstanding players had increased bargaining power because of competition between the ABA and NBA; players of more limited ability, or players whose ability was questionable, had greater opportunity for jobs.

My knee history had forced me to slip down in the draft, and my agent, Norman Blass, and I decided that the best place for me to begin playing was in the ABA. I was drafted by the Kentucky Colonels on the third round (Kansas City-Omaha on the fifth in the older, more established league), and it was there I hoped to begin my career in professional basketball.

But it didn't happen. The memory now resembles a nightmare, or a divorce, complete with happier moments that, in retrospect, clearly set me up for a big fall. I had come to Louisville for a week of tryouts. The workouts were competitive, but I thought I was winning. The Colonels first-round pick, Ernie DiGregorio of Providence, had signed with the Buffalo Braves. Second-round pick Ron King of Florida State, a forward who had had a lot of visibility after his team had gone into the NCAA finals before losing to Bill Walton and UCLA, was in camp, but I still thought I could make the squad.

I was filled with all the excitement of a young player on the brink of a career, at the beginning of a new job that would bring satisfaction and friendship. I had already begun forming bonds. The fabulous young player Artis Gilmore, a seven-two center who had led the Colonels to the championship final the previous season, had befriended me. He may have been the star, but he took me under his wing, and he and his wife Enola had me over to dinner, making me feel part of the team. I felt very positive about the team and my chances.

In our first intersquad game I played extremely well, scoring eighteen points and pulling down twelve rebounds. Enthused, I called my agent and gushed, "Norman, I was outstanding. I'm doing it. I'm making the club!" We were happy. We thought we had a future.

The next day I was called into the team office by the general manager, Mike Storen. I recall an element of doubt: I had thought about what I would do if I did get cut. But I also told myself that, based on my play, I wouldn't be. I was going to make it.

But I knew immediately that Storen had completely different news for me. It would have been one thing to have been sitting across the desk from a Jerry West or an Oscar Robertson, men who had played ball. Or looking at a Red Auerbach, a man who profoundly understood the game. But I was looking into the eye of a man who looked as if he had never bounced a basketball, and he was bringing bad news. It was a sickening feeling. As Storen began talking to me, I knew I was hearing reports of my darkest hour.

I listened to him explain that the Colonels wouldn't wait for me. He told me that a whole life spent playing basketball was over. At the same time, something inside me said I wasn't going to face that reality.

"M. L., we had to cut you..."

I felt like pleading, asking him not to do it. But I pulled back from that kind of emotion. Pride wouldn't allow me to plead. I did ask them to place me on the injured reserve, but the Kentucky Colonels wouldn't wait for me. To make matters worse, I did not have a no-cut contract, and only $10,000 of my contract was guaranteed.

"Thank you for the work you've put in..."

He kept talking, but I tuned out. I had gotten the message. Now I was thinking of the anonymous hotel room in Louisville waiting for me. For a young kid whose sense of self was totally identified with his performance in basketball, the universe had suddenly stopped. What Mike Storen told me that day was that my dream of playing basketball was only that: a dream. The love affair with the game was going to end after an afternoon workout in training camp.

In that hotel room there was total emptiness. I cried and cried and prayed. I had been brought up in a religious family; I called on that background as I asked God not to forsake me.

During the summer Sylvia and I had been married. Now I was going home to North Carolina a failure. The anger and frustration of my situation brought out the cunning in me. I knew what I would do: I would devise lies to make myself look good. I would tell my friends in college, my college coach, Jack Jensen, and my wife and parents that the Colonels' coach, Babe McCarthy, didn't like me. It was a personality conflict, I'd say. Since he had the power, he just eliminated his problem by cutting me. Or I would tell people that the Kentucky Colonels were a racist organization, a plausible reason back in the early seventies, when racial awareness was in its initial fervent stages. The ideas were flying at me like magnolia blossoms in a hurricane. But the lies were only adding to the confusion.

The lies weren't me, a fact made suddenly clear when an image from my past flashed before me. When I was young, my father was called to the door of our modest home to pay an insurance bill. He wasn't able to make that payment, but he wouldn't allow anybody else to meet that financial weakness. He met the inadequacy face-to-face. Very humbly, with simple honesty, he told the collector that he couldn't pay the insurance bill that week. Could the man please come back next week? The door closed behind my father as he returned to his family. He may have been worn down by the hard structure of the everyday world, but he had the dignity of his own courageous choice.

I am a man driven by feeling, and that image passed through me without stopping. I couldn't face the truth, so yet another escape suggested itself—drugs. Before going home to Greensboro, North Carolina, I would buy some drugs and get out of this trap of defeat.

I had given and given and given, and the result had been failure. I had never done drugs before, but somehow I thought they would bring relief. But that also was not me.

Drained, I packed up my clothes and gear and headed back to Carolina. I didn't have any answers, but I did make a decision on the airplane. Turning inward, I admitted to myself that I wasn't good enough at this point. I'd keep trying until I made the grade. As the plane carried me back I looked out the window at the blue sky and the clouds beneath the aircraft. I *was* confused, but the farther away I was taken from the tragedy of the moment, the more clearly I saw my situation. I was fortunate that I hadn't copped out, especially on drugs.

But looking back, I see clearly how I might have used drugs or lies to deal with my confusion. A kid of twenty-two, I had just experienced the high of playing great basketball in a professional camp and the low of getting cut. The despair of failing turned into a sharp feeling of shame. So I had a need to justify that failure—to myself, to those close to me. By manufacturing some distance between myself and the outer world— through lies, by using drugs—I probably would have been able to justify anything.

I know now there were reality-based reasons for being cut, just as there were legitimate reasons for my reactions. I didn't have a no-cut contract. For gate reasons, King was probably the better choice for them. And men do err. History certainly proved that King did not have the professional ability I had, but I had not been given a chance to prove myself. That was what really hurt. Although I played better under coaches less authoritarian than McCarthy, he wasn't the reason I was released. Were the Colonels a racist organization? Racism is something I've known since my adolescent years, when I was the first black player at Wallace Rose Hill High School. Obviously there are cases where people have been denied opportunities because of race and color. I'm not unrealistic. But in my life, my approach has always been guided by this controlling thought: I am as good as anyone, not better. I can walk in any circle as long as I am not looking to create a problem. Looking back, I don't think the Colonels cut me because I was black; after all, King was black, too. But I was looking for reasons to explain my failure.

As the plane landed in Greensboro that day, I realized that the Kentucky Colonels were an element of my past, and my world was at least something manageable. I admitted the truth to myself: I had been released. I knew I had to go to work immediately. I would find a way to play professional basketball. Sylvia met me and we embraced for a long time.

"I love you for you," she whispered. "I wouldn't care if you never bounced a basketball again."

No matter how unfortunate a situation is in life, I don't see losers. I see winners who haven't won yet. Too many times in life, people want to label men, women or young people as *outcasts*. I fight that. I want hope. I have been on the fringes often enough to know that a so-called outcast is often someone who hasn't been given the chance. I may have been an outcast after my tryout with the Colonels, but I was resolved to bounce back.

A month after failing in Kentucky, I was playing ball in the Eastern Basketball League, the forerunner of the Continental Basketball Association. At $110 per game, I was one of the highest paid players on the Hamilton Pat Pavers. Sylvia and I lived in her home town, Harrisburg, Pennsylvania. We stayed with her parents for three months while waiting to move into our apartment, a situation that contributed to my fears of not being able to support my family as a basketball player. Finally we moved into a one-bedroom apartment with an indoor swimming pool: that's right, when either of us flushed the commode a pool of Harrisburg's best toilet water turned our living room into a wading pool.

Obviously, you couldn't live life exclusively as an Eastern League player, although the EBL did give me the opportunity of continuing to play and to hope. I continued to have higher ambitions. Connected to the depressed Pennsylvania mining region, Harrisburg's economy was not fertile ground for ambitious thinking. Many late afternoons, with the sun falling quickly in the early winter sky, I had to wonder if wanting to play professional basketball was simply a case of chasing a dream. But I would counter that notion with the memory of playing against the ABA's Carolina Cougars when I was at Guilford. The Cougars used our gym for practice, and whenever I scrimmaged with them I held my own. Having played with them then, and having been productive, settled my fears about being able to compete if given the chance. In competition for a spot on a ballclub, I knew I would outwork anybody.

Meanwhile I had to scramble to survive. In the heart of the energy crisis in 1973, I persuaded a generous automobile dealer that I could sell cars without any previous experience.

"We don't have a position open for a car salesman."

"Maybe you don't for *a* salesman," I pitched, "but I think you'll keep *this* salesman."

If you're able to sell Dodge Chargers in the middle of a recession and energy crisis, I believe you can do anything. I was innovative; I went through the files and made a list of people who bought cars in the past three to five years. I called and asked if they were pleased with the vehicles and if they were aware of our deals. I predicted that they might be interested in buying again if they had been able to buy in a recession. I was able to bring a high percentage of those people back into the showroom, and by the time I had to move because of basketball, I had become a successful car salesman. Return customers were coming in and asking for Mr. Carr.

Even though I could have been successful in that business, the game took me to another place—Lewisburg, Pennsylvania, to play with another EBL team. My schedule remained the same: finding work by day and traveling the mountains of Pennsylvania for a game at night. Though I wanted to be a counselor at a penitentiary in Lewisburg, I was offered a job there as a corrections officer. The job seemed ideal for me. I would be working with people society saw as failures, and I might have some opportunity to do some good above and beyond earning a living. That was not to be the case. Failure penetrated that setting thoroughly, turning it into an unlikely place for an idealistic young man who saw his role as a helper, not a keeper.

A couple of incidents convinced me I was not in the right place. One afternoon I was meeting with a prisoner, trying to build up some of the rapport I saw as essential to my job. Treating inmates like human beings made my job and the system more human. I tried to be helpful; I avoided condescension. But some of my colleagues didn't see things that way, because as I was talking one of my fellow officers shouted at the inmate, "Come here!"

His tone was one of total disrespect. Surprised, I looked at him. My surprise turned to anger when I saw the inmate jump and prepare to follow the order. I knew what was happening here, and it did not fit my idea of what reform is all about.

"Stay here," I said.

"But..."

Naturally, the prisoner was confused, but I was making a stand. Again the officer demanded obedience. I could see in his defeated, middle-aged face that a lifetime on the job had made him as bitter as any of the people behind bars, but I was not going to allow him to exercise his will over someone with whom I was trying to establish rapport. So again I told the inmate not to move. I walked over to the officer and asked him what his commands were all about. He had not appreciated my actions, and we had a heated exchange. We went our separate ways, but it wasn't long before I was summoned to the captain's office for a meeting. I was told that my fellow officers didn't like my approach. I had also been to North Carolina for a vacation and had to return to work a day late, and that was also brought to my attention. I could sense animosity; I could sense a record being compiled against me. My own viewpoint was not regarded—this was not a discussion, it was a reprimand.

When I left that meeting I knew that a pattern had been established. Any officer who felt uneasy about my way of dealing with inmates could use any incident as an excuse to report me. I didn't have to put up with this treatment. I didn't deserve a slap on the wrist and I wasn't going to take one either. That so-called conference with the captain told me that there was a big gap between my ideals and the institution's approach. I prepared myself to leave.

Soon afterwards I walked out of the building and over to the parking lot. With the bonus I had received from the Colonels, I had proudly bought a red Corvette. When I got to it I found that someone had dumped hot coffee on the hood, an act of vandalism that forced me to get the entire car repainted. I looked at the cracked pavement, the gray building and the cold parking lot. That car was a symbol of where I wanted and needed to be; in violating it, someone had violated me. I had no proof, but my mind shot back immediately to the initial incident with my colleague. He had tried to establish a pecking order then, and he was sending me a message now. I didn't need this place. I knew I could never survive in that kind of environment and I left that day.

I look back on those days of rejection and struggle as a learning experience. In spite of my success since then, I try to keep the lessons I learned firmly in mind. These lessons were confirmed recently in a letter I received from John Poduska, the founder of Prime Computer and the Stellar Corporation. In response to a business proposal of mine he wrote and detailed his philosophy. I was gratified by his response. In part, he said:

> Thank you very much for your kind letter. We think alike. "Grabbing the brass ring" can only be done when you stretch to reach it. Somewhat like the drive and leap to the basket! We at Stellar do not doubt that we will, in fact, come away with the brass ring, we only itch to raise the winner's flag to the rafters.

Poduska may have been using the language of sports, but his comments summed up what my years of struggle in every area of life taught me. I did manage to rise from rejection to carve a career in basketball, and playing professional basketball was an ecstatic experience. I was totally fulfilled by all of it: the scoring, the thinking, the defensive challenge, the team ethic. Now that I have embarked on a business career, I have tried to carry over the same principles of positive thinking and teamwork that served me so well in basketball. On defense, I never waited for an opponent to go by me; I was the aggressor. In business I always "go for the brass ring." I go after clients and partnerships, just as I went after car buyers in Harrisburg. I feel I have something to give and I am willing to contribute my talents to make a program succeed, whether it is in business, a community-based drug rehabilitation program or a media responsibility.

When I thrust my arms into the smoky atmosphere of the Boston Garden that day in 1984 when we defeated the Lakers, I wasn't celebrating what I had accomplished on the floor that season. That year I had assumed the role of the twelfth man, providing leadership, encouragement, support and spirit. It's my belief that no player in that role has ever done it better. So when we won, when we had accomplished what experts across the country had said we couldn't achieve, when we had established our version of the Celtics alongside the great teams of Bill Russell, Bob Cousy, Bill Sharman and John Havlicek, I was genuinely able to celebrate a personal and collective achievement. In past ventures, I had known highs and lows. I had contributed significantly to the Celtics' 1980-1981 championship. I had played in obscurity in St. Louis when the ABA was disassembled in 1976. I had played in Israel during the years of the Middle East crisis, having to travel there because I was sent away by Mike Storen of the Kentucky Colonels. But this was my biggest high.

Winning and losing. I've known both, and through every encounter I believe I've come to know myself more thoroughly, with increasing detail. From the beginning. From my origins.

Chapter 2

Growing Up in Wallace

My father, John Carr, once gave me a very memorable parcel of advice. At age fourteen I had decided, under the Right of Choice law in Wallace, North Carolina, to travel across the city and become one of twenty-seven youths to integrate the high school at Wallace Rose Hill High. In 1965 this was a big decision for a teenager. My daddy never said too much, preferring to let his life be enough of a message to us five kids. But this time he looked me directly in the eye and said, "Look son. A lot of things might happen there that will be decided for you. You won't have to go looking for trouble. Trouble will find you." He was preparing me: for conflict, for trouble, for the possibility of violence. He was always the type of man who walked proudly the other way if he sensed violence was about to happen. "Don't want any part of it," he'd say. He preferred to deal calmly with people, the better to put his ideas into productive action. But he was a very wise man, and he knew that conflict exists side-by-side with security in life. His own background certainly contained both elements.

My father was one of six children, two girls and four boys. When the other children left his parents, John stayed to look after them, worrying about their safety and well-being. He viewed this decision as something of a sacrifice, but one for which he was blessed by the Lord. Grandfather Cisroe Carr was a sharecropper; he rented a farm (in North Carolina we grow corn, tobacco and beans) and worked the fields to raise crops and livestock produce, some for the owner of the land and most to sell at market. He was a strong man, able to raise a family and able to defend himself.

Sometimes he even had to defend himself against his own. My father's second oldest brother was *tough*; Uncle Willy would not back down, and one day he became embroiled in a particularly rough fight outside church. In the middle of it, he suffered a deep cut, so that blood flowed down his arms and legs. Willy went home and got the shotgun in preparation for some real restitution. But Grandfather Carr caught wind of his intentions and headed Willy off on the church lawn.

It was a hot summer day, with the sun shining down hard. They eyed each other, and Willy told my grandfather to get away. There was a hint of desperation in his voice.

"Put the gun down, boy," Grand-daddy warned him, and in a heart-beat they were grappling. It ended when Grand-daddy flipped Willy with a sort of judo throw, taking Willy by the wrist and turning him on his head. Willy lay there for a long moment as Grand-daddy reached over and picked up the shotgun. Lying there in the sun, blinded by the heat and his defeat at the hands of his father, Willy thought it over and shouted angrily, "I'm leaving! And I ain't ever coming back."

He never did. The last we knew of him he was in New York, living in the city somewhere. Uncle Willy had chosen one path that our environment offered him; my father chose another. Life in my home town at that time forced you to make stark decisions. This was the texture of the life my father matured rapidly in. He never wanted his parents to want for anything. Yet this commitment didn't prevent him from building his own life, either. John Carr was a tall, lean man with a composed, handsome face and a controlled gaze, the better to display a touch of joviality now and then. He worked hard, never earning more than five dollars an hour (and that amount came only at the end of his working career). He didn't bring home a hefty wage, but that never dulled his ambition. He worked in the shipbuilding business on the Carolina coast; laid off, he returned to farming, and after moving to Wallace, later he went to work for Davis Lee at Rose Hill Poultry Company. Around this time he met my mother, Lula Mae Kenan, of Chinquapin. They married in 1944 and went on to have a family of five, including me in 1951.

Family and work formed my parents' view of life. Mother was one of ten children, the daughter of a strict Holiness minister. My daddy remembers preparing to propose to my mom. He went to Grandmother Kenan to ask for her daughter's hand in marriage, and though Daddy wasn't a drinking man, on this occasion he took a few sips.

In the Chinquapin parlor, fifteen miles from Wallace, everything went well. Grandma Kenan welcomed my father into the family, gently urging her future son-in-law to take special care of her daughter. Daddy swayed and rocked from joy and inebriation and laughed out loud. He shook Grandma Kenan's hand and slipped some peppermint into his mouth. Obviously my grandmother recognized that my father was someone she could count on being a good husband to her daughter. My parents loved each other, and although they never had much in terms of material pleasures, they were extraordinarily stable. We grew up satisfied in our basic needs.

Mother was able to balance the demands of providing love to a family and working to give us clothing and meals. She joined Daddy at Rose Hill Poultry Company while we grew up. In my middle childhood years, they worked the four-A.M.-to-noon shift, placing difficult demands on all of us. Because they were working when we woke up for school, the oldest in the family, Cisroe, made us breakfast and got us out for school. Left alone, we were required by circumstance to cope, to find our own direction in life. But we turned out satisfactorily by anybody's measurement: my oldest sister, Mary, was valedictorian of both her junior high and high school graduating classes and is now a librarian for Burrough's Wellcome in the Research Triangle Park in Raleigh, North Carolina.

My youngest sister, Linda, took over the house we grew up in, so there remains a distinct connection between the life we experienced as children and our lives now, as adults. My sister Lavoice remains at home, helping to care for my parents. Though separated by geography, we remain a close family, and today we have reunions twice a year, in the summer and at Christmas.

Mother is a very reserved person, still very much the daughter of austere parents. Content to remain in the background, she has always been powerful enough to meet the demands of her working schedules easily (before she retired she worked for Davis Lee). Quiet, she nevertheless was resiliant and strong. Saying little, she spoke through her love for each of us. I have now what I regard as a very rich emotional life. When I'm sad, I'm not too big to cry. When I'm happy, I have a smile that lifts me up. My mom's care for me built up this ability within me and I'm a better man for it.

I was born in the back room of my home in Wallace on Route 41, then a long road that cut through the center of town. Our house was a white ranch-style with a porch in the front where my father would sit in his off-hours. He'd watch the traffic slowly meander by, the attitude then as now in Wallace being, "Why hurry the day? Like tomorrow there are twenty-four hours, so don't rush." My father and mother were extremely well respected by everyone in town. People would stop by the house and visit with John Carr, and he'd have something wise to to pass on. I'd take this all in, and the way these people got on with each other intrigued me. I wanted to find out just what it was that made people what they were. When I moved from the security of my front porch to the world-at-large, I took with me my father's advice and a healthy curiosity created by the world itself.

My earliest forums were school and the playground outside of class. We'd play and scrap, and on occasion matters would get out of control. I was always in the center of those kids' storms or somewhere on the periphery. I'd have early "meetings" with the principal, but I was always somehow able to escape the worst. Friends of mine would get into fights on the playground; getting the worst of it, they'd escape from a possible beating by saying, "I'm going to tell M. L.!" The adversary would immediately halt *his* part in the proceedings. "Oh no, don't tell M. L. Please!" And these kids were two or three years older. Even then I was a bodyguard type, an enforcer. I was tough, like Uncle Willy, but I was smart enough to struggle to stay within the system, where my oldest sister was already excelling. My instincts told me, just as my father and my whole background did, that going Uncle Willy's route was not going to get me anywhere.

Wallace was sparsely developed, though Main Street, down the center of town, was always healthy as long as Stevens Textile thrived. Running parallel to Main was a street we blacks called Back Street, where we'd walk in the darkness of the evening, cooling off during the summer while music streamed forth from the taverns and dance halls lining the byways. In a few minutes you would be out of the center of the city and into the rural pastures, where the cicadas sang throughout your journey. The screech of crickets was like my own developing consciousness, that unpredictable swirl of curiosity and confusion that marks puberty. Against a backdrop of hot summers, I lived a bandit-style youth until a few critical people helped shape and crystallize my direction.

The first was my grandmother. I was a mischievous child who continually tested boundaries—at home, in school and on the playgrounds. But I was the favorite of Grandmother Kenan. Others in the family, including my cousins, would regard my grandmother with apprehension, and they often did not look forward to her visits. She was always setting the rules and preventing anybody from breaking them. Except me. She'd wave her hand or lift her palms upward (to the heavens?) when I'd go on my mysterious, unpredictable way. "That's okay," she'd say to me when the others were out of hearing range. And to my mother and aunts when I had gotten into trouble, she'd say: "The boy must weed his own row." In other words, she believed in me, trusting I'd be able to find my own way and control whatever unforeseen circumstances might arise along the way.

Another influence was Mrs. Graham, my seventh grade teacher. I was bright, but I needed someone to guide me. Mrs. Graham was a slightly built woman who doubled as the school librarian. She wore glasses and a serious look but she was quick with a smile. Her distinctive characteristic was that *she would always listen*. I continued being mischievous—it was as much a part of me as my expressive face—but whatever the episode, Mrs. Graham heard me out. I could catch my breath and develop some composure there. Another teacher, Mrs. Henley, also helped me by giving me responsibility one year for running a ginger snap cookie sale, helping me mature and learn to operate within a structure. I always worked—for pride and the love of money. What I needed, often with desperation, was for people to help me rechannel my energy. I was fortunate to find my way toward people like these two wonderful women, whom I still see when I return home to Wallace.

Davis Lee, the man who owned the poultry processing plant in town, was another person who sensed my possibilities emerging as I began making progress within the limited setting of my black elementary school. I met him through my folks, and soon he invited me to caddy for him at Rockfish Country Club down the road from my home in Wallace. It was an opportunity to continue making money and refine my work ethic under a very successful, wise—and white—businessman.

Davis was extremely supportive while I was maturing. He sensed my humanness, stoked the fires of my ambition and soothed some smoldering resentments of an unfair situation at school and around town—namely, segregation. I sensed injustice in Wallace at an early age, and I was building up courage to challenge these barriers. I suspect Davis aided me tremendously here; he would always tell me, "You're as good as anyone else, M. L." When a successful and respected man in the community told me that, I felt I could walk in any circle as long as I wasn't looking for any problems. And later, when I'd encounter some difficult situations in a high school game, Davis would be behind me, saying firmly, "M. L., you just play basketball. I'll handle anything else that might come down." It was like the family and the church for me—a foundation of security.

Of course, the church was also a big influence on me. The Church of God of the Apostolic Faith, where my uncle was pastor and my father a deacon, was located down the road on 41. The church brought me into direct communion with the Lord and provided a place where we had a sense of community. Our lives were tough, but we persisted through faith and fellowship. Sundays were days we worshiped, shared meals and conversation and prayed for divine guidance. But I have to admit I'd hustle out of church on Sundays during the basketball season, especially when the National Basketball Association, deep into its playoff rounds, was featuring the duels between my two idols: Wilt Chamberlain of the Philadelphia 76ers and Bill Russell of the Boston Celtics. Watching those giants and teams go at it on Sunday afternoons from a distant place also shaped the course of things for me.

Given where I arrived myself, it's interesting to think back to those times. We'd watch the games on black-and-white television. Though I was a Celtics fan, most friends I grew up with were 76ers fans because of Wilt Chamberlain. Wilt was the essence of basketball back then. NBA basketball was Wilt the Individual and the Celtics the Team.

Wilt Chamberlain made basketball come alive in my neighborhood. He always struck me with his dominating play and staggering numbers. I was awed by the way he was able to combine speed, size and grace. But he always came up short when he played against the Celtics. The Celtics were outstanding, mysteriously so sometimes. With Wilt always putting the challenge to them, they had to discover different ways to win. It might be Sam Jones with a jumper or John Havlicek tirelessly outhustling everybody to lay a graceful shot in off the break or K. C. Jones making a key defensive stop. All was orchestrated by the traffic cop Bill Russell.

Their emotionally charged rivalry affected me. There was Wilt the Stilt—appealing to us because every southerner has a nickname—bigger than the game itself, dunking the ball, controlling the game. Although I was a Celtics fan, deep down I wanted Wilt to win too. My feeling was like the Celtics fans' response to Doctor J winning a championship in 1983. Whatever the fans' alliance, they were pleased when Julius finally won. And I think later I realized intellectually what I probably could only begin sensing as a youngster. Wilt was the first of the goliath seven-foot players. It was hard for him to move around in the society as a man. Of abnormal size, he had to cope with a lot, and he was always combating adversity. Like baseball's Reggie Jackson, he was often engaged in controversy, but he withstood the shots and succeeded. Wilt and Reggie had tremendous focus, great sense of purpose despite everything. I identified with this.

The Boston Celtics and Bill Russell had to combat this superb player. As great as Wilt was, Russell was always the underdog, even with the better team. But somehow he'd block a shot or come up with a score in the end to break the game open for Boston. There was something about Bill Russell that wouldn't allow him to lose. It wasn't a part of him, and that attitude was the core of the Celtics' philosophy. They'd be trail-

ing for an entire game but still manage to win. Outmanned they triumphed. Outplayed they won. And you didn't have to see to believe—the
championship flags were hanging from the rafters in Boston Garden for
everyone to see. Those games were classics.

I didn't watch much television growing up, although TV was our only
link to sports in a major city. I did, however, watch two other programs.
One was "Woody Woodpecker." He was a devilish little guy who used
trickery to get away from his enemies. And he'd be real cocky. You could
never box Woody in, never keep him down. That appealed to me. I'd
watch that bird, and as I grew older I'd practice my game with him. We
had a wooden floor, and while the bird was journeying through danger
I'd go through my dribbling drills—first the right hand, then the left,
keeping an eye on Woody. Later, when I'd conduct clinics and camps,
I'd call a drill that emphasized dribbling without looking at the ball
"Watching Woody." Woody Woodpecker would always bounce back.
He might lose some of his feathers, but he'd be around in the end, just
like the Celtics.

Our family would sit and watch "The Amos and Andy Show," too.
I watched it until I realized how we were being stereotyped. The character
Kingfish would try to pull the wool over Andy's head, tip the deal in
his favor. He'd tell stories to escape his trouble, but nine times out of
ten he'd get caught up in his lies.

I'd pull for Andy. He was pretty naive, but though he always appeared
to be the loser, I'd root hard for him! It was entertaining and it played
on the emotions. And somewhere along the line he'd pull together and
refuse to accept losing—also like the Celtics, and sometimes Wilt
Chamberlain, too!

But in a very important sense those Amos and Andy stereotypes were
not very funny, especially when I think back on those parts of my past
that were not particularly pleasant. Yes, I had my share of anger. I've
had doors slammed in my face, and I've had opportunities denied me
because of my race. I was a youth with an emerging consciousness of
the key question of right and wrong. I lived in my town, heard the music
suggesting freedom, but knew in reality that once off Back Street freedom
was an illusion. But increasingly, I was saying no.

In 1965 President Kennedy had been dead for two years, and the dream
of a New Frontier was supposedly extinguished with him. But Lyndon
Johnson's Civil Rights Act of 1964 had nevertheless produced a hopeful
climate. Within the spirit of the day, students black and white had equal
opportunity for as good an education as they could provide for themselves, building on the foundation established by the Board of Educa-

tion of Topeka vs. Brown, a judgment by the Supreme Court promising the end of segregation. But imagine a black-and-white newsreel of Wallace, North Carolina, in 1965: you move down Main Street past Dr. Blair's office, the general practitioner in town. Blair's office has two entrances, one for white, the other for colored. Doc Blair has two drinking fountains within, too: one for colored, one for whites. The camera proceeds to the movie theater in town; before we knew enough to rate our films for the sake of our children, we thought it proper to have two sections in the theater—upstairs for colored and downstairs for white. The film did not look the same from the different levels in the movie theater. The newsreel draws to a close on a recreational note: you see Wallace Stadium, where only Wallace Rose Hill High students may play. And since that high school is exclusively white, only white students are able to hear the crowd's cheers.

Yes, there was some anger. It didn't take a bright adolescent long to figure out what was right and wrong in this situation. So when Wallace courageously undertook to resolve the unjust conditions and integrate the schools (before being forced to do so by law), I stepped forth to be one of twenty-seven black students to attend Wallace Rose Hill High School in the autumn of 1965. A new era began.

Chapter 3

Dairi-O

I cannot justly say that times at Wallace Rose Hill High were terrible. Fittingly, I suppose, basketball proved to be a common denominator. I had played some pickup games with white kids during different summers in town, and I had seen that, regardless of what color people were, they laughed and cried. If they were driving to the basket and had a sudden fall, they screamed in pain. If they scored a big hoop, they celebrated. On the court people were the same, so I was able to carry this knowledge with me as I enrolled in the high school and engaged in the social and sports activities it had to offer.

Wallace Rose Hill High was a normal educational setting. A one-level building surrounded by a large field, it provided enough space for classes, social functions and sports. The idea to hold in mind about the place is that it was an institution embedded in the tradition of the small town of Wallace where people didn't think in terms of social change. Wallace Rose Hill High School had always been a white school. Though there were emotional people on both sides of the integration issue, the school remained exclusively white eleven years after Brown vs. Topeka because no one thought conditions would ever be altered in Wallace. Time moves slowly in my home town.

People get through change by finding strength within themselves and their family and friends, bonding together, helping each other. As the initial days and months went by in high school, I formed important bonds. George Keith, Randolph West, Donny West, Danny Newkirk, Thurman Williams, Joseph Lawrence, and cousins Willie Louis Carr and David Carr were all friends and allies. As my involvement grew stronger in basketball one of my best friends was David Wells, a white. David played point guard on the team and believed in me, both as a person and as a ballplayer. We hung tough versus everything that went down. We were tight. George Keith was the same. George's folks were like a second set of parents for me: Emiko Keith was Japanese, married to George's dad, a black man she had met during World War II and accompanied back home to Wallace. Emiko was persistent in her fight to have teachers and students view us as equal citizens around the school. I remember George's words to me: "M. L., you don't change. Be proud of who you are." George had been there; he knew what we faced. But though there was some tension beneath the surface calm, overall it worked itself out over the course of time. The first year of integration was difficult. We all understood we were pioneers in a sense. It's never easy for pioneers; you make mistakes, but the idea is to minimize them.

Our experience with integration was different from what urban students experienced. Life was different. Wallace was a rural agricultural town, where nobody was really highly sophisticated. And it was an early town; nothing much went on late at night, so you went to bed early. Likewise, if you got up at six A.M. to get some chores done, you went outside and found you weren't alone. People spent the majority of their time at work. So if integration was a focal point in the beginning, it didn't last as long as the problems remained nonviolent. People just wanted to go on with their own lives, and the school accurately reflected these values. As kids, we heard about places like New York, Washington, D.C. and Detroit, but they had no impact whatsoever on our behavior. We struggled with issues, but there was a sense of contentment. We left our doors open at home when we went downtown because we knew people respected each other's possessions.

This peaceful, rural atmosphere had a profound effect on us. We spent our after-school hours visiting, and on the weekends we'd go downtown. But there was always a distinct separation between town and country. The adults in our agricultural town worked the land and went to market to sell the produce. My daddy grew potatoes, peas, beans, watermelons. As I edged out of my younger years, I liked nothing better than going out into the field, dropping one of those watermelons and putting my hand directly into the center. What a *nice* feeling!

As a youth, you didn't dwell on repercussions, you lived through the time. The first time I bounced a basketball in a gym was my freshman year in high school. Before them I played ball on a dirt court, with the rim hanging down low over the front cylinder. We'd get dirty playing ball, but dust was a substitute for oxygen in the middle of spring. When it rained we jumped for rebounds, shedding mud as we did so. We had some great games, part of what still seems like a boyhood right out of a book by Mark Twain. We enjoyed our rural playground, eating watermelon, playing in the fields, sneaking down to the creek to swim. In many ways it was idyllic.

But there was also danger. The swimming hole was nicknamed "suck hole" because there was a location in the creek where the level suddenly descended and you could go under. One day while we were swimming word came back to the community that one of the kids had drowned. My mother knew that I had gone swimming and she trembled. She didn't know I had gone to a different swimming hole that day. She reacted immediately, driving right over to the suck hole, where she found out that the police had retrieved the kid who had drowned. They tried to revive him, but he had been under water for over a half hour.

But that didn't stop me swimming—or trying to. The people in our family were all afraid of the water, and I would stand on the side of the creek while my friends swam. One day they pointed up at me and said that I was going in. They threw me in the water. I beat that water to death, frantically trying to get out. But it was amazing; after that struggle I knew I could swim! I had survived. I was a swimmer from that moment on, and the swimming hole was important to me. It was the ultimate freedom. We swam naked with no fear of drowning—the death of the kid didn't deter us. On our way to the creek, I remember, we were fearless. We'd tease the bulls as we'd cut across the pasture. If the bulls weren't in the field, we'd ride the cows. Sometimes we'd see a snake and kill it. Then we'd swim and hustle back to our homes. There were tough times, but in moments like these, my vision was never any clearer. I was part of life. I had mastery and freedom. And I was learning the meaning of danger and fear—and how to handle them.

In my freshman year in high school I had to learn to deal with a different kind of fear. I call that the fear of the unknown, an uneasy feeling that you might be caught up in a situation where you'll be helpless. This kind of apprehension exists until something happens that gives you the chance to prove to yourself you have the strength to rise above it. Suddenly a situation will arise where, almost without thinking, you have done something that moves you beyond fear.

For me it was a fire. I was on the bus home from school in my first year when it broke out in the front of the bus. Although there was an immediate wave of fear, I wasn't afraid to seize control of the situation. I shouted, "Everybody file off the bus! People in the front first, one at a time. Fast!" Everybody filed off in an orderly way and there were no injuries. We kids could have panicked but didn't.

Situations like these sent messages throughout the community. We were trying to make the school a home. I wasn't thinking about earning any medals. I could have gotten off first. I was the biggest one on the bus. Hey, It was no march of dimes, but it was truly a march to victory of a sort. I was putting myself out front, as is necessary when a person is willing to take responsibility for any group. You can be a hero, but you can also be a goat.

Overcoming apprehension and relying on our smalltown values, we managed to make integration work. I'm not saying there weren't barriers—as the next chapter will show, there were plenty. But my high school experience was, for the most part, a good one. Wallace Rose Hill helped bring basically good people together. Wells and I hung together, while others went back to their enclaves. We were friends because we liked each other and color made no difference. We were pioneers, too, in that sense. We just liked each other for who we were. I had very good rapport with his parents. We took leadership roles in that way, and my friendship with David has remained very strong.

Of course, one of the things that helped overcome barriers and bring people together was sports. Sports created a cohesive school atmosphere, and for those of us who played there was something there after we started playing that helped us get on. The camaraderie was important. Personally basketball gave me something rewarding to latch on to. I could see the payoff from my labor, and I learned the importance of working with others.

My basketball ability developed gradually. I was a forgettable jayvee player, the third guy on the third team. But I loved the game and continued to practice all summer, intermingling practice hours with my jobs. I worked in the tire factory in town and for Davis Lee. By the end of my sophomore year I had grown to a full six feet and had shown enough promise and dedication to the game that Davis sent me to basketball camp at Campbell College in North Carolina. Pistol Pete Maravich headed those sessions and proved to be a key figure in my development. Pete took a real interest; he worked on my skill development. Among other things, he taught me the cross-over dribble; dribbling between your legs, you protect the ball with your body. He told me that if I worked at the game I had real potential. It was a significant boost to my commitment to basketball, and all summer I constantly worked on my ballhandling and my concept of the team game—endless sessions of change-of-direction, behind-the-back and between-the-legs dribbling; solitary figure eights up and down the Wallace Rose Hill High court. The coach of the team, Tom Edwards, gave me the key to the gym, and nobody ever spent more time there, shooting baskets into the midnight hour, the basket a constant focus for a slowly building dream. I averaged six points a game as a sophomore. After that summer of change, my average leaped to twenty-two. I had to shoot;

it was part of physically and mentally standing above. I was a post-up player, able to take my defenders down low. With position, a series of head-and-shoulder fakes got me two points. I had a sweeping hook shot that I used effectively from around the foul line. Soon college scouts were becoming interested. I was apprehensive at first, but their inquiries and presence weren't distracting. I was playing basketball, and that was fulfilling in itself.

We had fun, but sometimes the energy of our youth got carried away. As time went on, David Wells and I would emerge from the athletic regimen and take night trips. One night, after a visit to a neighboring town, I drove home over Route 421, tooling it up at a nice clip. The speedometer stretched past 60...70...75...80. I was flying, carried away by the excitement of the moment. Suddenly David looked out the window; on the other side of the highway, don't you know it, was a North Carolina state trooper. All right. I had a moment to assess the scene, and my split-second decision was based on this: the police were on the other side of the highway, so if I *increased* my speed they wouldn't be able to catch up to us, given the extra time they needed to reverse direction and cover our trail. I pressed my foot to the pedal: 85...90...David's mother was a judge in Wallace and perhaps because of this influence on his upbringing he saw things differently. "You're not in this by yourself, man!" he shouted through the tailwind. *"Slow up."* Between his protest and the justice of the situation, my speed slipped, and we were caught. We protested mildly, using excuses, fabrications and imaginative tales of despair, all designed to garner a reprieve. He didn't buy them.

"You'll have to come with us," the trooper replied.

My daddy had a rule: you'd better be in by twelve o'clock. If you weren't in the house, then you'd better have a night job, because you wouldn't be permitted entrance into our house. No help there.

We soon reached David's parents. His mom was our best hope of direct influence in this particular arena, but as sure as a sunny day in Carolina, as certain as the trooper closing his distance between our runaway car and his vehicle, Judge Wells had another perspective on the entire episode. The core of her thinking was that a jail cell might be a useful place to learn a lesson. We stayed there for part of the night, discovering that education happened in the most unexpected schoolrooms.

We left that jail considerably wiser, compliments of the justice administered by Judge Wells—like David, a true friend. The lesson learned, that incident became an adventure, one of several tales we kids would trade during our long lunch breaks enjoyed away from the rigors of school at the Dairi-O. The Dairi-O was a local hangout which I remember for its great shakes, burgers, kids, young love, fears and dreams that horizons might expand beyond Wallace, to New York City, Washington, D.C. or lakeside Chicago. Some of these vistas were talked about, others played out in an automobile version of the figure eight. At the Dairi-O we sat in the hundred-degree noonday sunlight and listened to Wilson Pickett, Otis Redding and Sam Cooke while cars entered the gray concrete parking lot, wheeled around the small enclosure and sped back out to the road. We were touring the Wallace Rose High universe, all of us wishing we were bound for greater glory—or someone to make us feel special on a Friday or Saturday night. While teachers and principals searched us out, we felt we knew where we were at.

I had two girlfriends then, a hint of love during my teenage years. I always looked around and enjoyed dating like other guys around school. We made promises and became caught up in our passions: fast cars, elusive tales, girlfriends, the Dairi-O and basketball under the lights. Around us the drama of integration unfolded slowly—and we had our parts in it, our battles and our resentments—but we were discovering so much and living with verve. Lord, I loved those years.

One of my happiest moments in life is sitting by the ocean in the evening in summer, the moon settled softly in the midst of the sky, its glow touching the waters so that a silver ribbon stretches to the horizon. When I am part of this scene, I feel that life is hopeful and happy, peaceful and sensible. The spectrum of life, from the grandchildren of my children backward through time to the father of my grandfather, appear before my mind's eye, giving time meaning and answering, if only temporarily, some of life's mysteries.

Yet as I settle in to watch this night, I know that with a snap of the fingers the ocean can change. The Atlantic, its waves rolling from the boundary where it joins the sky to the beach, can be like a song. But in the time it takes to turn away, the sea can become violent and destructive.

Chapter 4

Boundaries and Barriers

I understand the necessity for discipline and limits. I made a commitment to try and become the best basketball player I could possibly be, and I played ball every night during four summers in high school to make my future in basketball happen. My father imposed a curfew on us kids, and admittedly I was the one who had the most difficulty conforming to this household legality. But I was on time virtually every evening while growing up. I approached it as a beneficial time boundary. I slept well every night, developed a sense of personal discipline and learned to enjoy working hard. I had several jobs in my youth, including working in a tire factory, picking blueberries and doing various jobs for Davis Lee. I recognized early that there are needs for boundaries.

But there is a difference between a boundary and a barrier. A boundary is positive; a barrier, negative. People may bridle at boundaries, but in time, if they grow, they learn to accept them and use them. But even children sense that if unjust barriers are imposed, either through custom or the exercise of power, they are open to challenge. Yet teenagers are children of the culture they grow up in; if they learn from the beginning that they don't have to respect another human being because of differences of color or sex, then, if unchallenged, they will act on these teachings, however unreasonable.

At Wallace Rose Hill I had plenty of contact with unreasonable behavior, and I grew to recognize barriers quickly. It might have been a casual remark or a whispered insult, but the disrespect was there, and sometimes it even became physical. One day a schoolmate became engrossed in an argument with my girlfriend and reacted physically, slapping her in the face.

She cried, and I found out about it late in the afternoon, after school had been dismissed for the day. I slept on it, thinking about the attitude that led to this condescending manner, and in the morning I walked directly into the guy's home room and confronted him with his action.

I asked him why he had hit my girlfriend. I asked him why he had intimidated a girl. I asked him how he would feel if I had hit his girlfriend. I told him that if he needed to hit someone he should go ahead and hit me. I was trying to turn the other cheek, but the words were weighty and the message carried too much emotion. In the center of the room, hurt by the picture of the wrong imposed on the physically overmatched girl, I began fighting with him. I may have been young and impetuous, but I had an ethical leg to stand on.

Predictably, we were hauled down to the principal's office, and if the scene in the home room had been dangerous in its outbreak of violence, the ensuing scene in the principal's office was even more frightening in its ordered calm. When we combatants had finally been restrained, the teacher explained to the head of the high school what had gone down. I was still angry but willing to listen. The entire situation—the fight, my sleeping on it overnight, the guy slapping my girl—was described. The principal heard all of it, perplexed, uncertain. Then he restored orderly conduct. He told us that the whole thing was regrettable but that no punitive action would be dealt out this time. We were not to mention this to any adults. (How could they not know? We fought in view of the entire home room.) However, he admonished, if anything else were to occur, punishment would be enforced. A long, uneasy silence fell over us. Only for a minute, however. I gathered myself and stood up. "Listen, sir," I said loudly, piercing the silent enclosure. "This is not right. If he hits my girl, we keep it quiet and wait for the next incident. But if I had hit his girlfriend, you'd have had me arrested."

Nobody said a word. The principal knew I was in line.

As I went from day to day in my youth, my boundaries expanded, if only because my experience widened. As I looked to town for personal services and entertainment, I found walls. Around this time, I became increasingly frustrated with the conditions in Dr. Blair's office. Dr. Blair, who attended to my health concerns, was a very nice, well-respected Christian man, but his office depicted the times. For a black to obtain his care, he or she had to walk into the office through a door with a sign saying *Colored*. I became increasingly exasperated with the door. One day, I walked through the entrance labeled *White*. I needed to test what in my view was a myth of superiority.

This potentially incendiary encounter had both blacks and whites awaiting Doctor Blair's care extremely uneasy. But I walked through the small room and inside the brick building. Then I came across another challenge: two water fountains that bore the same symbols, *Colored* and

White. Hey, I went over to the water fountain (finally!) and took a long drink of the elixir. My reasoning: There must be something special about this water. It must taste better to cause it to be separate from the water we were drinking. More tension. Later we would do the same at the Danca Theater; at first my friends and I, seated upstairs in the colored section, expressed our resentment by becoming unruly. Later we took it a step further by simply sitting downstairs in the white seating. I thought I was missing something up in the balcony. Maybe the view was different, more entertaining downstairs.

Slowly but surely the barriers began to fall as we challenged them. Times were different, and sensing that difference we began to exercise our rights, almost instinctively. I'm not saying that the attitudes and ingrained beliefs of the townspeople were any different; I have no illusion about Wallace being different from any other southern, or northern, area in its individual and community biases. People's beliefs may or may not change, and I had limited control over that. But I was intent on attaining as much freedom that I had rights to.

Another day I was tooling around town with some of my friends when we finally stopped in at the White House Cafe, where service was broken down into two areas. White people were served in the main room while blacks were required to take their meals from a small area at the back of the diner. We had finished work earlier and were hungry. But I had a different hunger—as at Doctor Blair's, as in the theater, for me it was the time—and we walked in and sat down for our meal. The waitress, obeying tradition, passed us by for twenty minutes. We had to ask for service.

"Can't you see I have other customers in the restaurant to serve before you?" she hissed. There were two other customers in the place. We waited a moment longer; the delay invited further action. I pressed my fingers, soiled with tire grease, to the counter, fingerprinting the cafe for the sake of a message. "Ma'am," I growled, "can we please have some service and will you please clean our counter space?" She told us we weren't allowed to eat in the main section and insisted that we'd be told the same by her superior. She hustled to the kitchen and petitioned the manager. She paraded him for support, but to *our* satisfaction (we had altered the ritual), the manager pointed a finger at the waitress. "If they want a meal, you serve them. I don't want to hear anything different. From this day forward."

That evening was a victory. I had helped bring about a change, a change that any reasonable person would say was for the better. Within the short period of my growing up, inside the confines of a small rural town, I

had come into contact with century-old barriers that were in the process
of coming down. But that world was still one in transition, and I didn't
have to look far to see the irony of being a black youth in the South
in the 1960s. Across Highway 41, maybe a mile and a half from my home,
stood the country club where I worked as a caddy for Davis Lee. It was
a confirming time; as I developed a work ethic, I found myself and
discovered I could gain acceptance from people in the white community.
The feelings there were strong and positive. But on that same highway,
close to that country club and my home, where John Henry Carr sat
peaceably on his porch and offered his wisdom to the young, I met up
with the Ku Klux Klan. They held a march and rally that ended on 41,
and our group of guys went down there to see what they were about.
We went prepared; what we knew of them, we didn't like. The rally was
self-contained, however, and after that gathering they never openly met
in Wallace again. Maybe we appeared menacing (we certainly felt
menacing). When the state troopers saw our car, they hurried us along,
refusing to let us park.

When I decided to attend Wallace Rose Hill High, my daddy told me
that if I kept myself respectable and showed others respect, I'd get that
respect back. I've struggled against many barriers over the years, but
I've always been mindful of that advice. And following my father's advice
has given me a sense of pride, from the earliest years as a youth. I have
known many barriers: economic deprivation, doors slammed in my face
because of my blackness, knowing that blacks have been denied entrance
into institutions because of racial reasons. But I have pride in the progress
we've made as a people, in the difference between the days when George
Wallace denied the Black Man entrance into the University of Alabama
and now, when we have reached a measure of competitiveness in the
American society. Showing respect is key: I'll reach out and help a person
in need, regardless of his color. If two people are drowning do we reach
out to grab a hand or do we grab the hand that matches the color of
our skin? This black man would just reach for a hand; now perhaps two
people may survive, function and even find a way to save the other person
from drowning. I don't pretend to final knowledge, but I know that
through programs advocating progressive change, more blacks have
reached positions in where they can help and contribute in a better-
represented, multiracial society. We cannot allow progress to end. To
me, entrance is a first step; maintaining and even exceeding our
capabilities is necessary. Then we will be able to contribute fully as leaders.
My experience as a youth tells me that it is wonderful to attain, but

equally necessary, until the very end, to continue to give. I know I must not allow myself to become separate from these experiences. They illustrate perfectly the wisdom of my father's advice: give back so that others may experience the rights and beauties of life.

By the time I'd left high school I had gained a certain amount of confidence, a knowledge of the respect I was due as a man. I remember driving from Florida to North Carolina with four older ladies, right before I became a student at Guilford College. Midway through the state of Georgia, I was hungry. Very hungry. But these ladies had been conditioned in the malicious ways of the old South, and in Georgia they were terrified when I exited and headed into a truck stop. On the other hand, I had been fortified by my early experiences. Late afternoon, the angle of the sun was becoming more obtuse. Rural, remote and aged, the truck stop had people in there who seemed as if they where frozen in time—or in attitudes regarding race. I couldn't be absolutely sure, but I was on my guard. I could understand the ladies, tested by life, worn down in their wariness. We were returning from Eustis, Florida, were a friend of the family had died. Even down there they had been very cautious. When I wanted to go swimming one of them had held a finger over her pursed lips. "Be very quiet!" What she was really saying was, "Don't cause any trouble." She was worried about what might happen. She and the others were worried now as well.

I walked into the truck stop and placed an order for several cheeseburgers. "We don't serve *nigrahs,*" the man at the counter told me. "I'm not interested in having any. I need some food." I looked into his eyes firmly. But I wasn't interested in creating a disturbance. I was hungry, fatigued. I felt responsibility for the older ladies in the car. There was a stir in the truck stop, an uneasy silence. At that point I began saying that I had been to a funeral in Florida and had several women in the car who were hungry. I was apprehensive and a little confused. I didn't understand why I felt the need to go into this with the guy at the counter.

We were driving all the way back to North Carolina. It was 1969 and the drive still wasn't easy. But there wasn't any further discussion. Quietly, the man turned and prepared the meal.

The decade makes no difference: fifties, sixties, seventies; the barriers remain. They do not come down in a single generation: Sylvia and I were in Boston in 1979. I had just signed a free-agent contract to play with the Boston Celtics with five seasons' pay guaranteed, a dream realized. Headed to a dealership in Boston to buy a rug, Sylvia and I stopped to ask for directions. The young white attendant began to point the way; midway through the vocal map he stopped.

"I'd send you that way," he observed, "but you might get bothered. I'll send you another way..." He paused in reference to race. Thank you. He had given sufficient information before reaching his personal detour. We went directly to the rug dealership and made our purchase.

We continued establishing a base in Boston. We were looking at homes outside of the city, and the real estate agent brought us into a fashionable, upper-tax-bracket neighborhood. She opened the door with the key, but apparently the entrance was jammed because the burglar alarm blared its signal for a long time. In due course, through the expansive picture window, we saw a cruiser pull up at the curb. They walked up the path leading to the front door. I casually went to the front door to explain the error. We looked at each other, and in an instant the policeman had assumed a firing position, crouching low, gun pointed out at me over an extended arm.

Quickly I explained who we were and what we were doing.

"The next time something like this happens, send the real estate agent to the door," he advised. "Because I see this big black guy coming and I have to assume you are a burglar."

Later he said he had seen where I had just signed a contract with the Celtics.

"Good luck," he said as he left.

I deal with people every day in business, and my business competes quite capably. I believe that if we are prepared, competent and superior, we will win a bid for a contract, whether our potential client is black or white. Investors are usually color-blind when they invest their dollars. This is my conviction. But you don't forget the stories, the memories of inhumanity and disrespect. It might be Georgia, North Carolina or Boston, but the subtle reminders stay with you—and they continue to occur, never letting you forget that my father's words must always be kept in mind. It is when I am faced with these signs of disrespect that I think back to how I was able to challenge and overcome those barriers—and how I fell back on my religious background that has served me so well over the years.

Chapter 5

Religion

We had a simple lifestyle in our home. It demanded attention and encouraged devotion, and despite the hardships we were confronted with, the family was very close. We weren't materially wealthy, but we refused to allow the immediate conditions to thwart our hopes for the future. All of us in our individual fashion worked to improve ourselves: Daddy purchased tracts of land around the corner so that the kids might have a better place to live someday. My sister Mary was a serious student; just as I was determined to play to the best of my potential on the basketball court, she put in lengthy hours in school and the library to reach her goal of excellence. Cisroe had to make some sacrifices—as the oldest son he had to be certain that the kids were off to school and had some structure in their lives. I worked my jobs—in the tire factory, in the fields, in school jobs when I was evading the temptations of playground scrapes.

The family, as I look back, actually possessed a fragile framework. We were all working and battling the discouragement near-poverty imposes. But looking further, I wonder who's successful: my parents with their simple lifestyle, or myself, with my material needs substantially satisfied. A common complaint of basketball veterans is that the game loses some of its creativity and spontaneity when kids play only in formal leagues. They lose their capacity for creating individually and as a group because they don't play as often informally, on the playground, for fun. Is this a sign of the times? I have to call my neighbor, for example, to make an appointment for my son to play with his. My point is, who is actually better off? My parents' nuclear family, with the cracks in the walls but a zealous refusal to allow similar ruptures in the family nucleus, or a wealthy family so totally absorbed in its technological materialism that it has little sense or desire to know and love each other?

We secured our bond as a family through our reliance on religion. We had to allow time in our lives for gathering as a family on Sunday, morning through evening—and this after Saturday night's choir practice at the Holiness Church down the road from home, on 41. Daddy would pray before our Sunday meal of grits, eggs and sausage, but we didn't eat until he had completed his rejoicing and prayers. Sometimes he'd get long-winded; the family would be gathered around, eager to have their breakfast with the long day of worship before them and a peaceful Sunday ahead. Daddy prayed in his bass voice, spiritual. The hum of his prayer and song would often provide the only heat in the room, because the breakfast would be cold by the time he was through.

Daddy didn't care. He saw his communion with the Lord as a way of providing leadership for the family. It was his job to lead the prayers for us, and he never veered from that. His belief was that the family that prays together stays together. The characteristic I most respect about my father is that, though he had problems, he endured and continued to give. He was the motivator, the inspiring leader, respected in the whole community. As a kid in Wallace you would hear about dreams and lies, about hopes and plans, about leaving the South for New York, Washington D.C. or Detroit. People needed to get away. And when they did return home (some dreams fading into mere survival), the young adults would always find their way to John Carr's porch for a word of advice. I don't think my father has ever been booed in *his* life. His life was centered around giving, an attitude that carried over into business. He had a theory: if you have money in your hand and you squeeze it tight, you can be sure that the money will remain where it is. But open that hand a little, in several directions, and you'll always get some back while continuing to give to others.

My own family illustrated this paradox. From the outside our home appeared destitute, but I came up in a loving family. From the exterior we didn't appear to have much intelligence, but I see the brilliance now. The seed of contentment germinated because of the way we stayed constantly in touch with each other; that was the essence of our religious life. We would sit around the table and listen to Daddy's song; the words continue to echo in my head:

> *I will trust in the Lord*
> *I will trust in the Lord*
> *I will trust in the Lord*
> *Until I die.*
>
> *Won't you trust in the Lord*
> *Won't you trust in the Lord*
> *Won't you trust in the Lord*
> *Until you die?*

His meditative bass voice lured us into a soulful dimension. It lifted us and provided energy. We were able to carry on.

As I've grown older, that religious feeling has continued to endure, helping me grapple with the issues of manhood and understand the changes that families must learn to handle. We return home to Wallace frequently. Daddy is now afflicted with Alzheimer's Disease, an affliction that affects the temporal and frontal lobes of the brain, causing memory loss. Maybe it was caused by his work in the factories, I don't know; but it has been difficult. There are nights when we're back in the home we built for our folks, and Daddy will get up from sleep, mumbling and chanting. I'll get up with him and pray that he's praying still.

Church was at the center of our community. We'd pray, laugh, talk and discuss politics there. There were prayers and, always, the music: tambourines, drums, a piano. The musicians would generate a powerful beat. The congregation was brought together as the deacon and the brothers and sisters started shouting those songs:

> *How I got over*
> *How I got over*
> *Lord my soul looks back and wonder*
> *How I got over.*

My mind might wander late in the day, but the music, song and the Church's commitment to the spirit lured my soul. I sensed I was part of something larger than myself—some type of alliance that allowed us to survive with a peaceful outlook, even if progress was terribly slow. That heritage has been passed down over generations. A lot of spirituals were ways of communicating among slaves in the fields. As slaves were planning their exodus from the plantations, messages were sent along in song, and a chant, harmless on the surface, was actually a code for freeing our great-grandfathers from bondage.

The philosophical themes alone couldn't save us from the pain of coping in a culture that was extremely demanding. I knew people in the church who had a little money but lacked the cultural experience to invest it properly. They would squander it in short-term speculation and return to the Church every Sunday, smiling but insecure from defeat. There was a feeling, if subtle, that you still had to adjust to what was essentially a segregated society, that the greener pastures were on the other side of town. Yet, after I had graduated from high school and viewed the violence advocated in the Black Power movement of the late sixties,

I saw that the hatred engendered was partially caused by the militants turning their backs on the Church and the solidarity it provided. We needed change and we did need it "now"; yet however conservative the Church was, denying the very fabric of our heritage prevented the movement from becoming a long-term means of political change.

When I attended Guilford College I was fortunate enough to take part in an experience that, in a very personal sense, revealed the depth and richness of that heritage. Though on the surface the experience was of this world, I have to say that it moved me in a very religious way. The Guilford College basketball team had advanced to the NAIA championship tournament in Kansas City in my freshman year, and although we didn't win the championship on the court, we did win the sportsmanship award and a trip to Africa. The trip had many moments of cheer and humor, but it also led to a self-examination similar to the feelings I had had in the Holiness Church when I was a kid. We flew in old planes, and Coach Jerry Steele even had to drive a jeep across the countryside. In Senegal we slept in a village, eager to capture the feeling of being a native African, but in the middle of the night we heard enough of what we thought were noises from wild animals to make us abandon any intellectual ideals and find a safe place to sleep.

The most memorable phases of the journey took place on the basketball court and in the celebrations after the games. We had a strong club at Guilford, and though they had some legitimate talent in some of the African states, we won every game easily. But one night when we were playing indifferently and clung to a five-point lead in the early minutes of the second half. We were playing the games on lighted playgrounds with the tribal families gathered round, cheering and making all kinds of noises and gestures. The game continued at this pace, and though we still performed poorly by our standards, we should have been able to run out the clock for the victory.

But we faced a problem: regardless of the type of game we chose to play—our normal game or slowdown—we couldn't seem to run any time off the clock. The tribal fathers had changed the rules even as we played out our lethargy. They would allow the clock to run for as long as their team was in the game, so that we would play deep into the African night until our hosts were able to get the lead. Finally Coach Steele called a timeout and said to us, "Listen. They are *never* gonna let us finish this game unless we score the next twenty points and move so far ahead of them that they'll give up." He was adamant because he was exhausted. It was something like midnight, and we were still playing with five minutes left in the game. My teammate Teddy East, six-foot-two, 190 pounds of muscle, decided to reestablish us as a force out there. During an exchange, he went after their best player, a cat we had nicknamed the "Helicopter" because he could jump higher than any human being I've ever played against. The Helicopter went up for a fast-break dunk and Teddy went after him with a tackle any rodeo cowboy snagging a wild steer would have been proud of. They went flying into the crowd together and almost caused a brawl. After *that* was finally settled—we wanted to get out of there!—we summoned our concentration and won the ballgame. After the game we made a peace offering to the Helicopter; Teddy gave him a pair of basketball sneakers because the dude had played in his bare feet. He took them and flashed us a big smile. He handled them like they were expensive crystal and gave Teddy a big hug.

We were almost regarded as magic men in Africa; in our best moments we were one of them, but blessed with strange powers on the basketball court. Though young, I was able to gain a sense of my origins on this trip, a self-consciousness that was set on fire on one of our final nights in Senegal. At a tribal ceremony one of the fathers summoned our team around him and spoke to us at length in the tribal tongue. We were the honored guests, and the tribe's warmth was touching. After a number of sketches and plays we shared a dinner. Finally the warriors of the tribe began a ritualistic tribal dance. It was like nothing I had ever seen before. With the sound of many drums accompanying them, the dancers began pumping their legs up and down, slowly at first, then faster and faster. As their pace increased, the kids and adults of the entire village gathered around, experiencing the rhythm. I was drawn into it immediately, and for a period of time as long as a basketball game, I was transfixed. The drums went faster and the warriors continued dancing, at speeds that defied anything I had ever known about conditioning. It was an elevating experience that gave me a sense of pride and belonging. At the beginning of our trip I had felt a stranger; now I felt related to this land in a real, religious way.

As I grew older other commitments, particularly my commitment to basketball, entered my life. Sometimes there was conflict. My interest in sports wasn't easily accepted or understood by my mother and father. Mother was initially adamant about refusing my need for running shoes. "Why buy expensive sneakers when you have some already?" She said. The sneakers I had couldn't have transported me down the street, much less through the competition of a track meet. Like the Helicopter, I ran a couple of races in a track meet barefooted. Then we went out and bought a pair of three dollar shoes. As my interest in basketball became important to me, Daddy refused to support it. His attitude: if M. L. is serious about the game and it isn't a whim, let him prove it to me. He wouldn't watch me play at first, thinking I'd be better off studying so that I could get into college.

But I was grateful for the discipline the game imposed on me. My parents wouldn't drive me home from practice, and after some of those sessions concluded on rainy winter nights, one by one my teammates would offer me a ride as I stood waiting outside the gym. I refused each request—too much pride, even in a matter as minute as that. If walking home was part of what was required for me to succeed on my own, well, I was going to sling those sneakers over my shoulder and make it there. And back again the next day.

Soon I realized that my commitments to religion and basketball could support each other. The Church helped me come to terms with myself, helped me make productive use of my rebelliousness. This was particularly rewarding later, when my game began to improve dramatically. And over time my parents' stance changed, too. Mother couldn't bear to watch me head off to practice under those wintry conditions and she would follow me down the road and then pick me up after I had started walking. Always with that ball.

I can't really say what drove me those days, those years of some real inner conflict. I do know this: I'd go to bed around eight o'clock some nights, and on the nights when my parents weren't working at Rose Hill Poultry Company they'd retire early and set up for their prayers in the next room. Through the cracks in the wall I'd hear them praying, Daddy first, then Mother. And it was constant: after their entire messages had been offered up, they'd ask the Lord for special guidance for M. L. I'd hear those words and I'd contemplate them, words delivered specially for me from people I knew loved me to the Maker I felt to be a part of. I would do my share of rolling over throughout those years, but when I look back, it wasn't until my junior year in college that I was able to walk into their parlor in the old house and tell them that I loved them. It was an emotional moment, and I felt that I had matured considerably—even in the space of a single night.

Chapter 6

Guilford and Titles

Throughout my last year of basketball at Wallace Rose Hill, recruiters had been constantly trying to land me for their programs. It began in June of my junior year; although we finished with a mediocre 12-12 record, I had averaged 26.6 points per game and led the team in rebounding. After being named MVP of the team, the calls began coming in heavily. My family and I really didn't know how to prepare ourselves for this type of aggressive approach; the attention was gratifying, but after fifteen weeks of an average of five calls per week, we were bewildered. I think I managed to play through it decently. My scoring average remained the same, and my power game took me anywhere I needed to get against our competition. Our team had a strong comeback season, too, finishing with a 24-4 record. I played effectively until a game against South Lenoir, one of our traditional opponents.

The game was at home, and there was an uncommon electricity in the crowd. Rumors circulated that coaching legends had arrived in our small town. Scouts from Davidson and North Carolina State as well as Coach Tom Quinn of East Carolina were all supposed to be in attendance at the game. I hadn't had much formal contact with any of these men, so I knew I was being tested in this particular ballgame. I welcomed the spotlight, but still, I was only eighteen years old. The recruiting game was reaching its climax. I admit it, I was feeling the pressure. Part of it was because of the novelty of the experience; I had been brought up under trying circumstances, and the possibility of receiving a paid-for education threw me somewhat. I am honestly able to report that I received minimal illegal offers—only indirect aid through boosters—but even those offers contributed to the confusion. The whole process seemed part of that distinct clash of cultures in the South at the time, the clash between the rural background and the slick world of college basketball. I shouldn't have been intimidated, since I had helped bridge cultures by taking part in the integration of the Wallace schools. But I've kept my family's fate first, even in the most benevolent circumstances. The opportunity to attain a scholarship was one of the most important events in all of our lives, so when I heard that these coaches would be at the game, I quivered.

Predictably, nothing was different when I took the court for the game against Lenoir. On the first three possessions my play was so tentative and full of error that my coach, Tom Edwards, was forced to call a timeout. "Listen, M. L. You have to block all of this out or everybody'll be hurt. We'll lose the game and you'll have a setback in trying to get your scholarship." In times of tension, the most important tool for overcoming stress is to relax. I grabbed a towel, wiped my face and went to work. On the next three possessions I made two jumpers and an end-to-end layup after grabbing the defensive rebound. I had an excellent night, leading the team to the win. My college career was to be a reality.

I decided later that summer on Guilford College, a small Quaker school in Greensboro, North Carolina. The major selling point from Jerry Steele and Jack Jensen, the coaches, was their promise of comprehensive guidance toward the college degree. The scholarship was limited; my tuition and board were paid for, but I had to pay for my own books. I felt that there would be an opportunity to have an identity at a school that size (a thousand students). I was correct; I ended up with loyal friends on and off the court. Our gym, located on the edge of the campus, was affectionately known as the "Crackerbox." There was enough seating for nine hundred, and we were never sure who was in the gym at game time. The intimate atmosphere allowed me to grow at a deliberate pace. I would probably have known some degree of success at one of the Atlantic Coast Conference schools, but the school that best fit my needs at the time was that Quaker college. It was a logical continuity from Wallace.

College was an entirely new episode in my life, and I was determined to have as much of it under my control as possible. I understood this more clearly after I eliminated Oregon State as a possibility in February. I enjoyed the fantasy of being on the West Coast, and the program there was very interesting, but in the end I remained in my home environment.

The Guilford coaches sealed the agreement after visiting us at our home. Everything they presented to us was agreeable, and I told them they had themselves a player. They hesitated, reiterated their promise and told us they would go out and drive around the town for a while. If we still felt the same way when they returned, the agreement was settled. While they were gone, there wasn't much conversation in the room. Mother confessed that she really didn't know what to ask the men anyway. And all I knew was that I was going to be going on in school and that I'd be getting my college degree. It would fulfill my daddy's fondest dream.

We played some excellent basketball at Guilford; we could play both a deliberate pattern game as well as a running game that could overwhelm opponents. But it started slowly. We began my freshman season with an extremely disappointing 1-3 record that had the coaches totally befuddled. I walked into their offices late one evening after another uneven practice; we were missing connections on plays and simply going through the motions—inexcusable among a group of college athletes. We were out there because we wanted to play, but all that was resulting was a flat effort.

"Coach, we'll turn it around."

They looked at each other and eyed me.

"Coach, we're going to the national tournament."

More furtive glances.

"Listen. We'll be happy to finish at .500."

We pulled ourselves together, won twenty-nine straight games and finished fourth in the NAIA national tournament. Besides this achievement on a group level, I proved to myself early in my college career that I could summon an intensity that could be dominating. When I wanted to take over a ballgame, I could do it.

We defeated teams like Presbyterian, Lenoir-Rhyne and finally the Elon Christians to secure the Carolinas Conference title en route to the NAIA tournament in Kansas City. The tournament was a massive basketball celebration, with games played from morning to midnight. It was held at an old building in the downtown area with the letters ARENA chiseled out of the brick at the front of the old gym. The sports information director at Guilford, my friend Bill Buckley, visited Kansas City years later and stayed at a hotel on the same road where those games were played. The building remained, but the tournament is now held at the Kemper Arena, and only ghosts and barely retrievable memories are left there. It was another world, another set of feelings when we went to Kansas City that first year. My first national tournament!

Few media experts gave us any chance, but we were legitimate. We had a strong, six-eight center, Dave Smith, with a coldly accurate jumper from outside to complement his power game down low. Teddy East was a terrific, intimidating defensive guard. Jerry Crocker, a pure athlete, was a great shooter for us. I could control most of the games I played in. I sacrificed scoring to play a team game, with rebounding and defense setting an example for our guys to play team ball. We whipped through the tournament, defeating Stephen F. Austin, who featured James Silas and George Johnson. We made it to the semifinals of the tournament, where we were defeated by Kentucky State. That was the team with

Elmore Smith, a seven-footer with an outstanding vertical leap and excellent timing. He was able to shut off our inside game. And to make him even more threatening, the team also had Travis "Machine Gun" Grant at the power forward position. That man could shoot the ball. He stood outside and flipped up his jumper with a quick release, practically from a standing position. He was deceptively good. In the warm-ups and even in earlier games that we scouted, he didn't appear to be that talented. But he always got his points, and he had to be respected. And stopped.

In the pregame meeting I implored Coach Steele to let me have Machine Gun, but I didn't doubt that he would turn me loose on him. I had been doing it all season, playing superior ball for a freshman. I was having a blast in the tournament, too, shaking off defenders with stop-and-go dribbles, tossing in reverse layups without even looking at the basket. And my enthusiasm was understandable. By the time we broke up our meeting, we were ready to bury them somewhere out in the plains.

For most of the first half the game went our way. Travis led the country in scoring that season, and he had a scent for points—he was that kind of player—but in the first nine minutes of the game he not only had zero points, he hadn't even touched the ball! We were beating them, and we knew we were headed for the first of our titles. But something happened. We wore ourselves down—young bodies, emotionally drained—and suddenly Dave Smith couldn't find the lanes he had used only minutes earlier. Elmore refused to buy his head-and-shoulders fakes and swarmed him. And Travis simply stepped out farther; I wasn't able to close out the passing angles that far away from the basket. The man did not miss throughout the late stages of that ballgame, and he ended up with forty-two points. They scored seventeen of the final twenty points and defeated us by six. Still, it was a triumphant season, and we won the sportsmanship trophy and the trip to Africa. We always held our heads high at Guilford.

My sophomore year at Guilford was a maturing year—disappointing at the time but a learning experience in retrospect. After a season of highs we had a poor year on the court. Our center, Dave Smith, was thinking of transferring, which proved a distraction, and we had an inconsistent season. No matter what level you play at, getting back to where you were the previous season is hard. We did, however, have our good moments. Greg Jackson, an outstanding guard, joined the team, and he persuaded Lloyd (World B.) Free to come down and check Guilford out. Free would join us during my senior year, giving us what in my opinion was the best backcourt in the country at the time.

Personally, I had similar struggles. My freshman year had been exciting. Heady with freedom, I reveled in college life and our success on the court. When the team did poorly the following year, I got down from time to time, and I felt at something of a loose end. But I was learning. During my junior year I became more focused and got serious about school. I had my future to consider, and if I didn't make it in pro ball then I wanted to go to law school. You don't go to law school without paying some dues in the classroom, so I studied hard, and my life at college began to come together. Also I was beginning to attract the interest of the professional ranks; during my junior year the Chicago Bulls expressed an interest in drafting me in the underclass hardship draft. I did consider it—who wouldn't, given the money and prestige involved— but in the end my goal of earning a degree overrode all other factors. A far more significant event, one that really twisted my mind, was a knee injury I suffered soon afterwards. The date is coded into my memory permanently—January 23, 1972, just as Pat Williams of the Bulls, a classmate of Coach Jensen at Wake Forest (Jerry Steele had gone to the Carolina Cougars of the ABA after my freshman year, but that wasn't a problem for me—I had a strong friendship with both men), was discussing my chances for professional basketball. The Bulls had wanted to sign me during the Christmas break, which would have meant playing with them immediately. I weighed the alternatives and decided the money would be there after I graduated. But then came the injury.

At this time of my life, I couldn't get enough of basketball. I was constantly in the gym, constantly working on my game. On this day, we had finished practicing, but I decided to remain in the gym and continue shooting. Some others were shooting around, and we decided to get into a pickup game. There is a simple rule in these games: be basic. But I was tooling around and working on some moves. I drove down the right sideline and faked a pass. In the same motion I took off for the layup. Unfortunately, the plan depended on a normal reaction by my defender to the original move. But I had a critical problem. Completely transfixed by my advanced move, my defensive man stood completely still. I went up for the shot and came down on him, severely twisting my knee. The diagnosis was a tear of the patella tendon. It is often a career-ending injury, very similar to the one Toby Knight of the New York Knicks suffered against the Celtics in a 1978 preseason game in Portland, Maine. Knight never played again.

I was crushed, especially when the first two doctors I consulted about the injury told me I was through with competitive sports permanently. They advised me to be concerned about walking without limping in every day life. I refused to take their word. I made it back, but I still favor the knee today. I guess we were both right, although we had extremely divergent opinions.

In March I went to Dr. Frank Clippinger, the man who did most of the work on New York Jet quarterback Joe Namath's knees. He didn't rule out basketball, but he did acknowledge the extent of the damage. "It's one tough battle," he said. "If you want to play, you're going to find it rough to get back. If you can lift one hundred pounds on the extension machine, then I'll tell you that you can play." He arranged to have an operation to restructure the knee. After surgery, when I tried to life a *five-pound* weight on the machine, I screamed in pain.

When a basketball player hears his career is in jeopardy, he hears the end of the world. And when the knee goes, he's faced with the worst possible scenario. You do everything in basketball with your knees. You flex them for jumping, pivot on them for sharp cuts, extend them for faking and maneuverability on defense. But though I understood the severity of the injury, I was determined to make it back. My intensity, already high, was increased as I faced one of the turning points of my basketball career.

Of course, there was a lot more going on in my emotional life at this time besides basketball. I hung around with my buddies constantly during my college years. I grew particularly close to David Chesnut and Teddy East, and we were practically inseparable during my first three years at school. We laughed and talked jive; we called each other "Stick" and discussed cars, basketball, school and women. David was seeing a young woman named Sylvia Harris, a transfer student from American University. She was extremely attractive, with dark brown eyes and a serious expression that could quickly break into a glowing smile. She had a clear sense of herself, and her spirit was very alluring.

One night in the dorms I said to my man Stick, "Hey, what about this girl?" David quickly shot back, "You gotta talk to her Stick. She's too slow for me!" I arranged it so that very thing would take place. Within a week I bumped into her at the cafeteria, and feeling happy, propelled by youth, I gushed, "You sure have those jeans well adjusted!" I think she thought I was obnoxious, but that was my line. We exchanged small talk and negotiated going to a football game. She told me she had a date for the game but perhaps would break it. Okay.

It was a typical cold November day at the football stadium. I didn't care who was playing; I was concerned with scoring points in a totally different game. We were nervous and she was cold; we bought some hot chocolate, which she promptly spilled on my pants. My pants were the prized pair of my wardrobe: glossy black. Now I tell my wife that she spilled the hot chocolate to make sure I had no other thoughts. We started dating from that moment on, and she made me forget other women. I saw immediately that this woman could be my wife: she was very intelligent; I could sense quickly her very high morals. And as I said, she was very attractive. We fell in love immediately and planned to marry before our senior year in school.

Sylvia was majoring in Sociology and Psychology with a minor in Spanish, and after our junior year she decided to stay in Greensboro for the summer. We would be married in the fall and live in an apartment during our senior year. But the injury, to my way of thinking, changed everything in both of our lives. I had entered the courtship with upright ideals; I had optimism (the Bulls were interested) and I had talent (my senior season would be a winner). But when I went down in January, I retreated emotionally, uncertain. How did I know if I would *really* make it back? How does a man meet challenges in life when he has had his legs fold under him? The legs were my tools, my dreams, my entrance into the gates of stardom, but I had walked into the exercise room and couldn't even lift five pounds!

I had felt life ebbing that day, and I couldn't make a commitment to marry at that age, in that state, with the future so precarious. I had to make it back and resume my career. Then I could prepare myself for a future with a family. I did love her, but during the fall I broke our engagement. I had to make it as a basketball player. My whole life was centered around the game.

As I had vowed, I was back in the starting lineup on opening night of my senior year. I would average 18.7 points a game and 12.5 rebounds, helping our team to a championship season. We were a pretty undermanned team at the time, although in retrospect it wasn't the overmatch it seemed to be. We had senior leadership in Teddy East and myself. We had a third outstanding defensive player in Greg Jackson, who would later play a season with the Phoenix Suns. For offensive punch, we relied on a superb freshman, the dynamic Lloyd Free from Brooklyn. From the first time I watched Lloyd play up in New York, I was certain he would be an outstanding player. He had great jumping ability, a scent for the hoop and scoring, and an ability to play defense. We relied on only six players—a smallish (six-ten) center, Ray Massengill, and reserve Steve Hankins were the other two.

We may have had a small team, but we had a banner year. We edged our way into the NAIA championship tournament by defeating Winston-Salem State in the District 26 tournament. After traveling all day to Kansas City for the nationals, we continued to play tough, coherent, unselfish basketball. You wear down when you only play six men, but there's an advantage, too; if you hang around long enough in a tournament situation, you come to know each other's moves as if you were a veteran dance troupe going through the same routines for years. Outmanned? We had Jackson, Free and myself, all future NBA players.

The first three rounds of the tournament were preliminaries, we thought, to a rematch against Kentucky State. But they were eliminated by Valdosta State of Georgia in the first round. We swept by Keene State and Valdosta before nearly losing to Westmont College of Santa Barbara, California. Lloyd made a critical steal, and he and Greg Jackson scored down the stretch to give us the win.

The big hurdles were our final two games against Augustana State of Rock Island, Illinois, and the University of Maryland at Eastern Shore. Augustana, led by seven-foot center John Laing, had put together a 28-1 record that season, and they were tough. But we took the game inside against Laing, and I had one of the best rebounding and defensive games of my college career, pulling in twelve rebounds and helping out on the seven-footer. We shot out to a comfortable margin early and won going away, 98-81. We held Laing to 0-12 from the field in the second half. It was interesting: the play was extremely physical, but I had only one personal foul. In the game against Valdosta, on the other hand, I had fouled out because of a mistake in the scorebook. I actually only had four, but there wasn't anything we could do. Except Bill Buckley tried to stop the game altogether. Buckley got up from his chair in front of the radio microphone (in Guilford he doubled as SID and color commentator on broadcasts back to Greensboro) and screamed, "What do you mean? He's got *four* personal fouls!" He went on until he finally attempted to settle it by slamming his fist to the table. The result was a broken hand, all for the love of the game.

But we were headed for the championship, an all-consuming experience. Our final-round opponent, Maryland Eastern Shore, had a very fast team, led by Joe Pace, Ruben Collins and Talvin Skinner. We planned to retreat quickly against their fast break, but in the beginning they were on fire, and after the first eleven and a half minutes, they led, 36-25. At that point in the game we all started contributing and over the next twenty minutes we outplayed them to take a 76-68 lead. Collins led a flurry to get them within four, but Lloyd's scoring (our play-by-play man,

Tom Wall, called out: *"Lloyd Free hits from downtown Kansas City!"*)
was the final surge of energy we needed. I pushed the lead up to twelve
late in the game, and we held on for the championship. *That* solidified
me, I feel, as a potential forward in the professional ranks. I had sixteen rebounds and twenty-three points. Lloyd won the MVP award, and
for three days we commanded the headlines of the Greensboro news-
papers, heady exposure in the heart of Atlantic Coast Conference
territory.

In the meantime there was Sylvia to consider. Behind the scenes, the
life of a major athletic figure is complex. For a serious basketball player,
life is a roller coaster; if you're playing well and the team is winning,
you're up. If you're getting less playing time and the team is playing
poorly, it affects you and your spouse. I had given myself to Guilford
College basketball in the hopes of building myself up for the future, of
becoming physically and mentally capable in the eyes of professional
scouts. I had had feelers from the ABA (Carolina) and NBA (Chicago).
I had a terrific time in my senior season; we won, I succeeded in my
comeback attempt, and I had a good time. I wanted to renew my commitment to Sylvia, but it wasn't always easy establishing communication. So much of athletic training entails discipline, introspection and
commitment. Sometimes you need to find yourself before you can enter
into a marital commitment.

Sylvia went to Bogota, Colombia, for the summer to pursue her minor
in Spanish, a skill that would enable her to work in a women's prison
when I was playing in the Eastern League. Her bilingual expertise was
essential in establishing a communication link with a segment of the
prisoner population, although the Colombian dialect of Spanish she
learned is different from the prisoners' she was working with.

While she was there, I wrote her several romantic letters and promised her a gift when she returned. When she got off the plane I had a
dozen roses and a ring for her. It was an old-fashioned gesture but one
from the heart. We agreed that for the *second* time I would go up to
Harrisburg and ask her parents for her hand. Sylvia's parents are like
a second set of parents to me; her father is a career man with the postal
service and her mother is a social worker and teacher. They liked me
then, but they were affectionately skeptical; when I asked her father if
I could marry his daughter, he reminded me that this was the second
request. He said I could go ahead and use the same answer that I had
received back then.

I laughed and they laughed and we all had a memorable night. I knew the road was going to be difficult, but I wanted a wife like Sylvia. I was intent on fulfilling the promise I had written her when she was in South America. Dear Syl: What are you doing on August 11, 1973? I would like you to be my bride. Her mother laughed when she heard that.

"Do you think if you don't marry him now, he will be available later?" she said as she finally consented. "Do you have to get married before he goes to training camp?"

Chapter 7

Getting Ready for the Pros

During the 1972-1973 season, my senior year at Guilford, the Carolina Cougars of the ABA practiced at our gym, Alumni Gymnasium. In professional basketball there is a reciprocal arrangement regarding practice sessions. When a team is on the road, it usually practices on the same floor as the home team. This is how first the Cougars, and later the Kentucky Colonels, came to know who I was. The Colonels and their coach, Joe Mullaney, formerly of Providence College and the Los Angeles Lakers, were interested in me throughout my last year in college. They had me come down and scrimmage with their budding championship team, led by Artis Gilmore and Dan Issel. Then came that crushing decision during training camp, all the more devastating because of my strong senior year, good performance in camp and the positive feelings following my comeback from the knee injury.

After a year in the Eastern League, experience that contributed minimally to my progress as a player, I left to try out with Kansas City–Omaha Kings. The Kings had drafted me on the fifth round in 1973, but I had passed up their camp that year to try out with the Colonels. Though the atmosphere was considerably better, and though I was told I played well, I was caught in a numbers' game—I was competing against eleven players with no-cut contracts. On the way to Hawaii for an exhibition tour, the Kings didn't want to take me along if they were planning on releasing me. So I was released—again. Ironically, I was in the best shape of my career; after two-a-day practices, I would scrimmage one-on-one with Nate "Tiny" Archibald, then the best point guard in the game. Our games were full court, and I always gave Tiny a run for his money. Tiny loved to play and play—two seasons earlier, he had been the first player in the history of the game to lead the league in scoring and assists in the same season, and he was coming off a broken ankle that had limited him to thirty-seven games in 1973-1974. Six years later we would be teammates.

But not in Kansas City–Omaha (that season the Kings divided their home games between the two cities). Joe Axelson, the Kings' general manager, called me into his office, complimented me on my fine play, handed me a check for $2,500 and cut me. Disappointed, but more experienced now in the workings of the pro game, I still thought the praise and the money were a tremendous statement. The Kings' coach, Phil Johnson, was less visible after my release; he would go on to win Coach of the Year that season with a defensive-oriented, hard-nosed style developed under his mentor Dick Motta. But after that season he wasn't able to sustain a consistent high level of play with his teams. Yet he was rehired to coach the Kings in 1984 before being fired last season in Sacramento, where the Kings moved after bailing out of Kansas City in time for the 1985-1986 season.

I always made it a point to shake Phil Johnson's hand after every game I played against his team, whether he was coach of the team or an assistant. For me it was a matter of feeling proud to have made it after he had released me. It was a reminder to both of us that I didn't quit after he had decided back in 1974 that I wasn't good enough to play in the NBA.

Exiled again from the big leagues, I returned home to consider my options. I leaned toward playing another season in the Eastern League. Less seriously, I thought briefly about giving up playing and going into coaching. I was thinking about these options for two days when the phone rang. It was Red Auerbach of the Boston Celtics.

Red's voice has an unusual quality. It manages to reflect strength and friendliness; it enables him to be very persuasive. He's able to command—gently. He suggested I come up to Boston for a tryout with the Celtics. I was in Boston that afternoon.

In the fall of 1974, the Boston Celtics were back. The team had won the championship the previous season, defeating the Milwaukee Bucks in a stirring final series. Each game was totally dominated by defense; until the seventh game, the only two games where either team broke a hundred were the overtime second and the double-overtime sixth. Boston won that series by having guards Jo Jo White and Don Chaney press Milwaukee's Oscar Robertson full court for the entire forty-eight minutes. The Celtics also used John Havlicek as a pressing small forward and positioned Dave Cowens wide in their set offense so he would draw Kareem Abdul-Jabbar away from the basket.

These were the "New Celtics," but they were structured in the classic Celtic mold by their coach, former Celtic player Tom Heinsohn. Heinsohn built a set offense around the multiple skills of the small center, Dave

Cowens and maintained that defensive intensity, but his Celtics team also ran as well as any other great Celtics teams. In 1974 the Celtics had won a marquee series featuring some of the best players who have ever played: Robertson, Havlicek, Abdul-Jabbar, Cowens. As I walked into the Celtics' offices that day I sensed immediately the unique character and sense of communal pride based on years of success.

I signed a contract with the Celtics on October 9 and began working out with the team that day. It was an intense period of time for them, and for me it was a little tense, exciting and bewildering as well. Dave Cowens had sparked them to the championship the previous season, but that day he had gone up to block a shot by Cornell Warner and fractured his foot. The press began to focus on that situation. Meanwhile I continued working, but the prospects weren't promising. *The Boston Globe* had even reported my signing with the qualification that I would probably be sent to Europe by the team if I cleared waivers.

I played my first minute with the team in New York, the first game the team played without Cowens. Havlicek, White and Jim Ard played with intensity that night, pressured to play better in Dave's absence. My playing time proved to be a cameo appearance in a major theatrical production, Boston against New York in Madison Square Garden. I wouldn't back down, but Heinsohn pulled me out of there after a few times up and down the floor. It resembled a migratory pattern. Before the game in New York, Dave Sorenson, a free agent, told Havlicek he was leaving the team. Rather than taking the team bus to Madison Square Garden, he took a bus to La Guardia and a plane to Italy, to play over there. My fate was similar. Two days later Red called me in.

I walked into Red's office. Photographs of the champions composed the very wallpaper. There were black-and-white caricatures of Bill Russell, Satch Sanders and Bob Cousy; a color photograph of the team with President John F. Kennedy; and a Washington Capitols jacket, from the 1946-1947 team that won eighteen consecutive games in the NBA's first season. It was also the first professional team Red had coached, at the age of twenty-nine. I grabbed a chair in front of his desk, peering down at a small desk sign that read THINK. Red began talking and did give me something to think about.

"We have no room on this team for you, M. L.," he began. "Look at this team. We just won a championship. We have Paul Silas, Don Nelson and John Havlicek, three pretty good forwards don't you think? See. We don't have a spot for you."

I was stunned. But the way he spoke suggested to me that he had something else in mind. But my concerns were more immediate; if there wasn't a place for me, what had he brought me here for?

"But we think you can play. If you watched the final series against the Bucks, you saw the defense we play, and we think you can fit right in. You see, M. L., we know you had a bad knee in college. I want to hide you for a year..."

"In the Eastern League?"

"In Israel."

Two of his friends, Haskell Cohen and Herb Brown, both NBA people, were part of a group trying to form a league in Israel. Brown was also friendly with my agent, Norm Blass.

When Red said "Israel," I blinked.

I went back to my hotel and called Sylvia. "Honey, I'm going to Israel."

"What?"

"I'm going next week."

"M. L., for how long?"

"The whole season."

She was silent over the telephone for a long time.

But I was departing. I went to Kutsher's Country Club for the tryouts, and a week later I was on my way to the Middle East.

If I wasn't directly interacting with power circles yet, I was nearing the boundaries. Having dealt with Red one week, I was heading to Menachim Begin's land the next. I jokingly compared myself to Henry Kissinger. Kissinger, then the United States Secretary of State, was on a mission, trying to use shuttle diplomacy to negotiate a peace between Egypt and Israel. I was on a mission too: to get me an NBA uniform. And I wanted that uniform to be Celtic green and white on my back. Kissinger may have had his problems, but my mission was a success—though it took a few years to be accomplished.

My personal voyage to Israel confirmed my commitment to the game. I really wanted to play. I focused completely on my goal and didn't think much about the problems in the Middle East. My wife Sylvia joined me there around midseason and she couldn't believe how well I had settled in. We actually had fine living quarters, located in a country club out in the country. But it was easy to feel like a nomad. There were nights when the dream of playing NBA basketball was very distant, and the caliber of play wasn't top of the line.

The European League was an idea of several American businessmen who thought that since the ABA seemed to have a chance to survive, another league might also exist. As well as in Israel, they established teams in Belgium, Switzerland, Spain and Germany made up completely of

American players. They played a thirty-game season modeled roughly along the lines of a college year. Rookies and free agents who had failed in tryouts with the professional leagues in the States, or who weren't drafted at all, played on the teams. Players like Joe Dupree of St. John's, Ollie Johnson of San Francisco and big Roger Brown from the University of Kansas were in the league, helping to make it competitive. But it was definitely not of NBA or ABA caliber. And my team, the Israel Sabras (the name means "native son" in English), was not the most popular team in the world. In Spain, on one occasion, we had to deplane with an army escort when there were threats made against our team. The politics surrounding the state of Israel were volatile. There was still a lingering feeling of fear from the 1972 Olympic Games, when Israeli athletes had been murdered.

All to play basketball. We were representing Israel, and there was a constant fear of being the target of a terrorist group. In Israel itself, soldiers walked the streets. It was a way of life, as one armed guard explained to my wife. She asked him if there was a constant worry about being killed, with militant nations on their borders. He answered that the possibility of dying was a fact of everyday existence. The tragedy embedded in their culture affects me even now. I have always been interested in history, and I am a religious man. I would drive through places in the Holy Land, through Jerusalem and absorb the history and splendor of the religious meaning there. But I knew that just by living there that evil and war and conflict permeated the atmosphere, like a loud siren. It was a chore to manage the contradictions, but the possibility of war was always evident. There was always a feeling that conflict might break out at any time in the Holy Land.

But the Israeli people were spirited and had great pride in their country. They had constructed a modern nation in the birthplace of Western civilization, and the extent of their achievement never ceased to amaze me.

If you didn't have much time, the worse thing you could do in Israel was talk politics. The Israeli people talk about it all day. They have the highest taxes in the world, and everyone had an argument and a solution. I had a strong relationship with the people. They took pride in me. I played well and gave clinics for the kids. I'd walk through the marketplace and hear celebratory cries: "You are the Sabra! You are the Sabra!" I'd give some of the kids sneakers, which they treasured.

The Israeli people loved to bargain, and I was a willing participant. Sometimes I would purchase merchandise just so I could bargain. Once I bargained with a guy who had a little pottery stand. We exchanged prices back and forth on a little vase, and he finally won me over by claiming it was the only one of its kind in the state. I turned over the money. I left the shop, walked through the marketplace and discovered the identical vase on the other side. The only vase of its kind in the state! I turned around and caught up with my friend. He returned my money.

During the six months I was over there, there were often reminders of home—and my eventual goal. During warmups one night I heard some people calling out, "Wallace, North Carolina! Wallace, North Carolina!" It was the Fox family, who owned one of the largest department stores in my home town. We had a nice little chat. I was stunned to feel my origins in this foreign land.

I played well in a challenge game against the Maccabees of Tel Aviv, the national team, we proved ourselves. They had watched our team play and were certain they could whip us. Flying in from a game against the German team, we went out and defeated them easily, quelling that idea. I had thirty-five points in three quarters. The American game of basketball was still considerably better.

I was able to play well because I never lost touch with my purpose: I was using the Sabras as a stepping stone to the NBA. So when I was up in my room and heard the echoes of machine-gun fire out in the desert, I'd be able to stand it. That wasn't the case with everybody, however. Norman set up another player, Perry Warbington from Georgia Southern, on the Sabras. Early in the season Perry played well, pulling twelve rebounds down a game and shooting fine—but then he heard those guns. He got on the phone to Norman right away.

"Mr. Blass," he telephoned, "Mr. Blass, get me outta here! They're firing guns over here. They're shootin' people!"

Within days Perry was back in the States.

But if I lasted, it wasn't without some accompanying strain. The security finally got to me, too. Besides the army escort, we had constant security checks. During one of them, I was pulled over. They questioned me and let me go, but the incident occurred again and again and again. I didn't ask many questions at first, with the omnipresent machine gun staring me in the face, but finally, after we arrived back from Germany, I asked why. "I'm sick of this," I said to the guard. He said, "You don't look as if you have five kids."

I was startled. "I was just married last year. My wife and I are the only ones in my family." The security people had been pulling me over in a case of mistaken identity. A man had skipped the country while under investigation, and all the time they had thought that it was me. But I made it through and found my way back to the pros. I was the Most Valuable Player in the league, and I was impressive enough to sign a guaranteed contract with the ABA's Spirits of St. Louis the following summer.

In reconstructing these details, I always think back to the Wailing Wall in Jerusalem. I walked by there one day and saw a guy praying, offering prayers to God. He walked away looking serene, fulfilled. I leaned against the Wall. You can't get much better than the Wailing Wall in the Holy Land if you're praying for a dream to come true. I prayed and prayed, and I guess it does work. I was very specific. I prayed for a professional basketball uniform, with the number 30. My number.

John Henry and Lula Mae Carr.

With my cousin, Mary Lois Carr.

The key to our contentment as a family was the way we stayed in touch through the years.

Graduation from Wallace Rose Hill High with Kathleen Lamb and my friend George Keith (left), who said to me during integration: "Don't change M. L.; be proud of who you are."

My trip to Africa gave me a real sense of my origins.

Our championship team at Guilford, 1973. World B. Free is number 20;
Teddy East is number 15.

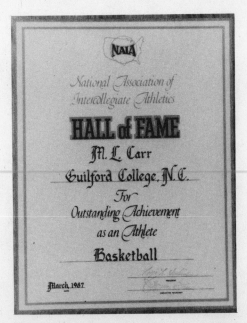

I was honored to be chosen a member
of the NAIA Hall of Fame in 1987.

My life revolved around basketball—in Israel, 1974.

My team photo as one of the Spirits of St. Louis in the ABA.

Courtesy of Steve Lipofsky

We knew our roles. Here we defeat Phoenix during our eighteen-game winning streak in 1982. Dennis Johnson, then with the Suns, is hot in pursuit.

Keeping my eye on the goal.

Courtesy of the Boston Celtics

The greatest mind in the game: Red Auerbach.

PART TWO
PROFESSIONAL BASKETBALL

Chapter 8

Making It in the ABA

The 1975-1976 season was my rookie year in professional basketball, but ironically it was the last year of the ABA's existence. The ABA, which had begun in 1967, was designed to capitalize on the increased attraction of the American consumer to both sports and television. The National Football League had recently effected a successful merger with the American Football League, and the two leagues had played the first Super Bowl in 1967. Much of the AFL's impact on the American consciousness was due to New York Jets owner Sonny Werblin's promotion of the star potential of that team's flashy quarterback, Joe Namath. Television advertising rates for a regular-season game had reached $75,000 a minute and were still growing. The success of the AFL proved that, in the modern era, a league could prosper on the strength of a few promotable stars who could carry teams that perhaps did not have the overall talent of an established league. The reasoning of the founders of the ABA was logical: with fewer players and greater visibility within the game itself, a new basketball league had at least as much potential for attracting a share of the increasing sports audience as the AFL had. The founders established an entrance fee of $650,000, and in the first season, the Pittsburgh Pipers with the great Connie Hawkins won the championship of an eleven-team league.

But despite the talent the league was able to attract, the ABA never succeeded. The league lacked a consistent core of owners who were committed to the league beyond their personal desire to have the ego gratification that goes with being associated with a professional sports franchise. Many of these owners had succeeded in business, but anonymously, and they enjoyed seeing their names in the paper daily. The owners were constantly moving their franchises, scarcely investing the time to build a core support in a city. The Oakland team drew Rick Barry away from the NBA's San Francisco Warriors but then moved the club to Washington. Barry, then the leading scorer in basketball, refused to play on the East

Coast, but he was forced to by the courts. The following season the team moved again, this time to Hampton, Virginia. Barry refused to play there, too, and the team traded him to the Nets. All sorts of machinations were going on.

I was fortunate to begin my professional basketball career in the ABA, especially as I got in for its last year. I had an opportunity to edge into the pro scene through the less established league, but I also got to play with some great players there. The irony was that the league, while aimlessly drifting from season to season as the media speculated it wouldn't last, attracted the best young players in the game. Julius Erving carried the ABA for five years, an age. Because of him, the nature of professional basketball became more spectacular, innovative and advanced. Doctor J averaged twenty-nine points a game in the ABA, won two team titles and three Most Valuable Player awards. I was continually hustling to keep up with Julius, never with tremendous results—but never for lack of desire, either. As a young player Julius propelled himself and his talent into the game: powerful muscles, long outstretched arms, huge hands—all perfectly coordinated. He brought an extra-human dimension to the game; the Doctor could fly. Besides Julius, Spencer Haywood, George McGinnis, Artis Gilmore, Dan Issel, George Gervin and Mel Daniels all went to the ABA in the seventies. An agreement with the NBA brought Billy Cunningham and Don Chaney to the new league; later, other great players went to the ABA even as the league's teams began folding during the season: David Thompson, Maurice Lucas, Bobby Jones, Marvin Barnes, Moses Malone. In my single season with the Spirits, my teammates included bona fide great players like Lucas, Barnes, Malone, Chaney, Freddy Lewis, Caldwell Jones and Ron Boone. We didn't have a strong season because we were constantly bringing players in and out against a backdrop of dwindling attendance and rumors of franchise and leaguewide collapse. But the dynamism of the players in the ABA transcended the insecure conditions of the league.

When the league failed to land a coveted television contract at the conclusion of the 1975-1976 season, it folded; the league champion New York Nets (with Erving), the Indiana Pacers, the Denver Nuggets (with Thompson) and the San Antonio Spurs joined the NBA. In the meantime, the Players Association, which was not going to allow the leagues to merge until the issue of player movement was resolved, had assured players' rights through what was known as the Oscar Robertson lawsuit, clearing away the final obstacle to the league's demise. But for that season I had my chance to prove I belonged on a level with professional basketball players—in the ABA with the Spirits of St. Louis, a team that had been moved from my neck of the woods, Greensboro, North Carolina, in 1974. I was ecstatic to be there, and I was determined to deliver on my opportunity.

But first there was the matter of the Boston Celtics. Red Auerbach had sent me to Israel with the understanding that I was "hiding" for a year and would join Boston on my return. That was my intention, but my agent, Norm Blass, convinced me to look at the ABA, where I had a better chance of playing quality minutes. Red felt I had not lived up to my agreement, though later he said, "M. L.'s agent double-crossed me." It would be a while before I would go to Boston. In the meantime I had a new home in St. Louis.

I signed with the Spirits in July of 1975 and immediately went out and proved I belonged. The team had had an excellent playoff the previous year, upsetting Doctor J and the Nets in the first round of the playoffs. Marvin Barnes, or "News" as he was known, had been spectacular; as a rookie he averaged 30.8 points and 14.1 rebounds in the playoffs. He was a superstar, but he was beginning to allow personal excesses to ruin his career. He met with the general manager, Harry Weltman, before the season started to renegotiate his contract; after the season began he was forced to return home to Rhode Island to deal with a legal hassle. Meanwhile, he played breathtaking basketball; in a game against Kentucky, for example, he scored forty-nine points with seventeen rebounds and three blocked shots. Another night against San Antonio, who featured the vintage George Gervin, Marvin scored twenty-four points with seventeen rebounds and continually broke their five-man pressing team with brilliant dribbling. But he was inconsistent off the floor, and he eventually distracted Maurice Lucas so deeply that Lucas, another great young player, was traded to the Kentucky Colonels for Caldwell Jones.

But we failed to make the playoffs that year. As our season was concluding, Marvin was asked if he would accompany the team to Utah if the team was moved, as was then rumored. He had just scored thirty-four points with fifteen rebounds and four assists. Marvin was a friendly man, but he was void of self-discipline. He replied, "Don't ask me if I'm going. Don't ask me. You smell this Pierre Cardin cologne? You see this red suit? You see this black hat? You see this Rolls Royce? Are they ready for me in Salt Lake City?"

While Marvin was the center of the storm, I had other ambitions. From the start, I played well in St. Louis and won a spot as backup guard and forward. I was determined to win a spot from the opening tip of the exhibition season: in the preseason, in a benefit contest against the NBA's Kansas City Kings, their starting guard Jimmy Walker went driving in for a layup. I crashed into him hard. "Hey, it's only an exhibition, man," he said as we picked ourselves up off the floor. But I was playing in my style, which was to win regardless of the cost. I didn't think of myself as a "dirty" player, but I would sacrifice my body for the good of the team. And I believed I was good enough to play.

My season began slowly; I pulled a muscle in my left leg in the opener against the Nets and missed some action. We played well at the start: Marvin was out, but we pulled together and had a .500 mark through our first twenty games. Then our team bond dissolved in the atmosphere of financial chaos that plagued our team. St. Louis failed to support us. That preseason game against the Kings was a benefit game for the school system in St. Louis. The Kings received a guarantee of $10,000, and for us to break even in any game we needed a draw of 7,000. Against an NBA team featuring Tiny Archibald, we drew less than 1,800. With the franchise faltering, there were serious discussions between our owners, Ozzie and Dan Silna, and the Utah Stars' owner, Bill Daniels, about merging the teams and moving to Utah. However, those discussions broke down, and Utah folded in midseason. In a desperate effort to make our team stronger, the owners made a major player purchase. That deal brought to our team the brilliant, raw, misunderstood twenty-one-year-old Moses Malone.

Malone was an imposing presence underneath, then as now. When Moses surged for a rebound, particularly on the offensive boards, he was unstoppable. A player who signed with the Stars immediately out of high school in Petersburg, Virginia, over Lefty Dreisell and Maryland, Moses consistently ran into problems with the press, always preferring to let his game do his talking. A black raised in a secluded environment in the South, he was extremely insecure. When he did talk, his eyes would be fixed on the floor, and he would stutter. He told a writer in St. Louis that year: "I knew I'd be hassled since I was just out of high school. I wouldn't want to be bothered by reporters, by the same old questions. And when I don't want to be bothered, I won't talk. It didn't bother me that I wasn't talking. The only people it bothered were the reporters.

"I've always had this philosophy. I've grown up with it. I just want to have the time to be myself. I have to accept that. It helps me in a lot of different ways. Not only in basketball, but on the streets. I keep to what I'm doing and try not to let things or people get to me. I thought it over very deeply before I joined the ABA. I know I've done the right thing. I didn't even think beforehand how hard the competition would be. I just came to play and let the pieces fall naturally.''

Moses was young, but he provided instantly for his family. He was consistent and self-assured in his abilities, but he never let that self-confidence overshadow his dedication to team play. His faith in the team mirrored Larry Bird's.

Moses's arrival affected me. After the team changed coaches at midyear from Rod Thorn to Joe Mullaney, Joe played Moses against the taller teams and me against opponents like Doctor J and David Thompson. Denver was the antithesis of our ballclub; they had Thompson, Bobby Jones and a complete dedication to the team concept under Larry Brown. They handled us throughout that season and actually put our playoff chances away after we had won three straight home games over the Nets, Spurs and Nuggets themselves. In two subsequent games on the road, Denver handled us with such ease that they seemed to make us realize our collection of individual superstars wasn't enough if we couldn't play together. I had some strong individual games (sixteen points, seven rebounds and three assists against Denver; twelve points and four rebounds in an important win over San Antonio; eleven points in the fourth quarter in a 99-95 win over the Nets), but we never did make the type of run we were capable of generating, and gradually our collective interest faded as we couldn't catch Indiana for the final playoff spot.

But my stock rose as a player. I won a spot on the All-Rookie team and finished second in the balloting for Rookie of the Year to David Thompson. I was also discovering how physical professional basketball could be. In a controversial game in New York I exchanged elbows during a fight with the Nets' John Williamson. I impressed Nets coach Kevin Loughery anyway, but the matter wouldn't rest with Williamson. The next time we played in St. Louis we went at it again. I still had the scar over my left eye from the first fight, and I wasn't about to let it rest. We had to be restrained by the officials, John Vanak and Rich Leber. Later, I would still not allow it to rest. It was an instance of letting my emotions overrule my judgment.

We may have finished out of the playoffs, but unlike the ABA itself and even some of the great players in the ABA like Barnes and Freddy Lewis, I finally had a future in the game. During the summer, I was exempt from the postmerger dispersal draft because I was a free agent, having concluded my one-year deal with the Spirits. I went on to sign with the Detroit Pistons, a two-year guaranteed deal with an option year at the end of the contract. The closest competitors were the Celtics, who offered a one-year guarantee.

The ABA sent many spectacular and efficient players to the established league. With the breakup there was also some sadness. There had been a genuine feeling of community among ABA players. They had had to pull together to survive, playing in places like Commack, New York, where the Nets once had to forfeit a playoff game because floorboards were ripped out of place and bolts were scattered all over the gym. That was the shadow beneath the glamor.

But you forgot things like that when the game began. The games were fun, and there was a tradition in the league of having wide-open play. If you got by your man, you took it to the hoop. Without defense-minded seven-footers to stop you when your drive was underway, a style of play developed that kept things moving. The league was colorful, literally and figuratively. Red-white-and-blue basketballs spun through the air, and the original three-point field goal kept the game exciting. The whole floor opened up with that shot. Teams couldn't pack it in, and long-range shooters like the Spirits' Freddy Lewis and Louie Dampier of the Kentucky Colonels had good careers. These were heady, smart players who were able to move around successfully in spite of their smallish size (both men were six feet tall).

Some of that color also came from controversy, of course. Freddy held out when the season began, reportedly because he was having financial problems back home in Indianapolis. He finally reported, but he was shuffled in and out of the starting lineup, partly because of inconsistent play, partly because of our coaching shift at midseason. Marvin had his feud with Maurice Lucas. When they faced each other for the first time after Lucas's trade, Marvin scorched him for forty-nine points. But Marvin was often distracted. One night he failed to make the team plane and was marooned. He solved the problem by personally chartering a flight from New York to Richmond for the game. He arrived ten minutes before game time and proceeded to star. The ABA was a professional operation, but we had interesting sidelights, too. We were the eccentric brothers to our more conservative counterparts in the NBA.

Some of the eccentricity we could have done without. Before what would be the final season for the league, the former Memphis Tams, then the Baltimore Claws, seemed to go in two directions simultaneously. They obtained Dan Issel, a six-eight power forward who could shoot the ball, and prepared to compete in the upcoming season. Then, days before the year began, they folded up operations. Utah folded in midseason, and rumors persisted throughout the year that Virginia was going under. We were rescheduling games constantly. Players were always talking among themselves about the possibility of the league folding up at any time. Naturally some of them were worried about whether or not they would be paid. There was confusion and there was tension.

But the sense of community did exist. Most of us took pride in the accomplishments of Julius Erving, who brought publicity to the league with his brilliant play and his position on a team in New York, the major market in sports. We understood that we had to band together if we were to have any possibility of surviving. At times you felt as if you needed something. I never played in front of less than a thousand customers, but sometimes I felt as if I were playing before a playground crowd. But even in that context I felt I was accomplishing something, that I was carving out a small niche in history. Some of the fans came out to the arena in St. Louis faithfully. They had seen the team overpower Doctor J and the Nets the previous season, and those who stayed behind the team weren't disappointed—we had some great players. And even if we did seem to be going in twelve directions at once, we were still committed to the game. The fans who came to the games nightly understood that the game was our life. Before our final game of the year a kid walked up to me and handed me this letter:

> Dear M. L. : We are sorry that today was the last time we will see you in person. My friends and I as you know are (were) avid Spirits fans. We loved your hustle and desire to win. But you are exceptional. You combine hustle and determination with being a great human being also. You thrilled us this year. We will really miss you and all the team next year. We're sorry David (Thompson) is in the ABA because otherwise you would be a cinch for Rookie of the Year. Wherever you end up next year, we are sure you will be loved and respected by fans and fellow players alike. We will always be behind you. Thank you.
> Mike Hunsicker
> P.S. Good luck!

This was the type of fan attachment that helped keep you going, even when the sounds of the bouncing ball were echoing against empty seats.

The ABA was not what you would call glamorous. The league began in places like that arena in Commack and Uline Arena in Washington, where Red Auerbach began his coaching career back in 1946. When the ABA's Washington Caps played there, they had to play fifty-four road games. In the *old* ABA, this was the way they were forced to operate.

But the modern player transcended this as the league grew up. We played an exciting brand of basketball, although we had no assurance of a pension plan or severance pay if the league went under. There was a standard conservative bias against our league. And without that major television contract we weren't seen—so therefore we were not good enough.

For all intents and purposes the Spirits franchise went down when the city failed to support the team after its great showing against the Nets the previous season. The owners, Don and Ozzie Silna, asked the city to purchase three thousand season tickets after they considered merging with the Utah team. But the city could only come up with twenty. The owners asked for help from a group formed by the Chamber of Commerce in the city but instead found itself, the team thought, shunted off to the Regional Commerce and Growth Association, which was more concerned with the financial problems of the arena than the team. In the end, the team lost over four million dollars in two years in St. Louis. When the season was finishing and the guys were making plans to go their separate ways, the team was reportedly going to be moved to Salt Lake City. Six-hundred thousand dollars was going to be put up by Booneville Corporation, a subsidiary of the Mormon Church. On that ironic note, the Spirits of St. Louis folded.

Chapter 9

Motor City

Our teams in Detroit had talent, flair, charisma and excitement. We didn't win much; our only playoff team came in my first year with the Pistons, 1976-1977, when we went up against the Golden State Warriors in the miniseries (until the 1983-1984 season, the first round of the playoffs was a best two out of three). That small series was emblematic of the type of team we had. The Warriors had won the NBA championship two years earlier, and although they were declining, they were still a classy team. Rick Barry, Clifford Ray, Phil Smith, Charley Dudley and an impressive rookie center, Robert Parish of Centenary, all knew how to play and win. But in the first game of the series, we handled them on the road in Oakland, 95-90. We thought we had them with the series returning to Detroit, but they turned around and kicked our butts at home. We were disposed of in the winner-take-all third game.

In Detroit I didn't learn much about winning, but I did learn something essential—that to play in the NBA you have to be physical. I had always played with a degree of strength, and I had refined my skills in this area in the ABA. In St. Louis players like Marvin Barnes, Maurice Lucas and Don Adams were both physical and wily. They were fearless players whose confidence led them into any situation with the ability to come out on top. Following in their path, I had my share of skirmishes in the league.

But in the NBA, the rough stuff was up another notch. In Detroit I learned immediately that I had better be prepared to defend myself. In the beginning, I drove through the lane and was flattened. I was a rookie in the established league and there were always tests. It didn't take me long to fight back. I threw elbows at everyone, including Tom Boerwinkle of the Chicago Bulls, a mammoth man. I fought him for territory, and I was determined to gain my share. My old teammate Maurice Lucas was one of several "enforcers" in the league that year. Kermit Washington, Jim Brewer, Dave Cowens, Marvin Barnes, Lonnie Shelton,

Paul Silas, Kevin Kunnert and Wes Unseld were others over the next few seasons. I joined their ranks. The interesting thing is that in Detroit, where I learned to play physical ball in order to survive in the league, I was a "hard-nosed" player. But when I came to Boston, the same man playing the same way, I became a "villain," a "dirty" player. But that was to be expected. Teams built their whole seasons around beating the hated Celtics, who were hated because they always found ways to beat you, and then in the end seemed always to win it all.

That first season in Detroit could best be described as a mystery, or a dark comedy. We had loads of talent. Bob Lanier, among the best centers ever to play the game, was powerful, but agile and quick. He would roll around an opponent, get a first step on him and hold him off as he went gliding in with a graceful lefthanded hook shot. That year he averaged over twenty-five points a game and over eleven rebounds. Once Bob-a-Dob had position on you, forget it. He was where he wanted to be for the duration of the play. You couldn't move him out. He was the lead player on a team that included Howard Porter, Kevin Porter, Eric Money, Chris Ford, Ralph Simpson, Leon Douglas, Marvin Barnes and myself. We'd have games where we were absolutely great, including a very successful trip to the West Coast, where Pistons teams normally died. Other times we'd play listlessly.

But the team did fight constantly. We'd start it up among ourselves or against other teams. There was a stretch of ballgames that had us fighting nightly. In one game in Kansas City, Lanier went at it with a reserve player on their team, Jim Eakin. There was some milling, and suddenly Bob just dropped him flat with a lefthanded swing. This brought Bill Robinzine charging at him off the bench. Those two started to square off, and both benches emptied. The fight went on for fifteen minutes. A few nights later we were involved in another fracas in Chicago with the Chicago Bulls. Kevin Porter had drawn Jack Marin on a switch and Kevin, a little feisty guy, played Marin chest-to-chest, trying to belly him out of the play. Marin took this pushing for several seconds, and then threw Kevin off of him. Enter Marvin Barnes. I knew from my days with the Spirits of St. Louis that Marvin could mix it up when he wanted to. News hustled over behind Marin, all the time checking over his shoulder to see if any of the Bulls' players were trailing *him*. Assured of his safety, Marvin wound up and blasted Marin with a powerful right hand. *Boom!* And again the benches emptied. I hustled over, able and willing to get my share. My target was none other than the most ferocious Bull, seven-foot, 275-pound Tom Boerwinkle. He was rushing over to the crowd, and trying to head him off at an angle was difficult. I tried anyway; I threw a long right cross at him, but as I did, he moved, unaware of my attack. I fell over his shoulder onto the floor and became vulnerable to a punch, stomp or kick. Fortunately he didn't know of my malicious intent.

"Hey, big fella," I shouted above the din. "Let's go over and break this thing up!" He didn't know.

From there we went to Washington, where another brawl broke loose. Leonard Gray cracked Ford with a slap to the face and we immediately emptied the bench to provide some defense for Chris. That one became ugly, lasting another ten minutes or so. Howard Cosell made the observation on his radio show, "There must be something in the drinking water in Detroit."

The fights were unlimited and came at any time, even between members of our own team. I remember one night Kevin Porter and Eric Money went at it over who should be the point guard of the team. They were both intense competitors, little guys who had to have the ball. And sometimes they didn't hide their feelings about it. Another night Howard Porter went off during halftime in the locker room. "Man, I am busting to fill the lanes and I'm never getting the ball!" he bellowed. Guys would mutter under their breath. And Marvin was falling; he had to leave the team during the latter part of the year to go to trial over a parole violation. Then he wanted to renegotiate his contract because of the increasing debt he was incurring. He threatened not to play in the playoffs. It was a volatile place.

The lasting impression I have of Detroit is that the team back then was negatively influenced by the environment. People assumed the Pistons would lose. They expected the team to fail, and management couldn't evade the criticism or the tempting fate of a self-fulfilling prophecy. We're losing, they'd say, so we'll have to make changes. So they'd bring in new guys, and because of the instability we'd lose some more. So they'd make more changes. There was a revolving door in Detroit; if players don't think they'll be around a place for very long, they'll never play with any confidence. That was what hurt us. Also, when teams "move" players, they aren't trading basketball bubble-gum cards. They're trading players' families, too. Guys' loyalties never had an opportunity to develop in Detroit. I think we had exceptional talent on some of those teams. Put those guys in Celtics or Lakers uniforms and they would have played effectively. Uncertain in the constant prevailing winds of change in Detroit, we could never win.

The effects of this attitude became very apparent over the following two seasons, as the team's fortunes dipped. Unable to achieve any peace among the fighting factions, our coach the first season, Herb Brown, was fired. He probably wasn't forceful enough with our emotional group. In the offseason, the Pistons' management decided to bring in the coach of the University of Detroit who had been politicking for the position, Dick Vitale.

Of course Dick Vitale is an important name in the game of basketball. He is now one of the dominant voices of college basketball as a color analyst for ESPN and ABC Television. He tirelessly pursues the college game at all levels and at all times of the year. Dick's loud and colorful on the air; you need experience to understand him, especially his unique jargon. "Players need more than just PT," Dick will point out about a young player. "They need QT!" Dick will then go on to explain that those terms signify "playing time" and "quality time." For the uninitiated, this translating might interfere with the actual game going on. Or Dick will bellow: "Bernard King just made a BP!"—a bad pass, that is. His descriptions are colorful, but they sometimes cloud the fact that he's the best-prepared college basketball analyst on the air. Dick lives the game; he's always looking for angles, tirelessly covering games from one end of the country to the other. He's a street-fighter; he understands the opposite of success, and he's unwilling ever to let go.

I thought he was a very good professional coach, a man who could compete intellectually with any of the coaches in the league. My major reservation about Dick was that he was often too intense. Among the coaches I've watched, I thought he was a major candidate for burnout. Dick worked hard and expected everybody on the ballclub to live the game the way he did. If a guy was fifteen minutes late for practice, Dick would spend the following half-hour of the practice session lecturing that player on how thankful he should be to be wearing an NBA uniform. That player's daddy wouldn't be fifteen minutes late for work, because if he were, he'd be fired, out of a job. These orations were pretty constant. He brought several players from the University of Detroit into the league with him, and he felt that he had major responsibility for their careers. Guard John Long was one of those; if John missed a few shots, Dick would go after him. "You should be in the gym for two hours before a game if you miss those shots." After a while, we'd be saying to ourselves, "C'mon Dick, enough." Pros can listen to just so much. Then they turn off.

Vitale ran the toughest training camp I'd ever been in. We'd go hours and hours per practice, in two-a-day formats. His belief was that we would break out of the gate fast and have a jump on the rest of the league.

But it backfired; we had several injuries, losing people like Lanier, John Shumate and Ralph Simpson. My minutes went up, and in my final season with Detroit I played the third most minutes in the league. But we fell out of the playoff picture, always hurt.

But Dick was always good to me. First, he played me all those minutes (QT minutes at that). Then he furthered my career and helped it flourish after I signed a free-agent contract with Boston. At that time, compensation was determined by agreement between the two teams involved. Vitale was up in arms about my having signed with Boston. "The Celtics are taking from us—at the worst—our second-best player. The hearts and guts of our team. Any time you lay [my $315,000 with a $100,000 signing bonus] on someone, the other guy has to get something of equal value. If it's not Bob McAdoo, we'll see you at the commissioner's office. M. L. had a better year than either Dave Cowens or McAdoo. Maybe we'll ask for both.

"There are only two players we'll even consider as compensation— [then rookie] Larry Bird or McAdoo. And I don't think Boston will give up McAdoo." Dick increased my credibility in the Boston market with those statements. Then, by building up his views of McAdoo in the press, he eventually lost out on the deal. Boston allowed McAdoo to go to Detroit in a separate free-agent signing. They didn't want Bob anyway; in exchange, Detroit was forced to give Boston their two first-round draft choices in the upcoming draft. The Celtics used those choices in a trade and wound up with Robert Parish and Kevin McHale.

The real lesson I learned at Detroit, the lesson that would be completed when I joined the winning tradition of the Boston Celtics, was that it takes more than talent to be a winner. The great talent of that team was never able to compensate for the inability to develop a winning attitude. We set records—the scoring record against Boston, my steals mark, Kevin Porter's assists—but after 1977 we were a team that could not dig in on the road and couldn't finish the season with any sense of purpose. I remember a Pistons play that occurred after I had moved to the Celtics. We were playing Detroit, and the game came down to the wire. They set up a play designed to get the ball to their shooting guard. We defensed him closely, denied him the ball and forced them into a situation where they had to settle for a bad shot, which they missed. We pulled in the rebound and called time, and as we were heading to the bench I heard that shooting guard shouting at his teammates: "Why didn't you pass it to me? Why did *you* shoot?"

That was a telling scene. More often than not the Celtics won in those circumstances—and we never lost our team unity like that. The Pistons had a tendency to unravel in pressure situations, and over those years they were perennial losers—which made the subsequent events in my career all the more fortunate.

Chapter 10

Valued Free Agent
Signs with Boston

In 1979 I was a free agent again, though this time the situation was a little different. In 1976, as a result of the Oscar Robertson settlement and the agreement between the leagues, there was a dispersal draft of the remaining players in the ABA. But I was a free agent; on the advice of Norman Blass I had signed a one-year deal with the Spirits and retained that contract midway through the year, compliments of Marvin Barnes's counsel. But the second time around, my bargaining power was better. The decision to sign with Detroit had been reached because of the strong relationship between Herb Brown, then coaching Detroit, and Norman Blass. Herb, who had coached me in Israel, knew my capabilities and urged the Pistons to sign me. But I had had no NBA experience, of course, so my bargaining power was limited. I still had to prove myself. The contract was modest, but I was glad to have some initial security. The three-year deal gave us $60,000 the first year, $70,000 the second and an option year at $80,000 for the third season.

I went out and proved myself from the beginning, and ironically my success caused some problems between management and myself. Early that first season the Pistons' lawyer, Oscar Feldman, called me in and told me how pleased the team was with my game. To that end, they wanted to pay me a bonus of $40,000. I couldn't have been more pleased. I had signed the contract, and I was prepared to live up to the agreement. But $40,000 was nearly my entire salary that first year, a substantial raise. So I suggested we renegotiate my contract. In good faith, I would be willing to agree to revised terms early. To me, it would have solidified the commitment immediately. But they didn't want to do that, though Oscar Feldman did say that they would continue to pay me a similar bonus throughout the duration of my contract.

We would have some better and worse times in Detroit, and my career was coming along satisfactorily. I showed I could play in the league, and my specific strength was defense from the small forward spot. By the third season, Dick Vitale had arrived, bringing with him some talented young players. There was a possibility that we could soon be a playoff team, during the years when I could be making my peak dollars. We were in contention for the playoffs until the final week of the second season, and again during the year the Pistons had paid me the $40,000 bonus, bringing my salary for the season to $110,000. At that moment in my career, my confidence as a professional player had reached its highest level, and I was ready to settle in both financially and professionally. Before my final year in Detroit, in an attempt to avoid negotiating at the end of my contract, we offered to close the deal at that time. Our offer before the season was $750,000 for five years with a $100,000 signing bonus. I remember Oscar Feldman saying in one of our meetings, "Listen, M. L., we're friends. The Pistons realize what you've contributed to the team and to the community. But when we're negotiating, I have to pull on my hard hat." The Pistons could have signed me early; I wanted the security of knowing that my family would be taken care of and that I did not have to worry about the deal all season long. But the Pistons preferred to wait until the season was over to finalize an agreement. I went out and played extremely well my last year there: I was third in the league in minutes played, NBA All-Defensive Second Team, NBA leader in steals. A forward leading the league in steals is something I don't believe will be seen again. The nature of the game has it that the ball is handled on the perimeter, away from the basket, so guards usually win that title. I was taking steals away from my own teammates late that season—I wanted it.

The pivotal matter in negotiations with the Pistons dated back to that initial verbal agreement regarding the $40,000 bonus they promised they would give me in each of my three years there. During this peak season in my career, I thought they would readily compensate me, as they had promised. But when I went in there, they told me they preferred to wait on that this season because we were negotiating the long-term deal. At the end of that season they did in fact make a resolute effort to re-sign me, and we negotiated a five-year deal at $1.5 million, *twice* the amount of our offer at the beginning of the season. But I had been put off by their reneging on that $40,000. It wasn't a question of money; it was a point of principle. My reasoning was that it belonged to the present contract with the Pistons, a matter of bargaining in good faith. I wasn't angry, but I realized I was a victim of a business decision. Throughout my postyear negotiating with the Pistons, I remembered how I had been a victim of this type of organizational decision-making before, and I started exercising my rights as a free agent by looking at other teams.

A number of teams were interested in me, including the New York Knicks and the team I had always dreamed of playing for, the Boston Celtics. When we opened negotiations with the Celtics I decided to take part in the discussions. I flew up to New York from Greensboro and met with Red Auerbach and Coach Bill Fitch of the Celtics. My agent Norm Blass and my business manager Phil McLaughlin were there with me as well. I saw right away that Red was a master of the art. Major corporations should hire this guy to handle their negotiations; he's that perceptive. But the meeting was tense. We were also negotiating with the Knicks. Since I would be in New York, Norman Blass, not the type of man to waste time, scheduled a meeting with the Knicks' Sonny Werblin. I was to meet with the Celtics early in the day, go to Madison Square Garden to negotiate with New York and then return to Blass's office to meet the Celtics again.

We were dealing from strength in the negotiations. There were three top free agents that year: Bill Walton (Portland), Larry Kenon (San Antonio) and myself. Earlier that summer, Walton had signed.

We sat down for the meeting, Red leaning back, puffing on a cigar. He was relaxed and telling jokes, and I recall thinking to myself, "C'mon, Red. I didn't come here to hear any jokes. Let's get on with the business." But amid the jokes, Red suddenly became utterly serious.

"How do you see your role, M. L.?" I answered calmly, but I was taken aback. He had me off balance; he began telling another series of jokes. After re-establishing the friendly manner, he looked at me and asked: "How much money do you want, M. L.?" At that Norman sensed the direction of the talk and began formulating my position—after an All-Star caliber season in Detroit, I was looking to be fairly compensated. Red listened and began building his position: that the team had recently drafted Larry Bird, that the Celtics had Dave Cowens, Tiny Archibald, that a great era was about to unfold. My thoughts were if they were *that* outstanding, why was the team 29-53 the previous season? And always, always, I was waiting for my statistics of the previous season to surface. My minutes played, reflecting dedication and desire. My second team defense and steals title, displaying my commitment to team goals and not the glory of scoring stats. But Red never mentioned these numbers. There were circles and circles around the negotiations, but through it all Red never mentioned those numbers. And I was becoming exasperated as he went on. "And M. L., you'd be only a part of the team, not the main focus. You see, Larry Bird..." Red continued. This was when Norman helped me out; he suggested we take a break for dinner, and he arranged for Sonny Werblin to meet with me during the break.

Sonny Werblin is noted in sports history as one of the key figures in orchestrating the merger between the National Football League and the old American Football League. Werblin signed Joe Namath when Namath graduated from the University of Alabama and Werblin was president of the New York Jets. As I noted before, Werblin had the insight to understand that Namath's skill and charisma could carry a team in the television age, and he utilized a similar approach with me after I traveled across Manhattan to talk with him. I went alone to that meeting.

In Boston Werblin is viewed with tremendous skepticism. In 1978 he very nearly hired Red Auerbach away from the Celtics after Red determined he couldn't work under John Y. Brown, a former ABA owner. Brown was flip, and he wasn't in the game for the game itself. Red had always conducted the Celtics' business that way, and he nearly left before pulling back and staying in an eleventh-hour decision.

In New York I had a totally different view of Werblin. I met with him for forty-five minutes, and in that short time we tentatively agreed to terms: $2 million for five years. People in Boston may have disliked Sonny, but I thought I'd found my best friend. Sonny was talking to me, with these numbers understood, and my mind was floating back to the Israel Sabras, to the days in the federal penitentiary, to selling cars. He explained that the Knicks really needed the type of player who would promote the team. In the past, with players like Spencer Haywood and Bob McAdoo, the players had played their games and gone home. New York needed a positive image. And that was acceptable to me; I saw the potential for marketing myself in New York City. We agreed to talk again and I walked out of his office flying. I *never* tip a cabbie (going back to my poorly paid days of working the fields), but this time I told my driver to keep a five-dollar bill. I was becoming a big spender because I was about to be a wealthy man.

We resumed the meeting with the Celtics back at Norman's office, and to this day I declare Red was psychic. Within the first thirty seconds he turned to me and said, "I know where you've been...over visiting with the Knicks."

Out of the countless places in the world I could have been, how did this man know exactly where I was? It was as if I were a teenager growing up again, walking in late at night, tiptoeing past my father's door. My father should have had no idea about where I'd been or how late I was. But he knew anyway. That was the feeling I had with Red in the office.

Phil McLaughlin handed Red a statement of our contractual requirements. Phil's a detail guy, and he's extremely comprehensive. He was prepared. But alas, so was Red...

"What's this?" Red bellowed, cigar smoke wafting through the air. "Who are you kidding? That kind of money isn't there for M. L. You see, you don't understand. You're not talking about a leading scorer. He's a role player!"

I had just finished negotiations with the Knicks; I could have consummated a deal a half-hour before.

"People will find out about this type of offer and nobody will want to sign you at these figures," Red went on.

The tension from the earlier meeting had resumed. I was taken again; somehow, if Red tells you in negotiations that you're not that good, you begin to wonder just how good you are. But whimsy aside, I again became angry.

"What the devil!" I muttered, and began to get up to leave. But Norman caught my eye and told me to sit down and relax. Meanwhile, Fitch began talking, conceptualizing the team, and the pieces seemed to make sense. I had the feeling that he knew the game and that Red had complete confidence in him. But I was still readying to leave for Greensboro, where I could have been sitting in the garden, listening to the cicadas, absorbing the peace of the green mountains. I balanced the conflicting feelings and arrived at a choice: I would have a deal with one or the other team by midnight of the coming weekend. Everybody shook hands all around and I flew home.

My wife and I waited through the weekend; I was attracted to the marketing potential in New York, but knowing Red, I envisioned myself part of the Celtics as they made their triumphant march back into contention. I knew there was some sales talk, but I also felt Larry Bird would be an outstanding player and I always respected Dave Cowens. Through Saturday evening, there were no calls. Sylvia discussed living in New York—White Plains, perhaps? New Jersey? Then at 10:25 P.M., Norman called and congratulated me. I had the deal and the dream. I was a Boston Celtic with financial security. I immediately called Don Chaney and told him we would once again be teammates. He said, "Oh really? Did you sign!" "We're teammates again, Duck!"

The Celtics arranged for me to fly into Boston for a press conference on the following Tuesday. Carl Yastrzemski was shooting for his four hundredth home run that weekend, and they didn't want to have our press conference overshadowed. To hide me from the media, though, they reserved a room for me at the Sonesta Hotel in Cambridge. But when are you able to hide anything from the media? The media may not see too well, but they always hear. They may not feel very well, but they're persistent, and they hear about things like player-signings.

I came away from the press conference the following day with a very
positive feeling. Red said all the right things: that I would do whatever
was asked; that my intent was to win. And that I was a winner. I repeated
his points, stating that my dream had always been to play with the Celtics
and that I would do whatever was necessary to contribute to winning
the championship. I also made another point. As a professional athlete,
I would become involved in the community. I wasn't the type of man
who would point angrily at a problem; I would go in there and do
something about it. The day was otherworldly; when Sylvia and I returned
to the hotel, we dropped down to our knees at the bed and had a long
prayer. We were genuinely grateful.

I reminisce and I dream. Looking back at the whole process, I recall
a little scene when I first walked into Red's office for the formal signing.
He looked at me, a directive in his eye, and tested me: "You're wearing
a sports jacket now; it's probably the last time I'll see you wearing one."
"I couldn't afford it before," I teased, "Now you've made me a happy
man, and I'll at least *have* them." But I respected Red Auerbach's
attention to detail. His teams used to have a dress code, and to me this
reflected the quality of the franchise. That quality ultimately swung me
in favor of the Celtics. I knew they were a quality team despite having
suffered so miserably the previous season. (John Y. Brown hadn't a desire
to understand the context of the Boston situation—namely that the
decisions about Celtics basketball had to be made by Red Auerbach. Dave
Cowens coached the final half of that 1979 season; when he heard that
Brown had decided he would sell the team, Cowens, his employee,
commented, "That's the best news I've heard all year!") You make
decisions based on quality and business perspective. I firmly believed
we would win in Boston, and I knew that despite the Knicks' slightly
higher offer, the basketball picture was traditionally most clearly focused
in Boston.

A postscript that took place three years later confirmed my decision.
Part of my contract—final terms: $315,000 per season guaranteed for
five years—included a provision that would allow me to test the free-
agent market for thirty days after my third season in Boston, the
1981-1982 season. Interestingly, the season was a strong one for me
personally, although we didn't win the title. Around that time Ted
Stepien, owner of the Cleveland Cavaliers, was flipping cash around like
it was popcorn at the movies. I felt I owed it to my family to go see
Brother Stepien. He offered a lucrative deal: $1.6 million for four years
with a signing bonus. I was thirty-two years old at the time, and the
arrangement was exceptionally tempting.

When I'm confronted with a major decision, I go out and gather my data for an informed decision. Two people I spoke with had contrasting opinions. Jack Satter, a wealthy businessman in Boston and a good friend of Red's continually told me, "Don't Leave Boston, M. L.!" But Red Auerbach calmly spoke to me about it: "Listen M. L., I don't want to lose you, but you'd be crazy to turn down that kind of deal." I spoke to different people, but Jack was like a fairy godmother whispering in my ear: *Don't leave Boston.*

"If you leave for the money," Satter reasoned, "that's it. You're essentially through. In Boston, people care about you. The money you would make in Cleveland you'll be able to make up quickly when you're through playing." I thought about that and how quickly we forget how much we want something in an earlier part of our lives. Growing up there was nothing more that I wanted than to play with the Celtics. Then three years earlier my dream had come true. You find you have a short memory. My family was set outside of Boston, and I began thinking I didn't want to uproot them. I wasn't sure they'd be able to adjust again so easily in another NBA city. So I stayed. Some things are more important than money.

And there were other factors. Back in February 1979, when I was designing my future, something important took place. Still a member of Detroit, I was having my greatest individual year, and I was a free agent besides. I felt strongly I could lead the NBA in steals and turn in excellent statistics. One night in Houston, near the All-Star break, I went in for a steal off of Calvin Murphy's dribble, and the ball rolled loose on the floor. I rushed over to get it, and as I did, my back almost seemed to crumble, a painful, eerie feeling. I couldn't get the ball. The rest of the night was terribly hard as Rick Barry lit me up for thirty-five points. The press let me hear about it. I suffered with that pain all season, but I was determined to play through it. Instead I took massage and heat treatment and fought for the necessary statistics and performance goals I set for myself at midseason. I didn't mention this during the free agent offseason; I had my doctor in Greensboro look at it after the year concluded. It turned out I had two cracked vertebrae, but thankfully they hadn't regressed to the extent that my future in the game would be endangered. But I wasn't risking anything. For the rest of the summer, I did absolutely nothing physical for the first time since I started playing ball. I had a sense of my own mortality, the limits to my career. I came to camp thirty pounds overweight, and I had to listen to some good-natured, honeymoon-period barbs from the press. "Hey, guys," I answered them, "It's not too much weight around my middle. It's my money belt!"

Chapter 11

The Celtics

I had grown up admiring the Celtics, and when training camp began, the history major in me sensed I was entering the realm of something unique and extraordinary. In professional basketball only one thing counted with me—having a chance to play on a championship team. It didn't matter how much time I'd play; the nature of the game is that you are able to help even by being a supportive voice. If we were winning, I knew I'd be a part of that. There wasn't a question in my mind. The Celtics would be back—as early as the summer of 1979, the ingredients for victory were already coming together in training camp, only three months after the team's most miserable season in its history.

The heart of the Celtics is Red Auerbach. Red is special. He always talks to his players on an individual basis, and not always about basketball. I believe that interaction has contributed mightily to the success he's had. The essence of his belief is that he can build winning teams by bringing in winning people. One of Red's proudest traits is his refusal to live in the past. "I live in the present and in the future," he's maintained, and I think that's true. In Boston Red has always been incredibly ahead of his time. In the eighties, experts discuss the Los Angeles Lakers' fast break glowingly, but the man who introduced the break to pro ball was Arnold Auerbach. Coaches like Dr. Jack Ramsay of the Indiana Pacers are challenging Red's coaching victory record of 938 wins, but Red's achievement was constructed under somewhat difficult circumstances. After beginning his career with forty-nine wins with the Washington Caps in 1946-1947—at age twenty-nine—Red moved around the league before finally taking over the Celtics for Walter Brown in 1950. He would never leave the Celtics organization, and in retrospect that deep-seated loyalty to the organization probably enabled him to keep going even when he seemed overmatched by circumstances.

At that time the NBA was a fledgling organization, coping with the burden of a gambling scandal that had nearly destroyed the college game.

The only athletes banned from the NBA were players who had participated in dirty college games (City College of New York, the University of Kentucky and Bradley were three affected schools), but though the pros weren't implicated directly, the sport nevertheless had to fight for credibility. Red Auerbach was winning as coach of the Celtics, but coaching wasn't all he was doing; he worked incessantly behind the scenes, doing what he could to help build a positive image for the league. The Celtics themselves needed constant work. Red worked without scouts or assistant coaches, so that he had to draw up game plans and draft schemes by himself. Traveling in the league was done on old, prop-driven airplanes or trains. Red set his coaching record as a pioneer on the American sporting scene.

Even geography added to Red's achievement; Boston adored hockey in the fifties and sixties. Kids growing up in New England at that time played and followed ice hockey, a passion that forced Red and the team to travel throughout the city and the New England region to give clinics. The Celtics taught the game of basketball personally, an impression that has endured over time with New England's young people. Now, basketball is king in Boston, but the foundation for this royalty was laid when Red and company drove the backroads when no one seemed to care.

But that was Red—always anticipating potential for the future. I maintain that there are certain battles you cannot fight alone, and an accompanying facet of Red's genius is that he always surrounds himself with people who are willing to put forth the extra effort to create a winner. And it goes beyond victory on the basketball floor. Red's wins sometimes seem to be inevitable because of the effort and care that led up to the Celtics being in the position to suceed. It's admirable what a group of people with integrity can accomplish when they work together, and in a sporting context, Red Auerbach led.

Professional basketball was always a complex experience for me, but the heart of my ten-year career came in Boston. I had extremely positive experiences with the Celtics, a team that transcended very real differences among individuals to win consistently. Ironically, because sports can be subject to such a diversity of emotion, ranging from hate to love, the Celtics' very real human virtues have been viewed with contempt *and* respect—because we played basketball. My time with the Celtics was characterized by people willing to give successfully of themselves. Red Auerbach's staff never sacrificed a Celtics-type person for talent. On the Celtics, you don't get traded—you trade yourself. If you go there willing to work, you can unpack your bags for good. The invitation is to deflate your ego and become part of a family-type environment. On the floor, this is translated into players willingly accepting roles; not becoming robots, accepting roles. I compare this mature acceptance of roles to parts of the body: your hands won't jump, and you want your nose smelling, not your feet. You want your heart pumping blood, not your eyes. Just as the body has perfectly designed parts to sustain life, a well-conceived basketball team is a unit made up of different role players. Your defensive specialist should not want to be the team's leading scorer. In our initial training camp back in 1979, if Coach Fitch had taken Larry Bird aside and demanded he concentrate on defense, he would have created problems. Winning basketball is very basic; roles are well defined, fundamentals are sound, and there's a harmonious blending of personalities. Fitch would say that in an ideal situation the players at the professional level are so committed to the team that the egos of these stars police themselves.

Carried further, the remarkable feature of the Celtics is that their basic system has withstood the test of time: from an unmarketable league, through no-cut contracts, to the present, where the big egos of professional athletes are further distorted by television, the Celtics have endured. The most responsible for this success were Red Auerbach, who constructed the system, and Bill Russell, who made it happen on the floor. More than any other athlete who wore a Celtics uniform, Russell combined pride and knowledge in his pursuit of victory. There was one man putting it all together: insurmountable defensive pressure, the inspiration for team play, the example to others of giving of yourself to make a teammate's job easier. Bill Russell—he's a special person, and his legend exists among Celtics players today; when a Celtic goes into a game, Russell has already helped him. It was Russell who translated Red's teachings into victory. He established the precedent for success for the Boston Celtics. As a Celtic you are *never* down and out, due to the established team concept, the firm foundation beneath the highs and lows of a given season.

Like Red, Russell is another person I admire tremendously. He's a giant, a man with tremendous intellectual capability and an un-compromising belief in his principles. In basketball and in life, the pressures are often so strong that you have to compromise, but Russell's inner strength has served as an important model for me. Within the Celtics' environment I would never compromise my effectiveness or my capabilities. I have had only light conversations with Russell, although in an ego-check, brotherly sort of way, he welcomed me to the Celtics in 1980 during my first season with the team. He came into our dressing room in Philadelphia before a game and introduced himself. We talked about a few things, the team, the city of Boston, nothing heavy. And then he looked at me—he was a color commentator then for CBS—and he said, "M. L., I'm going to make your name a household word in Boston." And he looked at me again. "And you know what that name is?" I asked him what, wondering what he was getting at. Russell answered his own hypothetical question, "Garbage!" He sought out my inner eye this time—could I take hard humor?—and exploded in that distinctive, high-pitched, cacophonous laugh of his as he turned and left the locker room. And this was before a pressure-filled game with the 76ers.

That deflation of tension was another characteristic of the Celtics. You never found a Celtics team that was tense—due to Red, due to Russell, and due to K. C. Jones, who coached the team when I finished playing. They regarded seventh games as challenges to go out there and positively parade with their best performance.

But I retaliated with Russell. Moments later, I walked out onto the floor, where Russell and K. C. were standing with Oscar Robertson, the Hall-of-Fame player and unstoppable six-five power guard. Oscar could drive, shoot perfectly from the outside, and play chest-to-chest defense. I looked at the two former Celtics enjoying a friendly conversation with their old rival, and I called out to them, "Hey, Russ, K. C.—I know why you're so happy. That's the closest K. C. has ever been to Oscar without yelling for help". My laugh is sort of a loud cackle, too.

I was a good pro player, not great. I was successful in Boston because I was effective under pressure, I learned quickly from experience, and when the time arrived to alter my role, I accepted the general conditions of the situation and adjusted. I was dedicated to going out and playing the best I possibly could regardless of the amount of time I was on the floor, whether it was for thirty minutes or for minutes or even thirty seconds. I pumped up my teammates as well as I could, as effectively as I was able to analyze their temperaments each game. It was the way I viewed my role, and I believe it was a Celtics view.

Our track record in Boston speaks for itself. It had costs—our first coach left and one of the starters on a championship team was bartered. But the professional game is a business. You adjust, you cope, you attempt to succeed.

We turned the franchise around permanently in my first season with the team. The Celtics had suffered through a 23-59 season and the turmoil of a chaotic year of ownership. John Y. Brown had been a successful owner in the ABA with the Kentucky Colonels, but by the time he had reached Boston his interests had changed. He acquired Boston by trading his share of the Buffalo Braves to Irv Levin, the Californian who owned Boston at the time. Citing declining attendance, Levin immediately moved the Braves to San Diego, where they became the Clippers, and as a result, he took a team from a city of superb basketball fans. When Brown met with the press in Boston, he sensed the media's skepticism about him and appealed to their business sense. "Gentlemen and ladies," he concluded at the conference, "if it were you, wouldn't you trade Buffalo for the Boston Celtics?" No one would argue; it was one of the few moments of credibility he would have in Boston. After a disastrous year, he went into politics and was elected governor of the Commonwealth of Kentucky.

By the start of training camp in 1979, however, this was all behind us, and the plans Red Auerbach had detailed in our meeting the previous summer materialized. Larry Bird instantly impressed me. Rookies just don't come in the way he did: making creative passes, joking confidently, and then going out and backing up his words with his play. He and Cedric Maxwell had several serious, competitive duels in scrimmages, prompting Max to claim later, "This white boy can play!" Maxwell, the outstanding player on the team, adjusted his game to the dynamic ability of Bird. Two other players elevated this workmanlike, comeback team to a multidimensional level: Dave Cowens and Tiny Archibald. Thought to be through, these two greats came back from age and injuries to have tremendous seasons. It was a Cinderella year, with the Celtics going at opponents from all sides. Bird won Rookie of the Year, Cowens came back to make the All-Defensive team, and Chris Ford was among the league's best three-point field goal shooters. I inherited the mantle of Sixth Man, and I played important minutes at the ends of games. Against Detroit, the Celtics trailing by three with four seconds left in the game, I grabbed a long offensive rebound off a Dave Cowens perimeter jumper and dribbled hurriedly into the corner to capitalize on the league's new rule, the three-point field goal. (I benefited from my St. Louis experiences; the ABA had had that rule from its inception.) I sank the shot as the horn sounded, giving our season a major boost, like a transfusion of blood.

As it developed, we needed everything we built up over the course of that season. We fought with the 76ers all year for the best record in the league. Los Angeles, with Magic Johnson playing well and Kareem Abdul-Jabbar having the best regular season of his Lakers career, was also lurking menacingly in the background. The final two months of that NBA season established us as a major force in the league for the next decade.

We had great talent and tremendous heart. We played to the furthest limits of our potential, and with a powerful thrust of emotion we beat the 76ers and the Lakers for the regular-season championship. Fitch won Coach of the Year; he confided to a friend that he didn't think the Celtics were as good as either the Sixers or the Lakers, but we won anyway. In the playoffs we went into the Eastern Conference finals against Philadelphia completely confident. During the regular season we had defeated them handily all three games we had played against them in Boston, so with the home-court advantage now, we didn't think we could lose.

But we did. Lack of playoff experience, fatigue and a worn-down inside game all worked against us. In Game 1, Jeff Judkins hit an amazing three-pointer at the halftime buzzer to give us a ten-point lead. It proved to be a dangerous illusion; we went into the locker room all pumped up, and then in the second half we were unprepared for the Sixers' intensity. They had been playoff-tested over three seasons, and they swept by us in the final six minutes of the game. They towered over us the rest of the series. The defeat had its painful memories and valuable lessons; in Game 3, I nearly fought with Julius Erving after I dropped him on a transition. We rallied from thirteen points behind after that play but lost, 99-97, when our offensive execution broke down in the final seconds. Experience—or lack of it.

There were frightening ghosts, too. After they handled us easily in Game 4, in Philadelphia, to go up three games to one in the series, I was standing in front of my locker talking about how we could rally in the series, when suddenly I heard a sickening crash and felt pain cover my back. A mirror had fallen from over my locker and shattered on me.

"Get a doctor! Quick!" shouted Chris Ford. "M. L., relax. Don't move. Just hold still."

Somebody suggested one of the Sixers had put the mirror there.

The ride home from Philadelphia was sad, and our exile from the playoffs in Game 5 was sadder. I remember sitting in the trainer's room before that game, anger and hurt welling up inside. I planned to get even that day—but the 76ers were too good that year. But this Celtics team had laid its own foundation and constructed its own identity. We were the dominant team in the East from that season on.

In the next four seasons, we achieved my dream of an NBA championship twice. The first win, in 1980-1981, was a passionate affair; for the second straight season we edged out the 76ers for the best regular-season record, and for the second consecutive year we were extremely confident against them going into the Eastern Conference championship. By then, we had made some changes; Red had worked out an imponderable deal with Detroit related to my compensation. He had finagled a first-round draft choice out of Dick Vitale in exchange for Detroit's signing of Bob McAdoo in 1979. The Pistons had been given clearance to proceed on that signing because of my having signed with Boston. In 1980, the year we would get their choice, the Pistons were a tragicomic crew. They shouted at each other, demanding teammates pass the ball. We'd be amused at them and handle them on the floor with ease, all the time knowing that with each of their defeats, we were getting money in our pockets. It turned out that the choice was the first in the entire draft. The three best players in the draft that year were Joe Barry Carroll of Purdue, a center; Darrell Griffith of Louisville, a guard who had led the Cardinals to the NCAA championship; and Kevin McHale of Minnesota, a forward/center who had played erratically during his senior season because of a young supporting team around him, but whose stock had risen in the postseason all-star games. Boston used that draft to rebuild its front line; Red and Bill both liked Robert Parish, a center for the Golden State Warriors whom they had hidden during the final half of the season, trying to trade him, wanting to start over. So the Celtics swapped the first choice in the draft for the Warriors' choice, the third in the whole draft, along with Robert Parish. With the rights to the best player in the country, the Warriors willingly let Parish go. But by letting Parish leave, they were leading us to the championship. The Celtics knew that McHale would still be available at the number-three spot, and Red came away with the steal of the century. Parish and McHale still form the heart of the Celtics' inside game.

If we were confident heading into the series against Philadelphia, it was not without reason. Bird had had an MVP-quality season with brilliant outside shooting and strong rebounding. Meanwhile, Maxwell became our defensive stopper, willingly shedding the spotlight on offense for a sacrificing, team-oriented role. Archibald, Ford, Gerald Henderson and Rick Robey contributed significantly. With Maxwell's emergence on defense, my role changed, too; when I first signed with the Celtics, Bill Fitch had said at the press conference: "Expect to see M. L. on defense against players like Dennis Johnson in the playoffs." (DJ was then with Seattle; later he was traded to Phoenix before coming to Boston in 1983.) After Maxwell's role adjustment in the 1980-1981 title year, I played guard almost exclusively, a transition that coincided with my recovery from a broken foot that I had suffered in an early-season game with Washington. The injury didn't deter me though; the first Monday after that Saturday night game, I was working out with weights and running the sidelines on my crutches. I refused to waste any time. And I thought that if the players working out on the floor saw me doing that, they'd stay committed to our team goal. I felt the same about moving to guard; if that was where the team needed me, that was where I would go. Everything came together for us in the Philadelphia series; ironically, we made it after it appeared we would be humiliated for the second straight year.

The 1981 Eastern Conference finals did not begin well; Philadelphia won the first game in Boston when Andrew Toney, their irrepressible rookie guard, scored two free throws with only seconds left after Maxwell had fouled him. It's a play you try to prevent; you don't want teams beating you from the free throw line in the closing seconds. But that was the opener, and the series was war throughout: again they went up three games to one, and in the first half of Game 5 (back at the Boston Garden, where they had closed us out last season), they jumped all over us again. After a close early game, Maurice Cheeks and Clint Richardson shot the Sixers in front. Late in the half, Doctor J, Bobby Jones and Steve Mix went for the kill. I remember this interval well; we filed quietly into the locker room for our meeting, trailing, time slipping away. Fitch was a great coach that year—he treated us correctly and sensed perceptively what we needed as a team.

"Listen right now," Fitch hollered to the group. "I don't mind losing, but I do mind seeing you guys go out and play passively. You're not doing anything out there, and you're forgetting what got you to this level!

"I'm warning you men. If you go out like this, you'll find it hard to live with yourselves all summer. I don't want to end my season tonight."

It took us the entire second half to regroup, but we did. Philadelphia rallied to go ahead, 109-103, with 1:51 left. But we stormed back to win. And we startled them. We overwhelmed them after we lost the ball.

I entered the game with 1:38 remaining and contributed a steal and two rebounds—and the two winning foul shots, one that tied the game at 109 and the winner on the following attempt. That game was the most memorable of my career.

From that rally, the series changed dramatically. For us, it was the best of times. We went down to the Spectrum and rallied from seventeen points behind to win, another crushing blow to their confidence as we hadn't won in Philadelphia in over two years. In Game 7 back in Boston, they again shot out to a twelve-point advantage, but we again wrestled the game—and the series—away from them. I played some of the best

ball of my career in this series; I teamed with Tiny or Henderson at guard
and had complete confidence in my outside shot as well as my defensive
game. When Houston upset the Lakers en route to the finals, we were
supremely confident, although we knew we had to play well to win. We
did win behind a powerful inside game by Maxwell, Parish and Bird.
It was as spiritually moving as any gospel I've heard, and I treasure that
first championship ring.

One day at practice during that championship year, Red was sitting
on the sidelines talking to friends. He pointed out at us—the players and
coaches laughing and talking, moving with the familiar rhythms of
practice like kids on the playground, happy just to be there. We were
winning and satisfied with our contributions towards the success we were
achieving. Red commented, ''I hope these guys realize what they have
and understand it. These types of feelings among players don't last that
long.''
As usual he was right.
The following two seasons were like a watercolor painting when the
canvas becomes wet and the colors run down the painting, ruining the
whole picture. Injuries, contracts and underlying tension dissolved the
bonds of that first team. But things started out well, and we seemed to
be having another outstanding year. We were sluggish early, but even
as Larry, Tiny and Chris went out injured, we scrambled back and put
together a team-record eighteen-game winning streak. We were at our
peak during that run, even though teams are usually fighting midseason
blues at that time of the year. With three starters missing, a starting unit
of Maxwell and McHale at forward, Parish at center and Henderson
and myself at guard evolved into a tightly knit unit. We swept through
a very tough Texas trip behind Parish's spectacular play. With Larry
out, Maxwell regained his dominating offensive inside game and basked
in the responsibilities of being the central focus of the team. McHale,
although at that point in his career not yet the best postup player in the
game, as he is now, nevertheless combined with Robert to give us an
impenetrable defensive front line. Henderson and I lacked Tiny's
command, but we contributed in other ways. We were intent on producing
something positive with each possession.
Then, when Larry and Tiny came back, we had unbelievable Sixth
and Seventh Men. Both didn't *like* coming off the bench, but we were
winning and we had fun. That season, we won the regular crown more
easily than the two previous years. But injuries caught up to us in the
playoffs and for the third straight season we fell behind to the Sixers,

three games to one in the final series. Despite rallying to tie the series at three apiece, something was missing. Tiny had fallen in the opening minute of Game 3 in Philadelphia and separated his shoulder. He was through, and in the final game in Boston Toney lit us up for thirty-four and we couldn't recover. Our championship had slipped away, and slowly our team cohesion followed.

The 1982-1983 season was a significant one for me in a number of ways. As a Celtic, I had been virtually injury-free, but in the exhibition season that changed. We were in San Antonio, and I was playing against George Gervin. In the final minute of the first half I went for a steal off of Gervin's dribble. As I did, he reversed his dribble suddenly, feinting, and my hand was left dangling out there. It jammed into his thigh, and my finger bent back severely. I screamed in pain; I thought it was broken.

That injury affected my play, but indirectly it led to the revelation of an even greater problem. My relationship with Bill Fitch was becoming increasingly acrimonious. Bill is an excellent coach; he studies the game constantly and works as hard as any man I've known in the game, and I respected that. He's a driven man who's concerned with execution on the court. He is extremely perceptive in analyzing his players' strengths and weaknesses. But he has an impulsive streak, and he is sometimes too quick with a critical tongue. I had walked out of a practice the previous season, resentful of criticism from him as he stood above us on a perch in the stands while we worked out in a hard practice. In San Antonio, I guess the resentment lingered. During our halftime meeting he asked, "By the way, did you hurt your finger?" I replied that I thought it would be all right, although there was some pain. He said that he hoped I had hurt it, because the play I attempted had been dumb.

That set me off. I shouted back at him, telling him that he shouldn't *ever* hope that a player was hurt—the worst possible statement a coach can make to a player! If an athlete is giving his best, whether the play is ill-conceived or not, he is still to be supported. I can handle just criticism if my assessment of a situation is off. My record with coaches I think bears this out. When a player who is giving an honest effort is injured, to be told that this injury is "good" is a rupture in the relationship between the coach and the player. It's a relationship based on trust and respect—both ways. A player refusing to enter a game when asked violates that. A coach desecrating the integrity of the athlete violates that, too. From that point on our relationship went sharply downward. We exchanged words heatedly two other times that season, and my days of playing effectively for Fitch had ended.

When I was fighting with Fitch at Hellenic College, where the Celtics train, I would occasionally glance over my shoulder and see Maxwell laughing and pointing his finger at the two of us locked in verbal struggle. "Froggy's going at it!" he'd scream. And he'd tell all the rest of the guys. They'd laugh knowingly. They appreciated the scenario; I was fighting with the man with power, power he wasn't wielding too compassionately.

Fitch and I would go round and round.

"Don't expect to play much from now on. You're not satisfied with your role? Does that mean you want to be traded?"

But I'd never admit that. There was no way I'd let him trade me. If he did that, I'd retire.

That struggle reflected the mood of the team the entire season. Though we played well during the first half of the season, it was as if from memory, as if we were walking in the path of the joy of a wonderful dream. But the time when we were champions, driven by pride and acceptance of roles, was gone. The second half of the year was dismal; despite the emergence of Danny Ainge and Henderson as our starting guards and Larry's excellent individual play, we were woefully inconsistent. We'd lose badly one night and then, aroused, come back and win big. But that wasn't the team we had carefully built over four years. We accepted our fates differently. Larry seemed genuinely hurt, puzzled. Robert withdrew, disgusted. Max played inconsistently. Rick Robey didn't play for six weeks; his attitude was that Fitch knew where he was, and that he had proven his mettle as a contributor. Meanwhile, we faltered.

The climax of the year came after Game 1 of the infamous playoff sweep by the Bucks over the Celtics. I'll never forget it; the Bucks won that game, 116-95, but the score didn't report the event accurately. It was a thirty-point defeat—at least it felt that way. When we walked into the locker room afterward I was thinking—"Gee, those cats really killed us tonight." There was no fire! No anger, just a resigned acceptance of defeat. That wasn't the Boston Celtics.

In retrospect, I contrast that game to the Game 3 loss at Los Angeles the following year, the season we regained the title. After that game in the Forum, we were stunned and shaken; when Larry Bird called the team "sissies" in the press, well, I was so ashamed that I looked down in the shower. I knew we had played badly, but I was certain I didn't want to be one of the ones he was talking about.

Without a collective goal, we were sunk early in that playoff series against the Bucks. I failed to get off the bench in Game 2; when Tiny Archibald and Harvey Catchings nearly fought in that game, I never moved from the bench. Quinn Buckner came over to me during the series and said, "You're not yourself. We need the fire from you. You're flat."

The following month, after the season had ended without a Celtic response in the Milwaukee series victory, Bill Fitch resigned and the Celtics named K. C. Jones head coach. We needed that change, and for me the following season was the most important year of my career.

During the summer Red called me up and invited me in for a chat. We had made some bold moves already in the months preceding the 1983-1984 season. We had hired K. C., and in a dramatic maneuver, Red had traded Robey to the Phoenix Suns for Dennis Johnson, one of the best players in the game. Red was reducing his time in Boston, but he was doing a lot of work behind the scenes. He was defining roles for the players again. From me, he explained, he and K. C. wanted veteran leadership, a player on the end of the bench who could play significant minutes if required, but one who would willingly subjugate his personal needs, including cherished playing time, and work overtime in promoting the morale of the team. I thought I could play those extended minutes, but I was willing to do what was necessary to help the team win again. I respect Red and K. C. that much. And apparently Red had viewed my diminished competitive fires the way Quinn Buckner had. "What's going on?" he asked. "You're being too nice out there. When a guy's been going to the floor, you're the first one to help him up. I don't think that's you, M. L."

I played a game for a living, and when it was through I was able to step away and see it for what it is. A game, a sport, entertainment. But Red was right. Doing my best meant competing hard and doing whatever the team needed to come away a winner. We had a productive year in 1983-1984, a latter edition of the turnaround season my first year here. Bird won the MVP award in both the regular season and the playoffs. Dennis Johnson fit in with the team without compromising his special talents. He was a strong off-guard with the inside ability of a forward but the ballhandling skills of a playmaker. Maxwell, Parish and McHale continued to give us productive stable minutes in the frontcourt, and Danny Ainge, Scott Wedman and Quinn Buckner all helped us win. The critical characteristic of that year, however, was that we all played a role in leading that team to victory. Relieved to be able to get on again with the business of playing, we allowed for individual differences and contributed to the common goal. K. C. has often said that he never felt more pressure as a man that season; he felt he *had* to win to satisfy Red Auerbach, the critics in the press and the critics in the inner circles whom he had perceived as preventing him from being a head coach. For another time in my playing career, distractions were minimized, and I focused all my efforts on winning a league championship.

That year came down to the great championship series against the Lakers. They defeated us in the first game at the Garden, and behind Johnson and Abdul-Jabbar they seemed to have us in the second game as well. But Gerald Henderson saved us; he stole a James Worthy cross-court pass and sent the game into overtime with a flying layup. That solitary act changed fate. Aroused, we won when Wedman hit a jumper from the left baseline. Defeated, Pat Riley presided over an absolutely stunned, despondent Lakers locker room. When we regained our composure and won in overtime in Game 4 at the Forum, 129-125, on a Bird jumper, we captured control of the series. Leading by that Bird basket, we clinched the game when I stole a Jamaal Wilkes pass and dunked. We had beaten the Lakers on their own floor. Two more victories and we would be riding in the parade.

But it wasn't easy, or uneventful. After Larry shot fifteen for twenty and dominated in ninety-seven-degree heat to lead us to a 121-103 win in Game 5, they got it back in L. A. by rallying from an 82-73 deficit to sweep us away behind Abdul-Jabbar. As we walked out of the gym, a fan threw beer down into my face, temporarily blinding me. I thought initially I would be out for the final game, but only for an instant. My attitude was, "Forget that, boys. Now there's a seventh game, and let's see who's better." The rest of the players thought the same way. And I found out later the coaches were scheming, too; they met immediately after the game at the Airport Marriott and decided I would be the first player off the bench. Glad to do it. K. C. called me early the afternoon of the finale, and I told him I'd be ready.

There is nothing quite like the seventh game of a championship series. Over the years seventh games have given fans their most dramatic moments. They have contributed to the popularity of American sports as staged entertainment. Suspense, conflict, joy, despair and reconciliation with one's fate draw the audience into the drama. Our series with the Lakers culminated in one of the best seventh games ever played. It was an extremely important win for both franchises: the Lakers hadn't beaten the Celtics since the teams began meeting for championships twenty-five years before; we desperately wanted to capture the second championship of our era. The first one can be lucky, the achievement of a team on a roll, unified by the emotion of its quest. The Golden State Warriors won a title like that in 1975 over K. C.'s Washington Bullets. But they never came back again. Second championships mean considerably more:

you've endured, you've proven yourself again, you've stared your competitor in the eye and triumphed. Often that competitor is your own gaze in the mirror.

I'm an emotional player, driven to my best effort by feeling. All that day I turned my career over and over in my mind, reliving the years at every level, looking at myself as if in a movie. I had worked myself up significantly by game time. I thought it time for some bona fide intimidation. I took my gear and told Wayne LeBeaux, our equipment manager, to tell me when the Lakers' bus arrived at the Garden. When they began walking in, I taunted them in the hallway, "You haven't a chance, Worthy," I screamed at their young player who had taunted Kevin McHale earlier in the series after McHale had dropped Kurt Rambis on a breakaway.

"You guys aren't leaving here alive," I continued. "There is no way you're beating us in the Garden, one game to take it all.

"There is no way." I continued, lifting my voice a level higher, the better to echo through the hall, trailing them as they disappeared into their dressing room.

Meanwhile, in our room we were reasonably loose. I walked up to the white board in the front of the room, where Jimmy Rodgers, our assistant coach, drew up the scouting reports, and wrote *Champs!* We were tense, sure, but we were prepared to hustle our tails off and take the game to them defensively. My approach as the first substitute was actual and symbolic; I planned to run and intimidate. I wore goggles to protect my still-aching eye (and to taunt Kareem).

It was a great game. We trailed early but rallied throughout the middle stages behind Maxwell, Parish and Bird. When the game became tense late, DJ and Parish made huge steals to seal it. We led, 91-77, before they made a final push (I suspected they would). But we did indeed win the most cherished championship. Maxwell had advised us to climb on his back, and he did carry us through. We hit foul shots—one after the other as the game wound down. When the Garden crowd overflowed, I felt I was part of something fun, but at the same time, something profoundly meaningful.

Of all the teams I played with in Boston, the 1984 championship team is my personal favorite. There will never be a team that had more fun, never a team that could talk as much junk as we did. We were a media delight. We talked about other players, coaches and teams; we made predictions; we won. One ignorant Philadelphia writer labeled us thugs. We were called the L.A. Raiders in short pants. They defiled our system, a direct knock on the greatest basketball mind ever, Red Auerbach. But though we were called cocky, dirty and many other things, when the season was over, everyone called us champions.

Chapter 12

The World Champions: Some Portraits

The best thing to do when the pressure is on is to relax, avoid panic and concentrate on the task at hand. The Celtics always played well under pressure. We were able to be serious when the game was going on within that ninety-four-by-fifty playing space, but before and after business, we were able to enjoy ourselves and enjoy each other. So when I think back to those championship teams, as much as I remember the unity and teamwork, I also remember the individuals, the way the Celtics' structure allowed for both the total team concept and individual expression, both on and off the court.

We were always kidding around. We'd ride each other when we went through stretching before practice. Kevin would be wandering around talking junk, a diversion from the serious business at hand. He and Max paired off in scrimmages with a covert agreement between them: not too much running around; not too much physical stuff underneath. They'd post each other up at either end of the floor, play loose and relaxed, and then repeat the waltz at the other end. We each approached practice differently, but we all worked very hard to prepare ourselves for the next ballgame. Guys like Larry, Tiny, Robert, Rick Carlisle and Greg Kite took practice very seriously. Henderson was very serious as well because he was climbing the hill, trying to win acceptance as a bona fide NBA player. Bill Fitch helped Gerald become a better point guard by constantly talking to him about his game. Tiny and Larry wanted to be on the practice floor all the time, so we'd almost have to force them to sit down during scrimmages. When Dennis Johnson arrived, he approached practice as the occasion demanded. If the team was really struggling, DJ would take charge with supreme concentration. Otherwise he was content to stay with the flow. But in spite of individual differences, collectively we always had a winning professional rhythm about the game. Every game was meaningful, so we'd concentrate, and there'd be no problem about it. But on a sunny Saturday morning in mid-

January—well, we'd discuss any and all topics. Nobody and nothing was sacred.

We'd approach playoff tension with a calm attitude. Once we were involved in a playoff game against Philadelphia at the Spectrum, where the Celtics always find winning hard. The Sixers are like any great team— they protect their home turf. Maxwell was at the foul line late in the game, and as soon as the referee gave him the ball, Larry yelled out from his position under the basket, "Max, you'll probably choke and miss both of them!" This was a key point in a playoff game! The Sixers probably thought there was bad blood between Larry and Max, but in actuality they are both true professionals, with tremendous respect for each other's ability during crunch time. In the Celtics' language, Larry was telling Max to forget the pressure, concentrate and stick those two freebies. As Robert Parish always says, Maxwell "shot those about as soft as a baby's rear end." Swish, all net, and the Celtics went ahead by one. Eat your heart out Sixers fans.

On and off the court, at home and on the road, we kept our sense of humor. I was standing at the American Airlines sky-cap station at Logan Airport when an older gentleman asked me to get his bags out of his station wagon when I was finished with the ones I was checking. Fortunately for this guy, I was in my usual ebullient mood, having a good time. But the unfortunate part of this incident was that my teammates learned of the request. A member of a professional team endures many things, and one of the most stringent is the cutting edge of his teammates' jocular abuse. For the duration of the West Coast trip, every time something had to be moved—the balls, the water cooler, even my teammates' bags, I, now known as "Sky Cap," was summoned. The summons was accompanied by laughter and a five- or ten-dollar bill. Maxwell would never let this end; that is, until we reached Denver, when our trip had reached its end and Maxwell ran into his own unfortunate incident.

McHale, Ainge, Maxwell and I went to the movies the night before we were to play the Nuggets; on our team we often did things together off the court. As we entered the theater, Max and I decided we didn't want popcorn, so we stood near the ticket collector while Ainge and McHale went to buy refreshments. As we stood waiting, a nice couple came by and offered their tickets to Max, obviously expecting him to take their tickets, tear them in half and return the stubs. Maxwell was stunned. First, he was crushed because he hadn't been recognized as a starting forward for the world champion Boston Celtics. But more importantly, I had a perfect angle on the whole episode, and Max knew

I would never let him hear the end of it. I laughed throughout the whole movie—and it wasn't a comedy. Even when the hero was killed I was in stitches. I still don't know what the film was about.

During a timeout the following night, I offered my man a cup of water and said, "Could you take this, sir?" Maxwell could only laugh.

So as great as those championship units were, my mind often goes back to the individuals, the men with whom I shared so much on the road to victory. We were quite a group—and here are some personal thoughts on the key figures of those championship teams:

Cedric Maxwell. I was never prouder of a teammate than I was of Cedric Maxwell in the seventh game of the 1984 championship finals against the Lakers. In Boston, the story is well known, but it bears repeating. We had just returned home the previous day after squandering a commanding nine-point lead down the stretch to lose Game 6. The series was down to a one-game, winner-take-all situation. We were confident, but in contest this tight, you never know. But Maxwell assumed control. After K. C. Jones had spoken to the team in our pregame meeting, the guys were sitting around the locker room, adrenalin flowing. Suddenly, Maxwell stood up—his locker was in the center of the rows of lockers—and looked at all of us.

"Well, boys, climb on my back," he declared, "I'm taking us all the way to the throne room."

He went out and backed up his talk with actions. Totally dominant, he scored twenty-four points and had fourteen rebounds. But as in many instances, those stats only point the way. Maxwell saved the championship for us that night with his positive approach and firm sense of purpose. All of us followed him. All of us climbed on his back.

Maxwell possessed a rare blend of comedy, camaraderie, instinct and intellect. He understood the game, and he had a unique insight into the players and coaches on the ballclub. We were not always a communal bunch, even though we resolved our differences once we went out on the basketball court. But Max had the knack of bringing us together, of coming up with just the right comment to loosen up when there was tension.

Early in my first season with the team, I had planned to meet my brother John, my agent Norm Blass and other friends at Charley O's, a restaurant located beneath Madison Square Garden in New York. But according to a team rule, the players had to take the team bus back to the hotel as a group. Then we would be free to dine or socialize on an individual basis. I thought the policy was absurd, and I began walking up and down the bus aisle, complaining loudly.

"I'm twenty-nine years old," I said. "Why should I have to take a bus across the city and then come back when my plans were to take place right here? Okay. But I will never do anything for this ballclub except bounce the basketball. Don't expect anything extra from me. Because I won't do it."

I stormed into my seat. At the front, Bill Fitch, Red Auerbach and the owner at that time, Harry Mangurian, sat, taking it all in. That was the point, but I kept repeating my basic theme until the message started to get a little tired. It was at that point Maxwell caught my eye, and I gave up pontificating. Instantly, Maxwell was on his feet.

"*I will never do anything for this ballclub,*" he mocked me, with the team his audience. "*This is ridiculous. I am a grown man.*"

By this time, the bus was cracking up in laughter, roaring away the discord such a protest might have had. The rich sense of humor that was background music throughout my career with the Celtics was often conducted by Maxwell in precisely this way. He understood that we needed to poke fun at the structure, regardless of how rigid it was. And his timing was always perfect.

I hated to see Maxwell traded from the Celtics. He made sacrifices to make our team champions, and when the games were on the line, he didn't back down. I remember going to his wedding, when he married Renee Sparrow in 1984. It was after we had defeated the Lakers, and Max had starred in that series. I remember how tall and proud he stood that day, a champion marrying a wonderful woman.

But like that ocean I often thought of in my youth, what was calm and placid one day could be the center of a storm the next. Max held out in the preseason the following year and never played as well for the Celtics. It was a tough call because he also had arthroscopic surgery on his knee in February. He didn't return to the team until early April, and by that time Kevin McHale had become an institution in our low-post offense. It was difficult for Max to begin coming off the bench. He was still young enough to be a starter and wasn't prepared to come off the pine so willingly. And there were some reports that Red was upset because Max didn't, in Red's eyes, work hard enough on rehabilitation. Johnny Most, our broadcaster, said that once Red becomes upset over something like that he doesn't forgive easily.

Sometimes trades are the best thing for everybody. The longer the falling out lasted into the summer after the 1984-1985 season, the more difficult it was to reconcile differences. So Max went to San Diego for Bill Walton, who came to the Celtics and played extremely well. Max continues to be a productive player in the league. I joke with him often. He thought when he went out to California that he would be going out to a camp-like atmosphere. Then the Clippers traded him to Houston, where he teamed up again with Bill Fitch. I tell him now that he's with Houston he's not going to summer camp. He's in boot camp.

Nate "Tiny" Archibald. When I tried out with the Kansas City Kings in 1974, and Tiny and I played those full-court games against each other after two-a-day practices, I was in the best shape of my life. For Tiny it was merely another day of playing ball. This is important to note. Of all the players I know, Tiny stands out as the one most dedicated out of pure love for the game. He played every day until his career ended. You don't see that commitment in many veteran players. Most players wear out, lose that youthful zeal. But Tiny played on.

Later, of course, we became teammates in Boston, and after Bill Fitch and Red Auerbach gave him a vote of confidence in 1979, he had a couple of beautiful years here. Tiny was small but tough. He played every day, but he had to fight back from a few devastating injuries, including a broken foot and a torn Achilles' tendon, to resurrect his career. Until Fitch and Larry Bird arrived in 1979, Tiny had wanted to be traded. But he came to symbolize the heart of our first championship team.

Tiny was an exceptionally exact player, accurate, elegant and fundamentally sound. Our first championship team was constructed with the idea that we would wear the other team down in a half-court execution game, and Tiny Archibald was our general on the floor. He had the total confidence of his teammates. He would always produce something for you in that scheme, by making the right pass, spreading the ball around, penetrating, hitting that lefty jumper.

Tiny was the best ever at creating points in the set offense. He took a direct path to the basket, and since defenders, unable to stop him alone, needed help from their teammates, Tiny was in the perfect position to utilize his passing skills by dishing off to the open man. And he loved to run, too; if we had an opportunity to get fast break points, Tiny would convert.

We played better with Tiny out there because he always kept us on our toes. Don Chaney said he was the toughest player he had ever had to guard because he always kept defenders back on their heels. If he wasn't going by you, he was beating you in the postup game. He was an amazing player. He could do so much so well.

He retired in 1985 after being cut by the Celtics before the 1983-1984 season. He ended up in Milwaukee because Don Nelson knew what people on the inside knew. Tiny's skills didn't leave him, and I'm convinced he could be playing until he's forty. His understanding of the game simply raised him to a higher level of play as he got older, like Julius Erving.

His emotions were sometimes difficult to read. To me, he could keep his feelings under control as well as anyone. You couldn't tell if you teed him off because he'd always wear the same face. But the truth was we believed in him, so any anger or frustration he might have gone through late in his Boston career was taken in stride. He had trouble at the end of his time with the Celtics because he loved to play so much that he couldn't cope very well with reduced playing time. With the nucleus of that first championship team breaking down, there wasn't enough communication, and Tiny retreated into himself, becoming subdued and probably angry. But the Tiny I'll remember is the quick, speedy guard so expert at breaking the press. Using the ball as bait, he would jiggle his hips and fly down the court.

As we were winning Game 6 of the 1981 Eastern Conference finals in Philadelphia, our first win at the Spectrum in over two seasons, we had possession as time was running out. Ahead by two with the ball and one second left, we had the game. I inbounded the ball to Tiny, who was standing twenty-five feet away from the basket directly in front of our bench. As the horn sounded he swept a hook shot up from that distance. The ball went straight through the hoop, all net. He stood there and it all came together for him. It was the pinnacle. Someone that everybody had written off was leading us to his first NBA title.

Dave Cowens and Chris Ford. Dave Cowens and Chris Ford were two veterans who provided our 1979-1980 team with a sense of purpose. Dave was coming off a couple of years of injuries and a year of coaching a very bad Celtics team, the team owned by John Y. Brown. But he had seen championship years with the Celtics in the seventies. Despite fighting injuries that year he was nevertheless responsible in a lot of ways for transforming us into a winner. Ford, on the other hand, had played for years in the aimlessness of Detroit. When the Celtics jelled that year, Ford was like a coach on the floor. What he lacked in talent he compensated for with experience and court awareness. Chris would be sitting on the bench and Tiny would have the ball: it would be almost as if Chris were inside Tiny's mind, helping that great playmaker see situations developing. Chris would call out, "Tiny, one-on-one!" and "T" would zip by his defender. Chris and Tiny were that much in synch. They had that much trust on the court.

Ford was a master of reading offenses and defenses, and he had an uncanny sense of the pace of a game. He knew when to press the offense or when to back off. When the three-point rule was implemented before the 1979-1980 season, Ford was one of the first experts. He immediately mastered spacing on the floor. He'd hide off in the corner, beyond the line, and wait as Tiny penetrated the defense. Tiny always knew where Chris was, so without having to look he would toss the ball over to Chris, who was deadly with that shoot. But Ford also used his expertise to draw the defense to him; using a head-and-shoulders fake, he'd shed himself of a defender jumping out at him. Then we'd have the defense totally out of position (particularly after Tiny had created the initial advantage). This quick exchange was extremely important when we were utilizing a half-court offense under Bill Fitch. Because he apparently lacked outstanding talent, people would ask, why is Chris Ford in the league? But he played a thinking game. He stayed within his limitations, knew his role and did the things we needed him to do in order to win, night after night. A team could depend on him. That internal coherence was absolutely vital to the team's success. Chris Ford is a winner.

Ford had a difficult time leaving the game as an active player. He was injured during the second half of the 1981-1982 season, and he never really returned to his former role. And it was hard on him. Chris had to battle every year, for a position, for playing time, and when he had his playing time decreased in order to start getting younger players like Danny Ainge and Gerald Henderson more time, he'd verbalize his anger. I would've been disappointed if he hadn't because it was a facet of his professionalism. He was an emotional player. One of the hardest things for an athlete to recognize is the time to go. We deal with it in different ways.

Dave Cowens was also an athlete driven by emotion. Dave never walked on a basketball court. Arguably he was the fiercest competitor ever to play the game. Cowens was often spotlighted for his trademark play: diving after loose balls. Some guys did this when there was four seconds left in a close game. But Dave did this four seconds into the game! That was how he established himself emotionally and physically from the moment the game tapped off. He wouldn't move around a pick, he'd run through an opponent setting it. And Dave went *after* rebounds: if the ball was falling off on the side of the rim opposite him, Dave would fly laterally to claim that territory as his. When he'd switch out on a guard, he'd get down in a stance that intimidated the smaller, quicker player. And Dave was quick, often quicker than those guards he switched to.

Like Ford, Cowens grappled mightily with retirement. He ended up that comeback season playing at 75 percent of his physical abilities, and in training camp the following autumn, despite Bill Fitch's continuous praise, Dave had decided he couldn't play anymore. He told the team when we were in Indiana, getting ready to take drive to a preseason game. Fitch and Cowens had remained in the hotel lobby for a long while, talking. When the two of them finally appeared, Cowens talked to us, standing at the front of the bus. He said he was really sorry, but he wouldn't be playing for us. He wished us the best of luck. He said he felt he could continue to contribute to a certain degree, but not anything acceptable to his standards. He felt that it was in the best interests of his family that he retire. He concluded by saying that all of us would reach a point sometime in our careers when we would have to choose whether to go on or retire. Continue or quit. At that moment the bus became quiet, the guys' thoughts filling the silent space. We realized that this was Dave Cowens, a player we had emulated in college and respected as a teammate. He had given everything on the floor. We were getting emotional.

I spoke up: "If that's all you have to say, then get off the bus." We laughed as a team.

I said that because it was a tough moment for Dave, for the players and for the coaching staff. It was a way of saying that we had heard what he said: that we'd go forth as a team, but that he had helped us realize that the glamor of the game is short-lived, and that of all the invaluable moments we had received from him this perhaps was one of the most important.

Dave and Chris taught me a lot about the aging process in athletics, physically and mentally. When I approached my own retirement I remembered their stories. Retirement is tricky. If you're not sensitive, the competitive spirit will tell you, *one more time.* It's a cruel joke because so many times you don't have what was formerly, preciously yours. As an athlete, you're programed to go on, to fight. Your instincts tell you that you can rise above insurmountable odds to make the grade and beat the best players or fighters in the world. Toward the end you're clawing, scrtching and fighting just to stay competitive, to savor the roar of the crowd. Yet even a man of the magnitude, grace and accomplishment of Muhammad Ali reached the end. I admire Ali's talent as an athlete and the things he did to help people. He was the most famous man in the world at the height of his power. But he is human. His skills began to deteriorate; he aged. He climbed into the ring for those last fights against Holmes and Berbick trying to grasp the sands of time slipping through his fingers. Having taken it too far, he's left with mixed memories and injury. We're left juggling the images of a magnificent champion and world spokesman with that of a man literally on the ropes.

Still, I say Ali's a true champion. He stood up for his beliefs and still won his cherished athletic prize. He was a true symbol of fire, fight and dedication. Standing up against overwhelming odds, he fought his battles and won.

The fact is, the competitive spirit can lie to you, and there's a time when you must walk away from it. But then you see someone like Kareem Abdul-Jabbar, one of the most amazing athletes I've ever seen, playing into his forties, driven to excel and place his records far beyond any player dreaming of approaching him. He made you wonder, as he must have made Dave Cowens wonder when Dave attempted his comeback in the 1982-1983 season with the Milwaukee Bucks. He saved a game against us that year in the Garden by leaping over a press table to keep possession for his team. But later he tore up his knee in Atlanta and his body refused to permit him to re-enter the gym. Dave couldn't hunt guards with the efficiency of twelve years earlier.

A player must prepare for the end of his career, even when he's starting out—that's why Dave's message was so important that afternoon in Indiana.

Robert Parish. I think one of the gravest errors we and the media have made over the past seven years has been overlooking the contribution of the Chief, Robert Parish. His impact on the team was underestimated for many seasons, and he was often criticized during the playoffs, a ridiculous criticism. The man comes to play every night. You can talk all you want about spokes of the wheel—the Chief is the hub. Day in and day out he works at an exceptionally high level.

I don't think anyone is happier to be in Boston than Robert Parish. For years he's felt that he was a scapegoat in a very bad situtation on the Golden State Warriors. He played hard in Oakland, but until he was traded to Boston he hadn't received any concentrated coaching at the center position. Most of the attention there was going to people like Rick Barry, Phil Smith and John Lucas. As they continued to lose Robert just became exasperated. Chief has worked hard since he's been in Boston; his attitude has been: They've made me a better player, and I think I've helped make them a better team.

Publicity has never mattered to Robert. He said once, "I think there's a class of centers in the league: Kareem Abdul-Jabbar, Moses Malone, Akeem Olajuwon, Jack Sikma, Artis Gilmore, Bill Walton and me. Pick any one, his team should win. The key to my effectiveness with the Celtics is that I'm willing to play a complementary role. All I care about is winning. I'm not so sure those others would come in here and play a role."

Like Tiny Archibald, the tough part about Robert is that he comes across as a person who is difficult to get to know because of his apparently glowering facial expression on the court. Like a mask, it creates distance. But it is misleading; Robert's personality off the court is one of an ideal teammate. He keeps the team loose. He's able to rescue a teammate who might be down on his game by being supportive. He does laugh, and he has the developed self-confidence of a man who's made it—professionally and financially. Occasionally he's impatient, but it is not easy being seven-feet and having to interact in public. Too many times we basketball players are subjected to comments regarding our height. People often ask me if I'm a basketball player, and I tell them, "Nah. I'm the governor." Or, "No, I am the chairman of the board at IBM." We are forced to deal with this taxing situation all the time. Over the years Chief has been in Boston, however, he's placed himself beside Bill Russell and Dave Cowens as one of *the* centers of the Celtics. His name will be talked of in the same breath.

Kevin McHale. I have to laugh a little bit about Kevin; I can never think of him without thinking of the famous incident that took place in the heart of the 1984 championship series. Kevin hadn't been playing well, altering the balance of our team then. He had won Sixth Man of the Year honors and we needed something from him. We got something, all right, but not what you would have expected from Kevin. And I had a part in the affair.

We were losing big in Game 3 of that series, with the Lakers storming by us with the intensity of a hurricane. All through the misery of the third and fourth quarters, I was watching alongside a younger, more impressionable McHale, and I kept saying after every basket: "Kevin, we have to slow them down and take them out physically if necessary. I'm telling you…" I couldn't *believe* how well he listened. In Game 4 (both Games 3 and 4 were played in Los Angeles), L.A. went ahead, but we were starting to catch them. Then came the turning point: Kurt Rambis went flying in on the transition and Kevin raced down the sidelines and caught up. Grabbing Rambis by the jersey while Kurt was in full flight, McHale ripped him to the floor. Big John Studds (a Celtic fan and a professional wrestler) couldn't have put a better body slam on a man. Well, Rambis got up, and he was exploding, ready to kill. Players started milling around. Kareem Abdul-Jabbar and Larry Bird nearly fought, that's how intense it became. Most observers looked at that play as the one that turned the series around. We had finally asserted ourselves, and we wouldn't be trampled.

But during the excitement generated by Rambis's fall, I looked over at Kevin. The man was completely shellshocked. He was looking at his arms and then looking around, his eyes glazed. He couldn't believe he had just done that! I laughed and laughed.

The following season McHale became one of the best players in the game. No longer tentative under pressure, he played so effectively through the final half of the 1984–1985 season the team had to sit Maxwell down when Max came back from arthroscopic surgery. McHale's post-up game had formerly consisted of position; he added slipping, sliding and darting moves. His jump hook was sensational and his shot-blocking skills made him a tough defensive player. McHale added something invaluable to the Celtics later in his career—an arrogance toward his opponents. He believed absolutely in his ability to score in the post. That confidence helped the Celtics. Knowing you have a player who has that ego-strength helps the group stay mentally tough.

Dennis Johnson. I am a Dennis Johnson fan. When I heard that we had landed Dennis in a trade in 1983, I was certain that we were going to go a long way in the playoffs. The man is tough and he loves to play the game. Before DJ came to the Celtics, I used to hear him described as someone who acted up. But when I was with him on an NBA Player Association trip, he was always having a lot of fun. When we were taking photographs, DJ was popping up in every one, smiling, laughing. His enthusiasm made the trip enjoyable for everyone. I liked him. Now, since Dennis and his wife Donna have been in Boston, Sylvia and I see them regularly, and I consider Dennis a true friend.

There is no way an opponent can press Dennis Johnson. Against hard defense in the backcourt, DJ rhythmically dribbles four times to one side, four times to the other, back and forth as he eases the ball into the frontcourt. I always found him to be one of my toughest opponents. Larry Bird, the team leader, called Dennis Johnson the best player he's ever played with, and that's saying a lot. DJ has made himself into a total player; he was always known as a physical, defensive guard who would accept the challenge of stopping the best offensive players in the league. He was also an excellent offensive player, but what caused him problems was his occasional inability to be the central focus of an offense. He played exceptionally well with Gus Williams and Fred Brown in Seattle, but often he would be sitting in the final moments of a game. In Phoenix he had problems because their system was set up to provide players with relatively equal minutes. In Boston, though, Dennis found the right place at the right time. He assumed the leadership role and gradually became the point guard.

Dennis did have a misunderstanding with K. C. Jones in his first year at Boston, but even that momentary disruption worked out well for the team and for DJ. Dennis apologized in front of the team. He declared firmly that he would not be a problem for the team or for K. C. He was here to win championships, not shouting matches. He was doing something else for the team, too. He was telling K. C. he respected him as a coach—and that he respected the team. I think that this set of circumstances helped Dennis greatly. He has been a key player in two championships in Boston, numbers two and three of his career.

Quinn Buckner. When Quinn was traded to us before the 1982-1983 season, there was a lot of insecurity about playing time among some of us (Quinn was the player we obtained through compensation when the Bucks signed Cowens). Quinn was the point guard of a championship-caliber team in Milwaukee, a strong ego, a powerful personality. We were strong ourselves, and we had players of comparable ability at the point guard position, including Tiny Archibald and Gerald Henderson. We also had Danny Ainge, an up-and-coming player who was beginning to prove he could shoot a basketball even better than he could hit a baseball. The result was we had too many quarterbacks and some problems. How would there ever be enough playing time to satisfy everybody? Our team struggled some that season; there was never a problem between the guys, but we all wanted to play. We tried to shuffle everybody in and out, but there wasn't any continuity.

But I always respected Quinn Buckner and what he brought to a team. There's a psychological barrier that a player has to deal with when he's traded. As a professional you accept it as part of the business, but you do have a feeling of being unwanted. Your team is moving somebody else into your slot and moving you out. But Quinn was a student of the game. He saw the game not only as he played it, but in its totality. That approach helped him deal with Boston. He didn't have it easy; he had to be asking on the way here: Will I be accepted? Will the others be comfortable? Quinn had been a bona fide player with the Bucks, in many ways the heart of their team. Ironically, on the floor things never went well for Quinn here. He struggled with a lack of playing time, and his skills were never showcased in Boston as well as they were in Milwaukee.

Quinn helped us tremendously when he stayed within his role, however. There were few better at hawking the ball defensively than Quinn. He was a master at being able to do two things simultaneously on defense: he was an excellent position player one-on-one, but he was so instinctively sound that he could jump-switch into the passing lanes to help make the steal. Quinn sometimes forgot the things that made him a top player in Milwaukee because he was trying so hard to have an impact here. As a shooter, sometimes he'd get the feeling that the shot was there—the feeling was right—but it wasn't going in the basket. All it was was a feeling. But Quinn was a winner as a team player, which is why Boston ended up with him. I think he has real coaching potential: his leadership abilities are definitely there—he is a success in business as part-owner of a software company, the Denver Group, and he is also sitting in as a member of the Executive Board of the NBA Players' Association. He has a grasp of the big picture and he has the ability to communicate it.

Quinn weathered his inconsistencies as a player in Boston. He was often the target of good-natured abuse from the guys, but Quinn took it in the interest of camaraderie. As we all took it. In the 1985 playoffs against Detroit, we were behind by three points with four seconds left. I hadn't played to that moment in the game, but I implored K. C. to let me go in anyway. I can shoot those threes, I told Case. So the guys supported me and K. C. put me in. Larry threw the ball to me in the corner and I fired up. I was envisioning this shot tying the game when, rudely, my romance with the ball's arc was shattered by a referee's whistle. I had been standing out of bounds when I caught the ball. I was the target, then. Quinn would never let me forget it.

Larry Bird. I used to say to Larry that he should be a golfer, a swimmer or a tennis player. Larry expects everybody to give what he does to the game, to have the work ethic he has. It's unrealistic; in a team sport, some players will be laid back, some will be gung-ho. Everybody has to approach the game in a way that will help him to play his best in one game and over the course of a season that may last a hundred games. Larry would love to have everybody the way he is.

The importance of Larry Bird to our team rests in intangibles. The man is a super talent, and he works and works at the game. Through practice, he has become an excellent shooter. If there's a critical rebound to take in, 80 to 90 percent of the time, Larry will get it for the team. When the pressure is on in a tight ballgame, Larry is able to concentrate harder and deeper, and he gets the job done against players who are fantastic athletes.

The NBA is made up of great basketball players, and Bird is one of the greatest ever. My first year in Boston was also Larry's first season in the league. We were both at Red Auerbach's rookie camp on Cape Cod, and I came away from that camp totally impressed with the man. As a rookie, he had complete confidence in his game; he wasn't fearful to try and create the play. He was throwing behind-the-back passes and over-the-shoulder flips. He was joking with the guys like a ten-year veteran. I'd tease Larry about his body. I'd say that if Larry and the proverbial turtle had a race, the turtle would beat him down the court. But Larry refuses to yield to nature's limitations. He beats the opponent down the floor because he runs hard every time. Larry doesn't pace himself. He has a threshold of pain equal to a John Wayne hero. He gets offended with his body when he's forced to miss games. For example, during the 1986-1987 season, Bird was angry because he missed eight games. So he undertook an extensive running/stretching/weightlifting program so he could play eighty-two games the following year. He always wants to be prepared. I remember sitting in the training room while Larry was getting ready to undergo a minor surgical procedure by Dr. Tom Silva, the Celtics' team doctor. It was classic Larry; he was sitting on the trainer's table with a beer in one hand, waiting. Doctor Silva was straining to get enough light, so Larry grabbed a small lamp and held it for the doctor to make the incision! Minor surgery, but surgery nevertheless. Cedric Maxwell or Kevin McHale would have been hiding under the table!

Gerald Henderson. Gerald fought a lot of odds to move his way up the ladder in the league. He has nice physical skills, and he works very hard on conditioning. Henderson worked incessantly with jump ropes and wind sprints as a younger player. Later he was always the last player to leave practice.

The pressure on him early on was tough. In the seventh game of the Eastern Conference final series against Philadelphia in 1981, our first championship season, I took down what appeared to be a clinching rebound in the final seconds. The crowd was shouting, and people were beginning to storm the sidelines at the Boston Garden. We were ahead by one point. Then Maurice Cheeks knocked the ball away from Henderson from behind, and we had to call timeout. Henderson was a young player, and he went over to Bill Fitch. In exasperation he said, "Take me out." There was a pause around the bench, and Maxwell and I said, "Shoot, *we'll* take you out, Henny!" In the early years he was almost overpowered by pressure. He hadn't accepted the fact that you can make a few mistakes. In time, he found a comfort zone. And he developed an instinct to make things happen. By the time of the 1984 championship opportunity, Henderson was the man who had the confidence to make the key steal. He saved Game 2 of the series and sent that key game into overtime, which we won.

Henny's career in Boston came to a rather abrupt end, the result of an angry holdout during training camp the following season. On the crest of bad public relations created over the bargaining, Boston traded Henderson to the Seattle SuperSonics for the Sonics' first choice in the

1986 draft. When I first looked at the deal, I was hurt. Gerald is my friend. As players, we're taught to care about one another. I have always felt that way about a teammate. But I didn't really think about the whole picture.

The Celtics traded a player who had come into the league as an older rookie. He was in his prime and at the peak of his market value. Teams need to build for the future, and the Celtics had an opportunity, as it turned out, to draft the best player in the draft. Tragically, Len Bias never made it to camp.

But the other question is, was it a bad move to break up a championship team, as we were in 1983-1984? Possibly, since we didn't repeat, and we could have used Gerry. But there were signals that the winning combination was breaking up anyway. Gerry and Maxwell had come in late, things weren't the same, and there was a feeling of increased pressure to play Danny Ainge. They were paying him a substantial salary, and there was a need to find out about him. Ainge had played exceptionally well over that summer.

We learned of the trade in Houston, and Henderson came down to my hotel room, crushed. "I've just been traded, M. L." He was quiet.

"Gerald, what are you going to do now?" I asked him. "You have to develop a game plan. The deal won't be changed. You have to make the best of it. Zero in on the nice things about the Celtics and the fans as having been a great opportunity, but don't take the Celtics to Seattle. Take the benefits of the experience to Seattle and go out and be the best SuperSonic you can be. Be open to this new challenge. You loved the Celtics, but that's over. Get Seattle back on track, be public, get involved. At the press conference be sure it's the right introduction of you to the Seattle community. Put everything behind you."

When a player is traded from the Celtics, it seems to me he has to shake that commitment out of himself. With Gerald Henderson, as with Cedric Maxwell, anger colored the way he responded to the Celtics months after his trade. The Celtics made a nice gesture to Henderson when he returned to the Garden for the first time. Jan Volk presented Henderson his championship ring from the previous season, and the fans in the Garden gave him a standing ovation. The players responded similarly. Henny had become affectionately known as "The Sarge" in his last season with us, a tribute to the angry tenaciousness of his game. When he went out to receive his ring from Jan, the players saluted him in military fashion. As Larry said to a reporter, when Henderson made the steal in the second game in the 1984 finals, "he saved us." Gerald played a great game against Boston that night, the steadying presence for the

SuperSonics as they defeated us. When it was through, and the players filed out jointly through the aisle at midcourt, Henderson took the ball from the referee and spiked it as hard as he could. He was making a statement with that gesture.

I think Gerald should have a respectable career in New York under Rick Pitino. He should benefit from the enthusiasm that Pitino will bring to that situation. He'll have an opportunity to use the experience that he has and build from there. No one was more dedicated to preparing for a game than Henderson.

Danny Ainge. When Danny Ainge came to the Celtics, he was greeted by the Big Chill. The guys were skeptical—he was coming in from playing pro baseball; he was a glamor player; he was going to be taking a player's job away. This was early in the 1981-1982 season, after Danny had finally freed himself from a contract with the Toronto Blue Jays. After he started playing, the guys began to ride him on poor shot selection. I believe this inauspicious start hurt Danny.

I always liked Danny. I viewed him as a sort of underdog, a guy who felt he needed to make a change and then followed through and did it. I was on the injured list at the time he arrived. When he was breaking into the lineup, before he was officially activated, I'd shoot with him at Hellenic College and then bring him over to my house to talk to him even though I knew my time would be cut. But I was in the minority. Even Bill Fitch was riding him pretty good. I went to Bill and said we should go easy on Danny, that Danny's mother had just died and he was having a hard time adjusting to the change from baseball. Bill said that maybe that was the problem, that maybe he'd been pampered all his life and become used to having the easy way. But Danny's sensitive. He's become a villain in a lot of arenas in the league. He brushes this off, but I think that being booed hurts him. What bothers me about Danny Ainge, I tell him, is that he was able to attract as much fan abuse in two years as it took me to get in seven.

In the beginning, when Danny was being compared to Pete Maravich and Jerry West, I pulled him aside and told him to look at those two. "Maravich and West didn't get to the Hall of Fame because they ignored their shooting opportunities. You have to shoot the ball!" Perhaps he was wary at first because he thought he would be taking opportunities away from other players if he shot more, but over time Danny grew on the guys and they accepted him. Three weeks after Danny joined the team, Maxwell finally offered him a friendly hand before a game. "Things are gonna be all right, Ainge!" Max said to Danny moments before the team was about to take the court for a game against Dallas. And they were.

Lately, Ainge has acquired the confidence to take charge of games. Now he shoots whenever he feels the opening. Now I tell him, "Hey man, you better learn that you have to keep the Chief happy. You better not pass over him. Get it in the middle and he'll get it back out."

Danny's reputation as a villain has been fostered because of his growing stature as a member of the Celtics and because he's thought of by some as a dirty player. I don't think Danny's a dirty player. He's an opportunistic player. John Havlicek was very much the same. If John was trailing a man on defense, he'd pull his jersey or hold his arm, but nobody ever heard that John was a dirty player. In rebounding action, John would step on an opponent's foot and then go get the ball. When the Celtics were running their fast break, John would hustle over to the wing and grab the defensive man's arm. Then he'd have the necessary one-step advantage.

Danny denies it, but he worries about reputations and about being booed. It's due to his always being in the middle, with his baby face and his growling. But that's him. I looked at it this way: let them boo me, and I'll stay happy about it. They'll remember me: when they go to the office in the morning, they'll all have sore throats. But I think Danny's fought through that. He's learned to make their booing an advantage to him. He's learned to use that negative as a positive and as a stimulus to play harder and better. He's booed now because he's good and because the Celtics are good. He's an embodiment of what the Celtics are: tough, tenacious, skillful and clever. He's a winner.

Pete Maravich. Pistol Pete Maravich played only three months with the Celtics in 1979-1980. His time in Boston was productive, however, for both sides. He shot us to the regular-season crown that year with twenty points in the fourth quarter of a late-season game against Washington. He was aging and aching by then, with bad knees. But he shed the weight of time that night. Pete capped the performance by hitting a thirty-foot jumper, a three-point field goal, in the final minute to save the title.

I badly wanted Pete to win a championship while he was in Boston. Guys play their whole careers searching for the ring. Peter had been the one who gave me my start in basketball, my dream. He had taken me aside at a summer camp at Campbell College and told me to work at the game because I had real potential. He was my first real hero in sports.

The climax of Pete's career was funny and sad. He quit during the Celtics' training camp before the 1980-1981 season, a camp in which he started off exceptionally well. But as the first week went by, he faltered. The day before he left, he said to me, "I don't need this abuse. I don't need the money. I want to have fun and enjoy the game." Training camp is a facet of the game in the shadows, an unglamorous part of the game that the fans don't see. An athlete gears up every muscle and bone for this workout and often becomes broken down, tired and sore, expecially if he is in the twilight of his career. You fight with your body physically and mentally. Worn down, you still have to concentrate on the plays, depending on muscles you haven't used all summer long.

I knew what Pete meant. Earlier that week I had come home from practice, and as I drove down the hill about a half-mile from my house, I started to cramp up. My entire lower body was lost, cut off from me. The car started out of control, so I dived down to the brake pedal and slammed it with my hand. I finally stopped the car ten feet from a tree.

One night during camp we had been running through an offensive series in an evening session. You become tired of doing the same drills, working out against the same guys, and you approach a breaking point. Fitch had turned his back, and I had reached that point, so I kicked the ball. It went rocketing all the way down the floor, smashing into a window, fortunately protected by wire mesh. When Fitch turned around, the first player he saw was Pistol. He cursed him up and down.

Pete didn't say anything. But a few days later he didn't turn up. We have a system of fines. If a player is one minute late, he gets fined five dollars; two minutes late, ten dollars, and so on. If you miss an entire practice, it tops off at $150. The morning Pete was late we began counting, joking, "Pete's late: five dollars!" Then, "Pete's late: ten dollars!" This continued until Pete had missed the entire practice. Then we realized: Pete's gone! Without a word, Maravich had left the game. No press conference, no fanfare. It was too bad.

The next time I saw Pete was at an old-timers' game in Denver.

Bill Fitch and K. C. Jones. When future experts assess this championship era of the Celtics, they will no doubt frequently compare the two very different coaches we had: Bill Fitch, who coached the team from 1979 to 1983, and K. C. Jones, who took the reins in 1983 and continues to guide the team through the late eighties.

Fitch was an excellent coach for a young team. No coach worked any harder; he drove us constantly. But as we grew and matured and gained experience, there was less need for his kind of policing. Some of us felt we were experienced enough to police ourselves. Athletes are temperamental; they are emotional. But he had to exercise control, and sometimes that need for control caused uncertainties and problems on the team. Maravich's attitude during the 1980-1981 training camp was an example of how a veteran athlete could become disgruntled under Fitch's eye.

I don't think Bill handled veterans very effectively. Bill is a much better coach for younger teams.

K. C. Jones, on the other hand, has a knack for leading veteran players. He gives players opportunities to excel within his more relaxed boundaries. But if you don't live well within it, K. C. will put you in a running drill and forget he told you there would be a limit to your running. He will let you know when he is upset.

K. C. has a wealth of knowledge about the game of basketball. The man knows how the game should be played, he knows how to put together a winning combination, and he refuses to allow his emotions to affect his desire to win. K. C. is a winner, and winners don't care what you say, they just keep winning.

K. C. Jones has won throughout his career. He won in the 1954 and 1955 NCAA championships; he won in the 1956 Olympic Games; he won eight championships as a player in the NBA; and he won the 1972 NBA championship as an assistant coach with the Los Angeles Lakers. He completed the cycle by winning two championships with the Celtics as head coach in 1984 and 1986. He waited for the head coaching position a long time after being fired too quickly from that same post in Washington.

One of the greatest statements of loyalty I ever heard in my playing career was in 1984, K. C.'s rookie season as coach. We were returning home from a Game 4 loss in Milwaukee, but still leading the series, three-one. The loss was particularly aggravating to K. C. He had practically gone to war with Darrall Garretson and Jess Kersey, the two referees of that fourth game. We couldn't get a call that entire game. On the plane, Larry Bird spoke out to the players sitting at the front of the plane. "C'mon you guys. Let's just win it all for Case." Somehow that sunk home in all of us. It was a heckuva statement from the lead player of the team, but it was the kind of loyalty K. C. could kindle in a player.

There were times when I had differences of opinion over game situations—with both coaches. But I remained silent. A successful concept demands that you do not question the coach during a game. On the battlefield, you don't disagree. You have to have faith. Afterwards, however, I always hoped I could bring my different opinion to the coach and have some input. I was more comfortable doing that with K. C. than with Bill. Perhaps I had reached an age where I was more capable of looking at the big picture, less emotionally involved with my own playing needs. But I just thought K. C. was a better listener. Many times I would be sitting on the bench, dying to be in the game. But I'd never question the coach's belief that he was doing what he could to win the game. I respected that. If you were called in for one minute, you did it. If you did not you were questioning his professional integrity.

When I was having tough times with Fitch, however, I violated that principle. He sent Henderson in to get me—and I shook my head. I was telling Gerald I wasn't coming out. The discord over things like playing time had put me in a bad frame of mind, and I regretted doing that because I was only adding to the discord on the team. It was wrong. The coach just doesn't have the time to worry about players asking questions about playing time during a game. He assumes (and is entitled to) faith in the system and his leadership. I never really apologized, but I'm apologizing now. I think that when you're right about something you stand up and fight. When you're wrong, you can't be a thickhead and refuse to admit it. It's a matter of respect: for the orderliness of the professional game and the way it's run.

K. C. doesn't always get the credit he's due. The system of selecting coaches for the honor of Coach of the Year has apparently become an award for the coach who improves his team the most. Don Nelson, who coached the Milwaukee Bucks through the 1986-1987 season, is a very good coach, and in 1982-1983 he was voted Coach of the Year for winning the Central Division championship with an injured veteran team. But overlooked that season was the superb job of Billy Cunningham, who masterminded the Philadelphia 76ers to the NBA championship, molding a diverse group of talents and personalities to win. That was the year Moses Malone had gone to the Sixers after signing a free-agent contract. Cunningham molded Malone with Julius Erving, Andrew Toney and Maurice Cheeks. Yet he didn't win the individual award.

K. C. is another coach who receives limited recognition in the voting; people assume he *should* win because he coaches the Celtics. In the past three years, for example, K. C. brought a team of injured players to the finals in 1985, won the title in 1986, and last season again led the Celtics into the final series, despite critical injuries to Kevin McHale and Bill Walton. The team refused to accept anything less than playing at their best, which reflects the commitment they felt to the coach, whose job is to lead the entire group to victory. Should K. C. be criticized for playing these injured players too many minutes? I don't believe so; if the player is in uniform and tells the coach he is able to play, then the coach's professional responsibility dictates he should play the man.

Pat Riley of the Lakers is another coach who is often overlooked in the balloting—another injustice. My rivalry with the Lakers never dimmed my respect for Riley as a coach. He is competitive, cunning and able to motivate his players. Like all excellent coaches, "good" is never good enough for him. He doesn't back down, and I have to assume that he got to where he is because of his competitiveness. Being the same way, I respect him. Many will think that since we exchanged angry verbal shots in the media that we're enemies. But in the championships, when everything is on the line, there will be fire.

Jimmy Rodgers. Jimmy Rodgers has been very productive since coming to Boston in 1980. As an assistant coach, he is very helpful to players. He works well with K. C. Jones and does a superb scouting report. The politics of coaching can be distressing; Jimmy Rodgers's name is always high on the list when candidates for head coaching jobs are reported. In recent seasons, Jimmy Rodgers has been a viable candidate for positions in Chicago, Phoenix, New Jersey and, most recently, New York. He has remained content to stay in Boston, at least until last season, when he apparently wanted to take the head coaching position in New York (he would have been paid with the top of the profession and commanded a team on the rise). But the Celtics demanded a first-round draft choice as compensation for Rodgers, and after some heated words on both sides, the offer to Boston's assistant was withdrawn.

I can only guess about the Celtics' strong demands. Apparently Boston felt that his contribution to the team is such that it dictates a substantial price. Rodgers is a winner, and the Celtics are comfortable with that. He's a no-nonsense type of man. The owners of the Celtics know that, and they know other teams know that. But it hurt Rodgers. Had his opportunity to achieve his cherished career passed him by? Regrets have to linger. Jimmy Rodgers's situation is the same as that of a player who's been traded. Coaches and players have to deal with the facts: if they're fired, traded, released or, as in Rodgers's case, blocked from advancement, they have to understand that there are negotiations and politics over which they have no control. But I think Jimmy is a true professional, and I don't think this will deter him.

I met Rodgers at the Celtics' rookie and free agent camp the summer after he had been passed over. He was still shaken by the turmoil. We had a long conversation after the night session had ended, and I told him that although he had been passed over, it wasn't the end of the world. We're friends; we could be frank. I told him he had to go out and continue to create opportunities, to continue to be part of a winning situation.

Jan Volk. Jan Volk became the Celtics' general manager in 1984 and immediately began working to insure that the Celtics would remain on top through the next decade when he helped make the Henderson trade to Seattle for that team's first-round draft choice. He learned the Celtics' system from the bottom up, participating in business, public relations, contract negotiations and legal counsel. Jan's job isn't an easy one; he follows in the footsteps of the greatest basketball mind in the history of the game, Red Auerbach. But Jan has real, tangible assets: he's brilliant, he's an incessant worker, and he's made himself into a student of the game.

I compare Jan's position with the corporate manager in business who puts on a final push to motivate his people when the fiscal year is ending and targeted goals have to be met. But Jan Volk's people are motivated this way every day, every game. He has helped to create team unity in the front office via his personality. If Red is a fiddler of the music of the emotions, able to play every note distinctly as he gets people to produce, Jan is working in a different era, when players are individual corporate entities as well as basketball players. He is a master of the business end of the game, but he hasn't ego needs when it comes to making basketball decisions in the coaches' province. I think he's universally respected for that. It's a form of strength, really.

Jan Volk is an important figure in the continuity of the Celtics. I asked him last year if he felt any pressure over not having his hand in the team recognized. He said that he doesn't need public recognition, that he doesn't feel that he has to prove himself to anyone. This is because he grew up in the Celtics' system, where achievement is rewarded internally by mutual respect and a type of brotherly love. The tradition of winning motivates him, not the money he's paid.

Organizationally, the team's corporate setting is an extension of team play on the court. There is a unity to the entire system created in part by the fact that everybody working in the upper levels of the Celtics' front office grew up in the system. Communication is quicker because it's likely that a particular problem will have been part of everybody's past organizational experience. Men like the director of marketing and communication, Tod Rosensweig, the vice president of sales, Stephen Riley, the director of sales, Duane Johnson, and the public relations director, Jeff Twiss, have all worked their way through the ranks. Red Auerbach remains a motivating force, and since he's away from Boston frequently now, the executive secretary, Mary Faherty, is invaluable as well. Mildred Duggan, the coaches' secretary, is also an important part of the organization.

Red Auerbach. What makes Red Auerbach and the Celtics special? I think it's because Red has built a system that has stood the test of time. He has a team and an organization which has a Team Ego. The individual ego defers to the team. The team's success perpetuates itself. In business and in sports everyone wants to be associated with a winning corporation. Most players who have been with the Celtics and other NBA teams consider themselves Celtics. I remember standing outside the Garden one afternoon after practice with Quinn Buckner. He sensed his days with the Celtics were numbered; after winning the championship his playing time had been cut, and he was falling out of the rotation. "If I'm traded from here at the end of the year, I'll still treasure my days as a member of this organization," he said. But that's the nature of the Celtic team—it creates a deep connection that is more than winning games. Red is responsible for that. His door is always open for players to go in and talk. Jo Jo White said this about Red: "Whatever criticisms anybody might have of him, what's most important about Red is that he's fair."

Red is always talking to players about basketball and about situations athletes face. He hustled all the time working his way up, because of his love for the game. He would conceive basketball plays and use kids on the playground on a Sunday morning to try them out. With the Celtics he'd talk about specific plays, ask you why you made certain moves during a game. You were always aware that he coached the best players in the game at one time. He might summarize a discussion by saying, "Well, K. C. did it this way." But he never threatened you with his experience. Red understands people with an uncanny perception. At seventy, he remains as committed as ever to the team's success. He's active in the team's draft, and he continues to find ways of combining the best elements of the past and present. For example, when the Celtics had the second choice in the 1986 draft, they brought center William Bedford to Boston for an interview with the coaching staff. Bill Russell was also in Boston that day for an award presentation, so while Russ was in the team's offices, Red summoned him to discuss the Celtics with the youngster. It works the other way too, of course; K. C. is always consulting with Red about basketball decisions.

Red would come into the locker room after a game, a Celtics tradition. Red would walk around the room. If he winked at you you were okay, you had played well. He might flick some ashes off his cigar if he liked the way you played. But if he asked you questions, it was a curse. You might not have liked cigar ashes, but they were a blessing.

Red's a tough but fair businessman. He's also a genius at building a basketball team and a system that withstands the rigors of time. He understands the game instinctively and intellectually. He stated in a 1981 article that the current critical issue in basketball was not on the court; it was finding a way to institute a system to balance the amount of money generated by the sport's financial boom without destroying player motivation. Two years later the union agreed to the salary cap. He tried to sign

Ralph Sampson when Sampson was a freshman at the University of Virginia, but failed. "I couldn't get a feel for the environment," he later moaned. So much of his success depends on chemistry. When he was asked at halftime of the heralded Georgetown-Virginia matchup about the effects of taller players playing the game, he suddenly became philosophical: "The kids on the playground are taking pride in being taller! They have improved diets. They have more complete role models, like Magic Johnson and Larry Bird. The game's taller and now it's better because there's an increased awareness about all the skills by players at every position." He has grown with the game; he has continued to learn. Though he enjoys visibility, I have to think he travels to do television assignments because he senses television is an important communication medium, and he wants to be out there.

Red's a friend and a trusted advisor. He says, "It's good to work hard. Hard work won't hurt you. But it's more important to work smart." He built the Celtics as a team and as a system because he understood talent, timing and patience. There will never be another one like him. Thanks, Red, for letting me be a part of the family.

Chapter 13

Playing the Game

I like to think that the winning attitude of the Celtics' system and the individuals who were part of it rubbed off on me. My own style of play, honed over the years, was always team-oriented, but with the Celtics it reached its pinnacle. I wanted to win, and whatever it took—from playing physical to understanding my role—I always tried my best to achieve that end. And winning is its own reward.

When I got the call to go into a game for defensive reasons, I would prepare myself mentally for the challenge. I would work on myself to be limber, relaxed and ready. I'd engage in rituals, like grabbing some resin from our trainer, Ray Melchiorre, to prepare myself for combat. Regardless of the minutes I'd be asked to play, I would extend myself to the upper limit of my potential as an athlete. The amount of minutes I played never really concerned me. Winning did.

At the beginning of the 1983-1984 season, when K. C. and Red asked me to play a support role, I was determined to make it an active one. I established other rituals: I claimed the seat at the end of the bench as my own to signify that every part of the Celtics' bench was a positive location. Attitude on a basketball team is very important. During a game, when a player gets taken out, he is often pouting, disappointed. He may be angry at the coach, and to retaliate he'll take the seat at the end of the bench. My thinking was that if a player came out and was upset, he should sit somewhere in the center, within the confines of the team. I remember the year I was third in the league in minutes played. Sometimes I'd come out and the guys on the bench at the time would give me subtle glances, as if they were saying that I was taking their time. I'd feel distracted, something that hurt the club.

But the days I take the greatest amount of pride in as a player are the days when I had that supportive role. The players respected what I was trying to do out there. I understood that the bench is a valuable facet of the game. The coach can't pick up everything during a game;

often he sees the game from the perspective of his game plan and scouting report. Players can pick up little things by concentrating while the game is going on, and the truth is that fifteen pairs of eyes are better than the coach's one pair. Sure I waved that towel, but I also assisted in other ways, valuable ways. Against the Houston Rockets in Game 3 of the 1981 championship finals, Larry Bird was having an off-day with his shooting. Predictably, Larry started passing up his shots, shots that we needed him to take and attempts around which our offense was designed. Our players were called for three-second violations twice, and we were getting completely out of rhythm. I pulled him aside and told him that he had to shoot. "If you miss five, ten shots, you have to keep shooting," I said. "Your role still is to shoot the ball. Your job isn't passing." Later in that series, Larry won it by coming in off the bench late in the fourth quarter of the sixth game and hitting five long jumpers. All net and all confidence. Encouragement and support from bench people can help make a winner.

"M. L.," Red told me, "be a morale-builder, a guide to our younger players. Smooth over conflicts and be a motivator." I tried to be the best there ever was.

I was a physical player. I established boundaries out on the floor against my opponents, and I used everything I could to establish an advantage. I'm not always certain I want to admit this deeply held belief, but I think everybody—in games, in life—is looking for an advantage. If possible I would have liked my opponent's basket to be tilted. In an individual confrontation I would play physical for an advantage; if I was fighting with a player and the contest became very physical, then I would become very, very physical—and so on. It was an advantage I had built up over time, and I refused to let any negative opinion change that because, simply, it was helping our team win. If I was staying within the limits of the rules, trying to be better than my opponent, well, that was the advantage I needed to win. It's the same in business; when I try to make a sale, do I shed whatever advantages I've developed over the years so that I will be equal with a competitor trying to make the same sale? Not in my company. I want to get that contract. The ideal is equality. The reality is that I want the sale.

I wanted to win. If this meant holding a guy, or blocking him out when the referee couldn't see so my guy couldn't score, I would do it. I suspect people can relate to that. They know it's true. In my career, I wanted the odds stacked in my favor. I wanted the best talent and I wanted the best blend of personalities. I worked hard to accumulate what was positive in order for my team to win. I'm just beginning to play tennis, and I operate with the same principles. I want to be better than deuce. I want to be one up and serving for the game. It's unfortunate but true: in life there are no ties. You win or you lose. In my high school game against Southern Wayne that went seven overtimes, we would have played until the following Christmas looking for a winner. The same applies to American automobile makers trying to get the jump on Japanese manufacturers, or medical laboratories researching a drug to cure AIDS. I think the nature of our culture prompts us to *create* an advantage—not have it be *given*.

So I played to win and I played physical. I never tried to hurt a player within the context of a game, though if a fight did break out I'd try my best to tag my opponent. I was willing to give and take my bumps and bruises. Players in the NBA were big, and they could take it.

I wanted a guy I was going against to be thinking about M. L. as opposed to fulfilling the task at hand—winning the game for his team. In the championship series against Houston in 1981, I was brought into the game to try and cool off Mike Dunleavy, a tough little guard who was shooting the devil out of the ball. I immediately walked over to him in front of press row and stood at his side. I said to him, "Mike, isn't this unbelievable? Here we are, playing for the world championship, in front of millions of people on television. And you are playing an unbelievable game." I was talking louder now, deliberately; I wanted the press to hear me, and I wanted Mike to know they could hear.

"You know what I'm going to do? When you guys inbound the ball, I'm going to kiss you and I'm going to grab your rump all the way down the court! As soon as you guys throw the ball in."

Now he looked at me as if I were from another planet. Get off of me, M. L. I played on his uncertainty and on the amusement of the writers. When they brought the ball up, I had my hand on his butt. I assure you, just for that one possession. But it had him thinking about M. L., which didn't help him put the ball in the basket.

I'd do other things. I'd walk over to a guy during warmups one night and shake his hand and ask how his family was. The next time we'd play I'd be ice cold; I'd ignore him so he couldn't figure me out. In the game I'd do the same thing: talk junk and create concern. If I went into a game at a free throw, I'd walk over to my man and stand directly beside him, staring him right in the eye. I would connect, mind to mind. I'd have him thinking, "What is Carr thinking of?" I'd do similar routines with our rookies in the Celtics' preseason training camp. I'd test them; I'd want to know just how much they wanted to play in the NBA. My attitude in every training camp was that I was going to win a job. *My* position was secure because I was going to outwork anyone to keep it. But it was more than that; if a rookie was worth anything, he had to be overly aggressive, overly determined to win a job on an NBA roster. If he had some of these qualities plus sufficient talent, then we'd want him on the Celtics. He could help us win. I busted my butt in drills and scrimmages to test the young guys. Larry Bird was the same way; we wanted to check out just what these guys were made of.

Toward the end of my career, I'd watch the "cool" approach by some of the young guys. They'd come to practice with Walkman radios, and as soon as practice was over, they'd have the radio blaring again. If I was rookie trying to make an NBA team, the opportunity of a lifetime, then I'd be all eyes and ears. I'd be talking to the coaches, the veterans, the trainer. I'd be listening, learning, making sure the coaches saw what I was doing. I was out to win a job. But maybe my strong feelings are a result of my having had to work my way up to attain an NBA position the hard way. Maybe that's always been a part of me.

Part of my game was politicking with the officials. They'd watch some of my rough stuff and say to me, "You better cut that out, M. L., we'll have to throw you out." I'd wait and see and establish my limits.

But I was on the receiving end of some violent play, too. In my rookie year I was trying to veer through a lane defensively when a player named Ron "The Plumber" Thomas set a thunderous pick. I bounced off him and thought about retaliating. That thought became reinforced the next time down. He set a pick and, it seemed to me, deliberately kneed me in the thigh, giving me a painful charley horse. That did it.

The next pick he set I went through. As I did, I threw a powerful elbow, getting additional leverage and power by winding up. I hit him flush and knocked him clear across the court. It was a blow that would have kept any man down for an eon, but not the Plumber. He was six-seven and 240 pounds, and he kept coming back. He went directly at me, and as I prepared to defend myself he pulled my jersey over my head. I tried to free myself by pulling the jersey off of me. He used the interval to whack me some of the hardest shots I've ever taken. I was trying to free myself. I thought about retaliating later, but I let that one go. We each had our shots. Good, hard shots.

I was fined three thousand dollars for hitting Bill Laimbeer the year we won my last championship. He was out there taking some phony flops for charges and antagonizing everybody. Sitting on the bench, I said to Maxwell, "When I get in there, he's not flopping down. I'm gonna put him down!"

I went in, and on the first opportunity I blasted him with an elbow that would have probably gone to the Hall of Fame if they bestowed recognition on such moves. I dropped him and immediately left the gym. I knew I was thrown out; I wouldn't contest that. I later apologized to Laimbeer. I told him I didn't mean for the elbow to be *that* flagrant.

At the hearing in NBA Security regarding the fine, Director of Security Jack Joyce said while watching the tape that the fine would be three thousand dollars because the elbow "appeared premeditated." I told him that it wasn't premeditated. It was calculated.

Of course I had always had my share of confrontations. I had a stormy career in professional basketball. I played hard and I played tough. I had a number of fights in the ABA, including two angry confrontations with John Williamson of the New York Nets. He was a confident player, even cocky. I refused to back down. I was younger then, and sometimes those arguments got out of hand. Soon matters between us became nearly uncontrollable. Finally the fight was over, but from that time on I had acquired something of a reputation as a fighter who fought for keeps.

In a game against the Nets, I tackled the smaller player Darwin Cook when he was going for a layup. I have regrets about the violent way I took him down, but it was an unexpected consequence of the way I played the game. There was a night in 1978, when I was with the Pistons, when I collided with Maurice Lucas of the Portland Trail Blazers. We started exchanging punches. Lucas is an old teammate of mine and a gentle spirit off of the court. After the game we went out and laughed about the fight. I played hard and I fought, but I disciplined myself to keep the fights on the court. After it was through, I walked away from it.

But in January of 1982 my physical style drew added attention. We were playing the Atlanta Hawks in a game in Boston, and midway through the second quarter I was trying to get through a double screen set by Dan Roundfield and Wayne "Tree" Rollins. Apparently, the Hawks had become angered by the physical play of our reserve center Rick Robey. An Atlanta paper reported that the pick may have been called to retaliate. Trying to get through, I was hit pretty good, and I was angry for the rest of the night.

In the second half Tree and I exchanged words, which only incensed me further. Robey tried to calm me down, but without much success. Rollins had been fined earlier that season after elbowing a Phoenix player, and he had been involved in a punching incident with Dave Cowens two seasons before in Boston. I suspect his behavior affected my attitude that night. Intimidation is a way of life on the court, and afterwards, I repeat, it is best to walk away. Tree tried to ignore the scuffling and its effects on me, but I was having none of it. After the game I walked out of the hallway where the locker rooms are located and headed toward the room where our wives waited for us after games. I waited for Rollins and exchanged words with him as we left. I was as angry that night as I had ever been.

Owing to my confrontation with John Williamson six years before, Rollins apparently went back to his hotel in Boston that night and called his attorney. Three months later, there was a report in an Atlanta paper saying that Rollins was thinking of filing a suit charging me with assault. In July he did just that—for an unbelievable $4 million. He charged that I pulled a shiny object resembling a razor or knife on him that night. According to the suit, it had caused him "physical and mental" injury. Ironically, I found out about it as I was considering the $1.6 million offer from the Cleveland Cavaliers. I looked at the newspaper story and joked to myself without laughter, "Heck I need four million. One-point-six isn't enough."

I scrapped plans to work on putting a swimming pool in at my home and headed into downtown Boston to meet with Phil McLaughlin and Dick Snyder. It was an incredibly traumatic experience. I was slapped completely off my feet. But I was absolutely certain that Dick Snyder could win the case; and Phil McLaughlin is a detailed, logical thinker, so I was sure he would guide me well. I'm a fighter and I won't back down. For these reasons, I felt better. But the suit was frightening.

In time it all worked out. We met that day and there was an air of confidence in the room from the outset. Because it was a negative situation, we couldn't parade our plans out front to the media. But we had conversations with the NBA. The initial investigation by NBA Security said: "The fact that nothing came out of this office [regarding the allegation that there was a razor involved in the incident] should tell you something about what we thought of Rollins's charges." Enough witnesses supported our case. Later we would take the offensive: the charges could not be substantiated and the case was settled out of court. But the incident remains a reminder of what happens when confrontation on the court is not kept where it belongs.

To me, everything about the game of basketball is part of a pattern. The individual, whether he is playing offense or defense, and the team, where each man depends on a sense of involvement in a unit, both depend on the disciplined repetition of certain forms. My strength was always playing defense. I established my earliest foundations defensively on the model of K. C. Jones, probably the best defensive guard in the history of basketball. Like K. C., I wouldn't wait for an offensive player to go by me. I'd establish my defensive stance and make jab steps at the player with the ball, keeping him off-balance. As Bill Russell said in his book *Second Wind,* there is a sense of geometry about the game of basketball. I always broke it down simply: the offensive man wanted to get from Point A, where he was with the ball, to Point B, the basket. My thoughts were consumed with preventing that from happening.

I constantly worked out there. I used trickery, showing my opponent an opening and then taking it away. I'd fake left, getting the man to go to the right, and jump back quickly to take the charge. On defense I dictated what my man would do. I wanted to be strong out there, but not too strong; basketball isn't a weightlifting contest. The game is fast and it helps to have speed. But quickness matters more, especially the critical first step. Defensively, if you beat the man to the spot he wants to go to on the floor, you have the advantage. Offensively, you're by the man with a quick first step. The game has reached an unprecedented level of play now. All players need now is a split second and they've beaten their man. The action in the game is constant, and it demands all of your awareness.

A basketball player's body is very fine-tuned. That's why pacing is important—although it drives coaches crazy sometimes. Coaches have to prevent their teams from "turning it on and turning it off," but pacing on an individual level is essential for success. If your body is fatigued you're likely to be a split second slow.

Soon after retirement I missed the conditioning I had as a player. I used to think I could jump over a canal! When I was walking through the city I felt as if I could run across town without missing a beat. The conditioning depended on pattern, too, the development of a workable routine. It assured me I would stay at the very top of my game physically, mentally and emotionally. The routine led to total involvement in my playing responsibilities, the game and the team. When we were clicking as a team, we were engaging in patterned activity, much as members of an orchestra interact to produce a symphony. Tempo is very important to a basketball team. When we were playing well, we all knew where we were supposed to be on the floor. What followed then was a co-ordinated sense of timing, and blind faith among the players. When I was at the top of the key and Cedric Maxwell was on the sideline, setting up his defender for a back-door move, I knew exactly where he was going to go. Maxwell would fake toward me, make a sudden move around his man's back and run to the basket. I knew he would deliver on the dash to the hoop, so I would make the pass. I had faith he would be there, and he accepted the pressure to succeed. He *had* to get clear of his defender, and inevitably we scored. But that didn't rule out patience, or improvisation, because we knew that the defense had patterns too. So we'd constantly be watching each other: eyes, hip fakes, sudden drop-steps in the low post for a pass and an easy score.

That fluidity created scoring situations: the reverse pivot, the back-door move, the strong move to the ball that got you into the triple-threat position, squarely facing the basket, where you could command the action by shooting, driving or passing. When you're one-on-one, your teammates adjust accordingly. You rely on balance and faith, but there's a delicate boundary between commanding the action and being selfish. One player out for himself will cause a team to lose some of that faith and team balance. This begins to explain why Larry Bird is such an outstanding player. He's one of the best scorers in the game, able to command action, but he is also an unselfish player, a man who helps construct the winning pattern. It also describes why players like Dennis Johnson, Magic Johnson and Maurice Cheeks will always have an advantage on the fast break. The Celtics, Lakers and 76ers have three-on-two or even four-on-one breaks because the teammates of their point guards fill the lanes, knowing that they'll get the ball if they're open. DJ, Magic and Cheeks are exceptional teammates and very unselfish players. They will always bust their tails to create an advantage. Not surprisingly, these three teams also happen to be the classiest NBA teams of the eighties. Selfish players, on the other hand, put strain on their teammates. There's really no secret to winning and losing. Players who look more for their own shots kill pattern and fluidity and create ulcers for the coach.

Patterns extended to my life off the floor as well, particularly during the playoffs. There was constant pressure at those times, and I wanted to minimize all distractions off the floor in order to focus on the task at hand. Athletes are generally superstitious. Some tape their right ankle before their left all of the time. John Havlicek was always extremely meticulous when dressing, hanging up his uniform the same way every time. Larry Bird nearly always shoots two hundred shots two hours before the game, usually alone, before the crowd fills up the arena. Adrian Dantley cradles the ball underneath his arms before shooting free throws, and Dennis Johnson bounces the ball one time for each year he's been in the league before shooting his foul shots. I would dip my knees four times on each free throw. You never alter those patterns because repetition creates a confidence zone. Bill Russell would throw up before every big game, and Red Auerbach would worry when he didn't. Of course, if I had to go up against Wilt Chamberlain, I'd throw up too.

In the playoffs the stress is high. For two months you get up in the morning thinking about the game and dream about it at night. I'd take an afternoon nap at the same time each day. But I needed it—the adrenalin kept me sky high. During the 1981 playoffs Chris Ford, now a Celtics assistant coach, couldn't eat. He was heading for his first NBA championship, and his wife Kathy, in a column for the *Boston Herald American,* wrote that Chris had no interest in whatever she tried to fix.

The playoffs have an extraordinary intensity. It's almost as if only basketball has any meaning for you. I would read the papers and use any quotes from opponents as sources of motivation. That would work with Danny Ainge. For Maxwell, however, it was different. Before a big game with the Bucks, I started pumping Max about Marques Johnson. Maxwell just waved me away. "It's too early in the day," he told me during the morning shoot-around. "I don't want to hear your pep talk, M. L. You'd be better off checking the athletic history of the guy who wrote the story. I'm not going against the writer. I'm going against Marques." Guys react differently under pressure, which is why coaching must allow for individuality. Coaches who have too much structure inevitably won't win much.

The game is emotionally draining. When you win, you're sky high. A championship intensifies the camaraderie. You respect each other and you bask in the glow of public recognition as you ride in parades and visit the White House. There's immediate respect, reward and gratification. If you lose, whether you played well or not, the response is usually negative. You have to maintain stength and consistency. You can't get too high when you win or too low when you lose. Experience helps there; when we were beginning our championship era in Boston, we were knocked off pretty easily in the playoffs by the Philadelphia 76ers that first year. We had beaten them consistently during the regular season, but they had us overmatched in the playoffs. It was eerie; the following year, they had us in the same situation. But we had been through it before, and we refused to beat ourselves, as young teams often do. As a young player, I'd play well and I'd call everybody back home, telling them the good news. I'd go out and buy every newspaper. It changes; when I was older, more experienced, the only time I'd buy every paper was when I *didn't* play well. Then I'd try to get every paper in town and burn them before anyone could read about it.

The intensity comes with the turf. The NBA is a high-level, demanding profession, and those demands can extend off the court as well. Sometimes, as in the playoffs, I was able to shelter myself from the outside world by having my family screen my phone calls. But afterwards I had to return to the real world, with all of the visibility that goes with NBA stardom.

Any time I wanted to be great, all I'd have to do was go out in the city. There, my image preceded me, making me the recipient of autograph seekers, smiles and applause. This off-the-court attention can be confusing. Athletes are often insecure away from the realm of the arena (where there's a small number of variables to manage). It's related to the perception that people have of you. The athlete seems self-aware, disciplined and decisive. But in everyday life, it's different. People often have a glitz-and-glitter image of you. In my last year as a player, I was driving to a Red Sox game. I drive a 1985 Oldsmobile, a fine automobile, but in the space between Kenmore Square and Fenway Park, probably a quarter-mile, four people shouted out to me, wondering why I wasn't driving a better car.

Those perceptions can cause insecurity. When I was being recruited by colleges I had no idea what to expect from the college life or even what questions to ask. I'm sure most kids and their parents don't. So early on you begin losing a part of your identity. It continues through college and into the pros. When I'd return home to Wallace to visit my parents, I'd often run into friends I grew up with. With limited time, I'd want to spend as much as I could with my parents. Then I'd hear: "What, M. L.? You too good to be with us, your old friends? We aren't good enough for you?" I'd be caught in uncertainty. Do I listen to these guys and give up what I really want to do? Am I forgetting my past, forgetting people who were and still might be important to me? These are small pressures, but they play subtly on your self-concept.

I channeled my uncertainties and coped with my fears by steadily increasing my interaction with people I thought I would work with in the future. The Celtics would laugh at me; when we'd go on the road for a trip I'd head up to my room to make a number of phone calls. I'd hear, "There's M. L., going up to his office." They'd laugh, but I knew the hotel was a good place to get work done. Dead time during the day of a game is the time that has led so many athletes off-course and into problems.

NBA players are special talents, high-powered personalities with specific ego needs. Under continuous scrutiny from the public, they are vulnerable, particularly a young player who has plenty of money for the first time in his life. Extra money and extra time can create troublesome choices. In the backgrounds of many players, there is a fine line early in life between surviving and falling completely off the track. That past accompanies some guys all the way into the NBA. The temptation that may have overcome previously can draw them in when money and time present opportunity. It's sad.

My friend David Thompson was a tragic case in point. I remember watching DT play basketball in Greensboro in the 1973 High School All-Star Game. David was a high school senior then, and he was a player with phenomenal ability. I recall one sequence where an offensive rebound bounced lazily on the rim, waiting to be grabbed by a defensive player. Suddenly David soared through the air and swept home a two-handed dunk over three defenders. I went over to him after the game and congratulated him. We spoke for a while and he described some of the recruiting pressures he had gone through. I encouraged him and found him—continue to find him—a nice person.

David went through the highs and lows, and he's struggling now. He encountered dependency problems, I think, because of the expectations that typically accompany a large contract. His statistics continued to be outstanding, his play outstanding, but because his team wasn't successful, and because David was the highest-paid player on the team, he was blamed for every failure. Apparently it struck deep within him.

I still believe in David. He's a fine person who's having trouble right now. When he was rumored to be having problems, I sent a note over to him when we played Denver. I told him that if he wanted to talk, I would be glad to listen. I just didn't feel comfortable approaching him directly. It's just a very sad situation.

I dealt with the highs of the NBA by always preparing for what lay ahead. I knew, probably from working outside of the big-time early, that regardless of how well-off I was as a player, I would still have to get up every day after it was over. I wanted to be involved in a business in which I could continue to progress. But that realization isn't an easy one for some athletes.

Toward the end of my career, I was on a Players Association cruise talking with some players, including Bob Lanier, Quinn Buckner and Junior Bridgeman, about the league and the changes it had undergone. In the late seventies, the NBA was suffering from an image problem. The game was too oriented toward one-on-one play; behind the scenes, there was antagonism between management and players. Drugs, of course, was another difficulty. We realized on the trip that there was a need to establish a better relationship with the owners, that players had to clean up their act and project a more professional image. Formerly, an NBA player was identified by the size of the stereo he was carrying through the airport. Over time, players began changing; they wore sports jackets and carried themselves with more pride. I firmly believe a major reason for this change had to do with player-management relations.

David Stern became commissioner of the league in 1984, and immediately a sense existed that a positive change was underway. From the beginning Stern has tried extremely hard to listen to both the Players Association and management. He has been able to get players and owners to see that we are involved in the same game. Symbolic of this is the salary cap in the NBA, as well as a plan that provides for sharing of game receipts. The overriding factor in a better working arrangement between the players and management is that the league has made a concentrated effort to promote the player and the game.

Over the last three or four years, there's been a priority placed on positive things. Before the 1987-1988 season, the NBA hired Tom Sanders, the former Celtics coach and player, as director of player programs. Sanders's most recent position was associate director of the Center for the Study of Sport in Society at Northeastern University in Boston. Sanders's role is to work with veteran players and rookies in designing programs to help them take advantage of their status as players as well as assisting them in coping with some of the pressures they face as athletes. In another innovative move, the league has recognized some of the problems attendant with entertainment and high visibility and is formally trying to manage them. The drug rule in the league, which allows for a player to come forward for rehabilitation while retaining a position in the league, is another attempt to combat a problem in the professional basketball business. All of these changes are excellent; they ensure that the focus remains on the game itself, and not on the external distractions that can so easily plague its stars. They help players and they help fans. And they help everyone enjoy the magnificent individual play and teamwork that is the hallmark of NBA basketball.

Chapter 14

Some Individual Memories

I have thought of basketball from a number of different perspectives, depending on the memory, depending on the time of my life. As a player I was totally involved in the game, totally dedicated to doing my best and helping my team win. The highs and lows are intense, and objectivity is lost in the passion of the game.

Yet, from a distance enforced by retirement and its conditions, wins and losses seem an altogether different reality. I remember that feeling of needing to be victorious, but the collective memories of a playing career suggest something else to me now. I recall people, ironies and unusual twists to events, as much as the heartbreak of defeat as a young player. I treasure the championship rings, but I also go back repeatedly to the people and moments from the everyday game that made my career so interesting. So here are some memories from my sixteen seasons of basketball:

Most Talented Teammate. Marvin "Bad News" Barnes. Marvin had nights of twenty-five rebounds and thirty-five or forty points on a regular basis, often after hanging out on the town for two or three straight nights. I remember the night he lit up the Kentucky Colonels for forty-nine points, a team that featured Artis Gilmore and Maurice Lucas. It was after Maurice had been traded to the Colonels from the Spirits because, according to Marvin, there wasn't enough room in St. Louis for both of them. When the press came into the locker room after the game, Marvin told them, "I have one thing to say about our duel. Fifty-one went into the hole and two jumped out." News was referring to a shot at the buzzer, a step-back set from thirty-five feet that didn't count. News's point: if the game had continued, he would have continued scoring to prove he was the better man. When it comes to pure talent, very few could even come close! However, though I still consider us to be very close friends (Marvin guided me through the rookie season), I remain upset with him for messing up what should have been an easy walk into the basketball Hall of Fame.

Marvin, you're still *number one* when it comes to helping others. I've always wished you were a little more selfish when it came to life in general. You still are a caring, witty and bright young man. You must forsake all who now say you will never make it.

I will never forget that Bad News Barnes was the most powerful rebounder in traffic I have ever been associated with in the game. Marvin dominated the boards, had exquisite touch inside and could go outside to hit the jumper or do the ballhandling for the team. Marvin carried the Spirits over Julius Erving (his idol) and the Nets in 1975 and virtually was the St. Louis team for two years. But hangers-on and a financially demanding lifestyle created problems with his professional attitude. His original contract wasn't as secure as it could have been, and he was constantly plagued by worry. His talent and his past were substance and shadow; a fight in college in Providence ended violently when Marvin allegedly slugged a teammate with a tire iron. He was in and out of court for the next three years, and I suspect this drained him of some of his mental toughness. He was always unable to etch out his individuality.

Barnes had to grow up too quickly, though ironically he guided me through some delicate contract negotiations with the Spirits. Midway through my rookie year as a pro I was asked to sign an extension to my one-year contract with the Spirits. But Marvin advised me not to do it unless they gave me a $100,000 signing bonus because the league itself might not be in existence beyond that year. It was an uncertain playing environment—players around the league weren't sure if they would receive their next salary check. News's reasoning was that if the ABA folded and I had signed, I would be property of the Spirits, killing my negotiation rights with other teams if there was a merger. I should make the Spirits pay to retain my services.

When I presented this plan to the team, I thought I had made the biggest mistake of my life. Within three days, I went from starting to a very limited role. It was very scary for a first-year player with no security. But Marvin understood my position, remained loyal to me and acted to correct it. Marvin took me under his wing, saying, "Don't worry, Bro. News'll make sure they understand." We were in Denver and Marvin went out on a limb for me, acting perhaps with questionable ethics. But in the context of premerger basketball, within rules that were being created day-to-day, I think he was right.

In a tough ballgame Marvin suddenly came to the bench, saying to Coach Joe Mullaney, "I'm hurtin'. Can't go. Put Bro in. He can *do* it." He was faking the injury to place me back in the lineup. I went out and had one of my best games: eleven-for-fifteen from the floor, twenty-six points, and a solid defensive game against David Thompson. Marvin followed this up; he told the team's hierarchy that he worked better with me in the lineup as opposed to the recently arrived Moses Malone, who had come to the Spirits after Utah folded. "Moses and I get in each other's way," Marvin told Joe. "Bro and I do much better." I was returned to the starting lineup, except for some specific matchups, and went on to have a fine rookie season, making the All-Rookie team and getting runner-up honors to Thompson in Rookie of the Year voting.

I was also declared a free agent after the ABA folded. Given the right to negotiate with any team, I was signed to a secure contract with the Pistons during the merger period in the summer of 1976.

Marvin, nice call, and I will never forget. News, forsake all of those self-destructive tendencies and go for God's best!

There was a recent postscript in my relationship with Marvin: in the 1985 playoffs against the Pistons, I ran into News in Detroit, where he had stayed after failing a number of NBA trials in the late seventies. Marvin was a shell of who he used to be; even his stylish clothing had lost its luster. Marvin and Larry Bird introduced themselves to one another and had a long, friendly conversation. For all their similarities in ability, I couldn't help notice how different they were.

Most Inspirational Teammate. Don Chaney. I played with Don Chaney at two different times in my career. When I broke in with the Spirits in 1975, he had also joined the team as a free agent after playing on the 1973-1974 Celtics championship team. He played the veteran role to my rookie part, and he was always talking to me about defensive strategies and ways of becoming consistent. Later we joined up again on the Celtics, where he was completing his career, back with Boston for a second term in 1979-1980.

Don Chaney was incredibly stable; he broke into the NBA as a tall, strong defensive guard under Bill Russell when Russ was coaching the Celtics in 1968. Having played under Guy Lewis's free, running system at the University of Houston, Don was able to adjust easily to the Celtics' running attack throughout the early seventies. I emphasize *adjust* because Chaney's strongest characteristic is his emotionally stable personality. Chaney was a splendid combination as a player: hard-nosed on the court, to the extent that he could regularly defend other team's top guards out of their game, and amiable and genuine off the court, an ideal teammate. He taught me how important and helpful a loving family is when an athlete is trying to cope with the strains of a professional sports career. The NBA lifestyle can severely test the fabric of a family. Don has a lot of time for his three children, Michael, Donna and Kara, but he reserves most of his attention for his loving wife, Jackie.

Don Chaney's NBA career took some further twists and turns after he completed his playing days with the Celtics. An assistant coaching job at Detroit led him finally to a head coaching position with the Clippers, a tough situation. The ownership at San Diego would not supply him with the type of team and players necessary to win; at this level, a very surprising phenomenon. Why would an ownership procure a team, with its costs and operations, and then not bring in compatible talent?

Though I have known Don well for twelve years, I have to say I misread the man. I didn't think coaching was in his blood, but he threw himself into coaching totally, and he developed into a strong X's and O's guy. A coaching maxim says that the coach isn't any better than the talent he's managing. In Don's situation, the Clippers made a bid to become competitive in Los Angeles by bringing in marquee-type talent. Players like Marques Johnson, Norm Nixon, Darnell Valentine and Cedric Maxwell represented either direct links to Los Angeles (Marques was an All-American at UCLA; Nixon helped lead the Lakers to two NBA championships) or All-Star quality (Maxwell). But injuries brought this program to a halt, as did the team's investment in hardship center Benoit Benjamin from Creighton. Benoit, only nineteen years old, showed flashes of mobility and power for a seven-foot player, but according to Don he lacked the aggressiveness underneath the boards. "He's too nice," Chaney told me during his last season as Clippers' coach. Too often that means passive play, and the NBA doesn't accommodate itself to this type of player. When injuries struck and Benoit didn't work out, the Clippers failed miserably. Don was fired in 1987, but I believe he'll get another shot. He'll continue working at it, I know that.

Most Dedicated/Disciplined Teammate. Larry Bird. Contrary to much public opinion, the choice is not Cedric "Cornbread" Maxwell, but the player from French Lick, Indiana. Larry will not expect anything short of his best every time out. If he goes out and has a seven-for-eighteen shooting night, I'll bet he will be the first one at practice the next day taking shots. It isn't an accident that Larry Bird has emerged as the best player in the National Basketball Association. To be a professional takes discipline, talent, drive, hard work and then more hard work. This cannot be overstated. To reach the NBA, a player has to be great; to rise above the rest, as Bird does, requires that he polish that talent continuously through his faith to his game. No one works as hard as Larry.

Larry would never be denied his opportunity to be the best. And some of his best games have come in practice. I recall a pair of games that illustrate his drive. In 1980-1981, the year of our first championship,

we lost a game miserably to Golden State during the Christmas West
Coast trip. For the only time in his career, Bird went scoreless. His
rebounding game was there and he passed pretty well, but he got zero
points, an insult to a scorer. The next game was in Portland: he was
unusually silent during the trip up to Oregon, and in that game's opening
minutes, we understood why. He took over completely, rushing through
the pack to grab loose balls, seemingly to take the ball physically from
our guards for shooting opportunities. He swished his first five long
jumpers, finished with thirty-five and led us to an important road win.
But that win reflected the practice and the time before games, the private
times not open to the public that are the true tests of dedication. It is
said that a great team player makes his teammates better. Larry Bird
made me a better player. Retirement brought one subtle gratification:
I don't have to figure out any longer how to perform the impossible,
I don't have to figure out how to stop Larry Bird in practice.

Most Courageous Teammate. Bob Lanier. I played with Bob Lanier
for two years in Detroit. He was a giant of a man, six-eleven and around
270 pounds, but he was quick and agile, too. His skills took him to places
other less talented players equally built couldn't reach. But he paid a
price physically. I walked over to Bob one day while waiting to board
a plane for a road trip. He was rubbing his legs, probably as much from
habit as from need. I asked him the last time he had played a game without
pain. It was his seventh year in the game. He pondered and then answered
that the last time he could remember one was his junior year at St.
Bonaventure.

Men in this game sometime endure tremendous physical punishment
to bring themselves out every night. Lanier wore heavy knee braces at
the end of his career. He had Achilles' tendon injuries that prevented
him from jumping repeatedly for offensive rebounds, or jumping two
or three times to block shots under his defensive board. But he still carried
on, pursuing an elusive championship. His closest attempt came late,
after he had been traded to the Milwaukee Bucks. The 1981 Milwaukee
team with Marques Johnson, Sydney Moncrief, Junior Bridgeman, Quinn
Buckner, Brian Winters and Harvey Catchings came very close, losing
the seventh game of the Eastern semifinals by one point to Philadelphia.
That was the season of our first championship. Lanier retired without
a ring in 1985, but he is a certain Hall-of-Famer.

Most Difficult Player to Score Against. E. C. Coleman. Not many
people have heard of E. C. An outstanding defensive player for the Jazz,
he would never give you an inch to move. He was consistently able to
play you aggressively off the ball. The Celtics sought Coleman a season

before they began their decline in the late seventies; he was a player who had little publicity, but was respected within the scouting and coaching networks. He was strong, quick and agile, and he had a burning desire to make people have a bad game. That takes a special type of approach to the game because recognition and money is usually given to offensive stars. This was particularly true in the late seventies, when there was such a priority on scoring and one-on-one play.

Most Difficult Player to Defend. Julius Erving. Doctor J had a score of overpowering offensive games against our Boston team in the early eighties. He scored forty-five in a double-overtime contest in 1980, a career high. Another one of his most significant outputs against us was in 1982, when he scored thirty-one in Game 7 in the Boston Garden; Philadelphia dethroned us as champions in that game, 123-107. Erving was great that afternoon, stopping us after we had rallied from a three-games-to-one deficit to tie the series for the second straight season. When the Doc took the floor against us, we always knew we were in for a battle. He was a grave competitor when our teams took the court.

Dr. J's talents, written about widely, have astonished fans throughout the league. He had spectacular jumping ability, a powerful righthanded driving game and, after he took command of the 76ers as captain, a much-improved outside shot. He was tough from the top of the circle and deadly accurate from the sides, when he used the backboard with superior effect. But forget about his extraordinary talent for a moment. Julius was incredibly intelligent on the floor. He knew all his opponents' strengths and weaknesses, and he was a master at exploiting them, especially one-on-one. But he would never encourage the one-on-one confrontation away from the basket unless it was in transition. One memorable break came in the 1979-1980 Eastern Conference final series between the Celtics and the Sixers, the season they defeated us four games to one. I was brought in during the third period specifically to try and stop Julius, who was defeating us singlehandedly. In the middle of a 37-26 Philadelphia run, Julius took off from the top of the key on the break, and I went under him, attempting to draw the charge. He knocked me over and slammed the ball home. We had words after that. My feeling at the time was that it wasn't an occasion to retreat, to back down. But it was a perfect example of Erving in his prime: he forced you to crouch down low, to match his quickness, but then he'd sweep by you or shoot over you. And he would always go hard after the offensive rebound when you'd overplay him. Doctor J was smart enough to know that he had me at a disadvantage in close to the basket because of his superior leaping ability.

Late in 1985, my final season, Artis Gilmore and I had a chance to reminisce about Julius's days in the ABA, when Artis was with the Colonels, Doctor was with the Nets, and I was with the Spirits. Artis swears that Doctor J went up to dunk against him and he was able to get up with Julius to block the shot—all palm against ball.

"But he takes the ball while in the air," Artis insisted, "and switches it from his dunking hand to his other hand. Still up there, he slams the ball back down through, lefthanded. It was the most awesome play I'd ever seen." But that was Julius—physically capable of doing whatever had to be done to make the play, he could overwhelm a team physically, all by himself. He was a challenge.

My Most Memorable Game. Game 5, 1981 Eastern Conference final series, Celtics vs. 76ers. In 1981 we had everything necessary to win a championship, including size (Robert Parish, Kevin McHale and Rick Robey), a superstar (Larry Bird), superb playmaking (Tiny Archibald) and players like Cedric Maxwell, Gerald Henderson, Chris Ford and myself who were excellent support personnel. Yet in the latter stages of the series against the 76ers, we had played tentatively, fitfully; against a team as great as the Philadelphia 76ers, playing in this manner is tantamount to suicide, and we trailed the series three to one for the second straight year.

They were playing hard in that fifth game at the Garden (we had the home court advantage in the series), attempting to close us out. They surged to a 57-47 lead and controlled the game for the first twenty-four minutes. But we came back, pride forcing us to shed our submissive role. Late in the third period we led by six. But they regained their composure and used the hot shooting of Andrew Toney to grab the lead late in the fourth. They had us reeling, on the edge of elimination. With 1:51 remaining, trailing by six, we called timeout to set up an option play for Larry. He would either drive to the hoop or toss it into the low post to Robert. Larry had the ball in the left corner and immediately threw it to Chief. But Darryl Dawkins sensed the move and leaped in front of Parish to steal the pass. He cuffed it triumphantly. Philadelphia had the ball and led by six points with less than two minutes remaining. But against all odds we fought back with such fury and passion that we not only overtook them in that game, we changed the entire series around. They worked the ball up slowly, and when the rookie Toney went for the basket Maxwell leaped in from the weak side to block the shot (body completely extended, arm and fingers outstretched); Tiny immediately took the ball in on the right, pivoted in an expert low-post reverse and flipped the ball in. With a foul. We were within three, and the crowd began roaring. At that juncture, our defense became very aggressive. Chris Ford said everybody was out there overplaying. You just could not ask for better defense from those guys. They didn't want anybody to make or receive a pass. They really wanted it. We forced a turnover, Larry drove for a baseline basket at :47, and the lead was down to 109-108. I went into the game with thirty-eight seconds left.

I was ready to play aggressive individual basketball. Although I won't make the claim that I could dominate that game the way I did in 1973 in Kansas City, the internal power was identical. Our Celtics team this night was consumed with victory. Nothing else existed.

On my first play I was defending an out-of-bounds play (Philadelphia had called time after the Bird basket). I waved my arms frantically and tipped the ball. They called another timeout. After the teams lined up again, they set up a triangle with Dawkins in the post and Doctor J and Bobby Jones on the wing. But they lost the ball, and Larry picked it up and drove directly for the basket down the left side. Bodies collided underneath and I saw nothing but the basketball. The shot missed. Running down the center of the court, I reached for the ball, sliding off the rim. Erving, Hollins and Dawkins were there, but I had it. I gathered myself for a turnaround jumper and Erving fouled me. I made both free throws and we had the lead.

The final twenty seconds were unforgettable. By now, I was attached to Toney defensively (I said to him, "Andrew, they're going to Doctor J on every play! They forget about you?" I was talking junk to him). Hollins brought the ball up on the left. They worked the ball to Erving, and Bird and Maxwell doubled him, forcing him to give it up. Bobby Jones took it and drove left; because Bird was out of position, he had a clear lane to go up with a soft, lefthanded floater. Robert went up to block the attempt but pulled his arm back at the last moment. The arc was too high and it would have been goaltending. But the shot missed. I had been in the low post with Toney, and when the shot fell off, the ball was mine! I forced my way past Dawkins to grab the rebound and the game was ours. I was fouled and it was decided that I should make the first one, then miss the second. There was one second remaining and all we would have to do was bat the ball around to secure our win. I did this. But the final shot was too hard—Jones grabbed it and they called a timeout. Now, if they were able to score on the half-court inbounds play, we were going into overtime. But Bird swarmed Jones inbounding and Parish stole the pass. Ford and I embraced and we hustled into the locker room.

When we were in the locker room celebrating, there was a moment of of controversy. Fitch, who had instructed me to miss the final free throw, was taking some heat. Red, as well as some of the other former Celtics greats, believed the decision could have put us in a bad position. We should have made the free throws, taken the points and put them out of winning position.

Most Memorable Offensive Play. In my first game back in Detroit as a Celtic, we were down by three when Coach Fitch called timeout to set up a three-point shot for Dave Cowens. The shot was short; I got the rebound, and instead of putting the missed shot in, I dribbled out to the left corner and fired a three-point field goal up and in from the left corner—with no time left on the clock. Instead of losing by one, the result of tipping in Cowens's miss, we had created an overtime situation, which we pulled out. At that moment, I knew I had found a home.

Most Memorable Defensive Play. Game 4 of the 1984 NBA finals. In this key game against the Lakers, I was able to anticipate an inbounds pass from Jamaal Wilkes to James Worthy and make the steal that sealed the necessary road win in that series (we had lost the first game in Boston, apparently relinquishing the home-court advantage). The steal probably shouldn't have mattered to a man who had once led the NBA in steals, but it did; I had predicted a victory in this game and was told by some members of our national media that in light of the 137-104 Laker runaway in Game 3 such a prediction was crazy. This play was also gratifying because I was an older player looking for other ways to contribute as my playing time diminished.

Most Embarrassing Moments in Sports. Losing that aforementioned Game 3. The nationally televised game was a torrid display of fast-break basketball by the Lakers. We viewed ourselves as a disgrace—to ourselves and to anyone who had been a part of the Celtic Family. In fact, headlines in the Los Angeles papers the following Monday morning proclaimed that we showed no heart. "We played like sissies," Larry Bird said. Larry was our leader; I believed our leader, so when I went to take a shower, I looked around me to see who he was talking about.

My Dumbest Play. In the fifth overtime of a seven-overtime game at Wallace Rose Hill High, we were ahead by two points and I had the ball with four seconds remaining. Someone in the crowd made a sound imitating the final horn, and I dropped the ball and started celebrating. An opponent picked up the ball and called timeout. After the timeout the same player made a shot at the buzzer to force a sixth overtime. We finally lost the game in the seventh OT when I fouled out with over a minute left. I still cringe when I think about that one!

Most Unusual Shot. As a Piston in a game against the New Jersey Nets, I found myself in a sitting position near the foul line with the ball. The twenty-four second clock was winding down, and there was no one to pass to, so I took the shot. All net! Funnily enough, that day I was having particular trouble putting the ball in the hole while I was on my feet.

Most Physical Teammate. Teddy East, Guilford College. I've played with a lot of physical players in my day, but nobody matched Teddy. Teddy would bump anyone off a screen and go after players sailing in for an easy basket. There weren't easy buckets against Teddy East. He was so intimidating that the commissioner of the Carolinas Conference made a special trip to the Crackerbox in Greensboro to check him out. That night, Teddy was the sweetest young man in the sport. He didn't commit a foul. In casual contact with an opponent, he was certain to help the stricken gentleman up. After the game I had to double-check his numeral to be certain it was my man Teddy.

Best Big-Game Teammate. Dennis Johnson. I knew the DJ for Rick Robey trade would send us over the top. DJ was a constant in our multidimensional attack, and when the game was on the line, he was absolutely fearless. He's one of sixteen kids, and before starting his collegiate career, he drove a backhoe for a year. Maybe things like this help him keep some perspective on matters like ballgames. A list of Dennis Johnson Big Games would probably stretch from Lenny Wilkens's home in Seattle to John MacLeod's in Phoenix. Who knows why those coaches traded Dennis away. From the time Dennis took over the point guard for our team, we had a leader.

One night in March of 1984, Dennis took over down the stretch against the Knicks, leading us on a comeback to almost win that game. He had the ball with time running out and the Celtics behind by one. Out of a one-four offense, he drove the lane and got stripped of the ball. We ended up losing. It was his first season here and we were still building; we walked into the locker room after the game and there was some uneasy tension. But nobody was angry with Dennis. We knew we finally had a player who had complete confidence with the ball down the stretch. The Celtics are always angry and tense when they lose. Dennis quickly felt at home in Boston; his intensity matches that of the team's.

Greatest Rivalry. Boston Celtics-Philadelphia 76ers. This rivalry originated in the fifties, when the 76ers were located in Syracuse. Then, the Celtics had Bill Russell, Sam and K. C. Jones, and Bob Cousy. Syracuse had Dolph Schayes and George Yardley. They played a seven-game series in 1959 that many of the Celtics of that team called their toughest. After the Nats moved to Philadelphia and became the 76ers, the rivalry continued, especially when the Sixers acquired Wilt Chamberlain from the San Francisco Warriors. That was the rivalry that so entranced me when I was growing up in Wallace.

Through the eighties, there has not been another rivalry in sports that can compare to the classic battles between these two teams. The media would always quiz us before each game with the 76ers—about the history, the significance of a game during the regular season, the matchups, and so on. K. C. and the rest of us would patiently explain that the games had pertinence *every* time we played. We genuinely went after each other; from the beginning of our own Celtic championship era, it was either the Celtics or the 76ers who dominated. And we always wanted to win.

So many fascinating games! In 1980, they defeated us in the Eastern Conference final series. The following season, they defeated us in Philadelphia in November in that double-overtime game in which Erving scored forty-five, and Bird scored thirty-six. But we won the regular-season championship on the final day of the season by defeating them in a one-game showdown. Both teams finished with identical 62-20 records, but because we won that final game, we had the home-court advantage in the playoffs. It was a war in that playoff final one month later, as we kept rallying from double-digit deficits to win. I remember the final game, Game 7 back in Boston. We were skying, on an emotional high coming out of the locker room. During the warmups, with about a minute to play before we were to be blown off for the introductions, we started dunking, high-school style. At first slowly, Henderson, Maxwell and Carr. Then, in a cascade of dunks Bird, Ford, McHale and Parish followed slam, slam, *slam*! The crowd began applauding and screaming, and we needed every reserve to win by one point, 91-90.

In 1982 they dethroned us, winning Game 7 back at the Garden after we rallied to tie the series at three-all. At that game several Boston fans showed up wearing ghost costumes, reminding the Sixers of the previous year. Unfortunately it sparked them. Julius laughed later, saying he thought the Klan had entered the Garden. Billy Cunningham, their coach, did a very intelligent coaching tactic; with three minutes left in the warmup, he took his team out of the arena and regrouped in the sanctity of their locker room. The crowd continued roaring, but there was something convincing about them as they walked back onto the Garden floor. The filed in, separate, independent, powerful, against over-whelming odds. And they took the ballgame. As the clock wound down on our season, the fans started shouting, *"Beat L. A.!"* a classy gesture to the 76ers as they went to the finals.

Nineteen eighty-three was our down season, but we did defeat them three times in Boston, even as we were unraveling as a team. The following year, we won the championship and again split the season series, although each team won a game on the other team's home floor. The teams always went at each other, even in preseason games; that year, there were several fights in our exhibition in Boston (Moses against Maxwell, Henderson against Sedale Threatt, and Red Auerbach, descending from his seat, swinging an elbow at Billy Cunningham). Without three starters, we still carried them into double overtime in Philadelphia.

Nineteen eighty-five ended the rivalry for the present teams. We defeated them in five games in the Eastern Conference championship and they seemed to be strangers out there. Toney was injured, Moses was fighting the owner, and they hadn't yet assimilated Barkley effectively. But it wasn't pleasant; earlier in the year, Bird and Erving had a violent confrontation even during one of Bird's best shooting nights. Suddenly after bumping, they were at each other's throats! I ended up being fined for trying to wrestle Malone off of Bird.

But that was fitting perhaps. Cunningham would resign after the season and the teams began changing. Yet through the present, every time the teams take the floor to oppose each other, it's a special game.

Chapter 15

The Fans

An attractive woman in her early thirties had the best seat in Madison Square Garden for games between the Celtics and Knicks. For each game we played there, she would arrive early, reach into a Gucci handbag for her eyeglasses, and proceed to act in a way that made me want to use earplugs. From the moment we headed onto the floor for warmups, she sent a steady cascade of catcalls, abuse and epithets in our direction. Her shrill voice filled the space behind our bench like fire. The most visible target of course was M. L. Carr. I finally had to retaliate during the 1984 playoffs.

Bernard King was in a zone that season—a frighteningly quick first step on the drive and an even quicker release on his jump shot. His driving game was relentless, unstoppable. They would take us to seven games in that series. In Game 4, King was driving and there was a collision. Our bench stood up to see what had happened, and in the tense atmosphere, the young lady's voice began bellowing out. Again.

"Sit down Carr. Be quiet you cheerleader! You don't have any class. Sit down! *Sit down!*

I waited.

We returned to New York for Game 6 and I plotted my move. We filed out to the floor, and before she was able to mount an offensive (this woman was waging war), I walked over to her.

I said to her: "Now you act like you don't know me." She was stunned. I looked at her friends sitting alongside of her. "You think people don't know about our affair?" I constructed a plausible scene that had her friends wondering. She was quiet for the rest of the night.

Another group of kids in New York used to carry a sign around the borders of the court that read, "M. L. Sucks!" They held the signs over their heads and shouted at me, "C'mon over M. L. If you're not a chicken." So I walked over to them and initiated a surprisingly friendly conversation. I caught the eye of a photographer from Boston and asked him to shoot a photograph of all of us standing together. They gazed at me, bewildered, "We're friends, fellows," I advised them. I took special attention to put my arms around all of them in a series of pictures. After that ordeal, I never saw the sign again.

Sports audiences invest their money and emotions in athletic events. In a way, they're as committed to the outcome of a particular game or season as the players themselves. The Boston Celtics are important to Boston and the New England region because of the players, the manner in which the players play, and the institution that the team has become in a tradition-oriented region of the country. They have a strong influence on the outcome of games in Boston; they certainly inspired us in my two championship seasons, and beyond: in 1985-1986 and 1986-1987, the Celtics won 100 of 103 games played at the Boston Garden.

Waving the towel has become something I am identified with. When I sensed the team needed prodding, I would grab a towel and thrust it into the air, inviting the fans into the game. I led the cheers—no question about it. But only because I sensed the fans were so deeply invested in the outcome. I understood it mattered to all of us—the players, the Celtics organization and the fans. The fans in the Garden were representing a much larger rooting base, in Boston and nationally.

But fans in opposing arenas are often just as vociferous, which can make for some abuse for players on the road. Yet a remembrance from my past shielded me from taking this abuse too seriously. During the time when Wallace was first integrating her schools, I would lead our team out on the court, even on the road. The road wasn't always such a friendly place when you're a pioneer in race relations. I took the court at South Lenoir one night and looked up in the bleachers behind our basket. A big black dummy hung by its neck from the upper level. It had a Wallace Rose Hill jersey on it with the number 30 across its chest—my number. The worst epithets I ever heard in L.A. or in Madison Square Garden couldn't affect me after that experience.

But the fans are a major reason why the NBA's brand of basketball is so exciting. They are also as individual as the teams they root for, so here are a few personal observations on the fans throughout the league.

Boston. The Celtics are more than a team. They are an institution. They give many people around the league an opportunity to be part of a winner. This is their team and they are proud it. It's almost like a cult. Generations are brought up with the Celtics. They have learned how and when to push the team and they know how the team wins. One day I'd like to see a banner lifted to the rafters of the present or future Boston

Garden that reads: *America's Number 1 Fans*. It would be fitting. In my opinion, they've paid their dues in helping the Celtics become the most successful team in professional sports.

New York. New York fans are frustrated because they had such great teams in the late sixties and early seventies. Since that time, however, attempts to purchase (George McGinnis, Wilt Chamberlain), rebuild (three draft choices acquired from John Y. Brown of the Celtics in 1979 failed to make a dramatic improvement), or demand continued success (Hubie Brown) have met upon hard times. When I first came into professional basketball, all that was being said about the Knicks' fans was how loyal and emotionally involved they were, how Madison Square Garden was always sold out. It seems to me that with the number of people living in New York, win, lose or draw the Garden should always be sold out. I've never seen sportswriters as hard on their team as the New York writers, and I suspect that hinders the support of fans in New York. They haven't been as committed as I had been led to believe. Only when the Knicks made a pitch to sign Red Auerbach away from the Celtics in that 1979 season did I finally believe what New Yorkers had been telling us throughout the years: that they had the makings of the next dynasty in professional basketball. The Knicks did win two championships in 1970 and 1973, but the lack of any harmony between the front office and the coaching staff has hurt that team. The Knicks really needed someone like Red to take complete control of all basketball matters. Instead there has been chaos; communication breakdown has plagued the team, and they probably reached their nadir in the Dave DeBusschere/Hubie Brown era, when, ironically, they were finally able to produce a playoff team. Then, the fans were genuinely involved; later, even after Patrick Ewing arrived, they seemed to lose interest and become cynical. It is an unfortunate state of affairs.

New Jersey Nets. The fans there are confused because they don't know whether to pull for New York or New Jersey. They are caught in a tough situation. It appeared as if the Nets were clicking in the early eighties; they had Darryl Dawkins playing extremely well, with Mike Gminski in a more-than-adequate backup role. Buck Williams was one of the best offensive rebounders in the game and an ideal support player. Micheal Ray Richardson, Darwin Cook and Ray Williams were crowd-pleasers, effective guards. Larry Brown was a smart and energetic coach. But Brown left the team and injuries descended on the players. The fans quickly filed out of the gym after that, and since that time the marketing strategy of the Nets has changed. They promote visiting teams, hoping that fans will come to see a Larry Bird, a Michael Jordan, an Isiah Thomas. It'll take some time before we see die-hard Net fans.

Philadelphia. Sixer fans are lively, enthusiastic, knowlegeable and hurt. They're hurt by a team that has achieved a number of playing goals, including an NBA championship, yet still isn't quite up to the standard of the Lakers or Celtics in the eighties. The fans and the team suffered for lack of a main ingredient in team success: loyalty. Forget about the Lakers, the driving force behind the 76ers' competitive urge is their desire to beat Boston. I think the Sixers' audience marvels at the player/management/fan loyalty of the Celtics and how that's been sustained over decades. Philadelphia fans would love to see that in the City of Brotherly Love. Instead they have witnessed great players like Andrew Toney, Moses Malone, Clint Richardson and even Julius Erving, the great Dr. J, look down the street of loyalty and find it wasn't two ways. And it certainly wasn't located on Broad Street, where the Philadelphia Spectrum is located. Admittedly the Sixers have been among the elite of the league. But controversy has been the Sixers' Sixth Man and it has worn on their fans.

In the late seventies, they attempted to win a title with "superstars" at every position: Erving, McGinnis, Free, Collins, Dawkins and Caldwell Jones. But that team lost its best shot in 1977 after leading Portland two-nothing in the finals. They never recovered, destroyed by infighting. They rebuilt the team by adding role players (Bobby Jones, Andrew Toney) under the excellent coaching of Billy Cunningham, but they still fell short. Later, they acquired Moses Malone via free agency; that was the turning point, because after finally winning the title in 1983, the controversy intensified instead of fading out. Harold Katz criticized Malone and finally ended up trading him. To a man up in Boston, we felt that the Sixers had blown it.

Fans of the Sixers talk more junk than anyone else in the league. I loved the interaction with them as much as any, though they really gave it to me every game. It was a nice love/hate relationship because they were very vocal. They helped carry the classic battles between the Sixers and the Celtics to new heights. Sometimes they went a little too far. Cedric Maxwell reported that after he was pushed into the front row by Darryl Dawkins in Game 6 of the 1982 playoffs, he heard such racial abuse that he had to charge back in there and fight (he drew a hefty fine for that one). But we understand that all is not perfect in Philadelphia. Even the Liberty Bell is cracked.

Washington Bullets. Their fans were very hard for me to judge because I could never determine whether they were cheering because they appreciated their team or because it was a required governmental stress reduction procedure. Or maybe it was because their tickets were federally subsidized. Whatever the reason, the games were always well-represented.

Milwaukee Bucks. The Bucks play in a collegiate arena, the Mecca, home of Marquette University. The fans in Milwaukee love their Bucks, but they are like a big unit; if one of them stands up, they all stand up. If one goes to the bathroom, they all get up and go. To say the least, they are all of one accord. It was absolutely incredible to see their response to the rumors, eventually true, that Don Nelson would be leaving their team as coach after having that job for ten years. They showed support for their coach in a way that hadn't been displayed in this league for a long time. Don Nelson made the first coach's curtain call in the history of the league after he coached his last game in Milwaukee. Bucks fans have a small family feeling, helped by the team's small arena.

Portland Trail Blazers. You have to be a fanatic to pay to see your home team play on closed circuit television. The legendary Blazermania began in the Bill Walton-Maurice Lucas championship season and created an excessive demand for tickets. The Trail Blazers have sold out the Memorial Coliseum for over nine straight years; the Paramount Theater in Portland is utilized to allow Blazer fans to see the team play when they're at home. It's one thing to watch games on cable TV. It's another to travel to a theater to watch your basketball team. That's dedication and need. Of course, Portland will always have great fans because it's the only thing to do in that town. Other than watch it rain all the time.

Los Angeles Lakers. The only Lakers fans who care about the players are their families and Jack Nicholson. The only reason the Lakers get great fan support is because it's the most expensive ticket in town. If the event were two frogs competing in a high jump and the tickets cost two hundred dollars for the cheap seats, you would still have fans driving up in their Mercedes, Jaguars, Rolls Royces and limos with their designer sunglasses on. I could never go to the Forum without thinking about Disneyland.

Golden State Warriors. After several years of organizational aimlessness, the fans there will finally have a number of reasons to cheer again. The Warriors lost several fine players because of free agency (Rick Barry), trades (Robert Parish) and management (two weeks after winning the 1975 championship they traded a key player, Butch Beard). The fans, though sparse, have always impressed me as being interested and enthusiastic. The team, in my opinion, has consistently had a young following as a strong part of their support base. The Warriors reached the second round of the playoffs last year and refused to quit against the Lakers, rallying from twelve points behind in the second half of the fourth game of that series, trailing in games, zero-three. Most teams give up in that situation, and the Warriors' comeback sealed the support for Don Nelson, the general manager, and George Karl, the coach. Both men know how to construct winning teams. It will be a long road, but I think both from the fans' and from the organization's perspective, it's a very positive situation in Oakland.

Denver Nuggets. The fans in Denver have been loyal over the years, both when the team was in the ABA and through good times and bad in the NBA. They had and still have the dream of one day putting it all together and really making that mile-high altitude an ally in the NBA finals. But to me, the team and the city still live on the memories of the glory days in the old ABA, when Bobby Jones, David Thompson and Dan Issell comprised an exciting front line and their running/pressing game led them to the brink of an ABA championship. The team drew over 17,000 per game in that final ABA series agaisnt the New York Nets and Doctor J.

Atlanta Hawks. Though Atlanta gives strong support during playoff games, in the past the city generally found it more convenient to watch "the fabulous superstation" telecast of games from around the league. But I think that's changed recently; fans have taken a closer, more dedicated look at their present team because of the youth, vitality and direction it's getting from a bright young coach, Mike Fratello. The team also finds joy in pulling for their exciting little guy, Spud Webb.

Spud Webb is my favorite player in the NBA. He's five-foot-four, an unprecedented height for a player in the league. He was cut quickly from his first team, the Detroit Pistons. But he was an outstanding push man on the Hawks' fast break from the beginning—K. C. was an immediate supporter of Webb from a performance perspective, not merely as an entertaining sideshow. The Hawks struggled in 1986-1987 when he was injured, further evidence of the little guy's ability. Webb beat all odds to play in the league and wouldn't be denied his opportunities.

Cleveland Cavs. I predict serious title contention will finally happen for these fans. With the leadership of Lenny Wilkens and the drafting of excellent young talent in 1986 and 1987 (Brad Daugherty, Ron Harper, John Williams, Kevin Johnson), the fans will soon have something to cheer about. On two occasions Cleveland had excellent crowd support: in the 1975-1976 season, when they won the Central Division championship, and in 1985, when we knocked them and my old teammate World Free out in the first round. All of the playoff games sold over 20,000 seats per contest. It's amazing how many people will show up when a team starts winning a few games! I suspect there are probably more Cav fans than we realize—it's just hard to get them to admit it. But the team will one day stop being the laughingstock of the league.

Dallas Mavericks. The only thing bigger than a Maverick game in Texas is a weekend dance at Kings Ranch. These fans take their team seriously! Formerly the town belonged to football, but that's not the case anymore. The fans have been patient while the organization built a solid team through the draft. I think the NBA is proud to have fans like these in Dallas.

Houston Rockets. Their fans are tired of the "Dream Teams" that are so heavily promoted: Moses Malone in the early eighties; the Twin Towers, Akeem Olajuwon and Ralph Sampson, now. The dream teams do just that—keep the fans dreaming. The fans keep on going to the Summit and finding the well dry. The city of Houston is blessed with a super place to watch the Rockets play; they must not abandon ship because if the team stays together and adds a couple of guards, it may eventually happen. Fans in Houston may go home at night and be assured that their coach, Bill Fitch, and forward, Cedric Maxwell, know what it takes to win.

San Antonio Spurs. Spurs fans still talk about the "good old days," much as fans in Denver do. They recall fondly the years when George "Ice" Gervin was scoring thirty-plus points per game and the ABA was still a league. There are some wild fans in that city, beginning with the famous, or infamous, "Baseline Bums." This is a group of tough-looking guys who come and jeer opposing teams mercilessly. In the Spurs' best seasons, they combined a home-court advantage, a raucous country fiddle and the sniping of Ice and Larry Kenon to intimidate teams. The Bums love the Spurs nearly as much as they love doing that great Texas dance called the "Cotton-Eyed Joe." If San Antonio is fortunate enough to get David Robinson, the noise level will probably be measured on the Richter scale.

Detroit Pistons. No NBA fans have suffered more long, cold winters than Pistons fans have. The conditions are finally beginning to look bright in the Motor City because Isiah Thomas has his talented teammates clicking on all cylinders. The toughest thing the Pistons have to figure out is which arena in the city they should go to for the home games. There soon will be *five* in which the team can play, with proposed plans pending on a new arena downtown. Currently the Pistons play in the Pontiac Silverdome, an arena twenty miles outside of Detroit.

Detroit can boast that it has the NBA's most famous fan: Leon "The Barber" Bradley. He's a distinguished-looking, middle-aged, gray-bearded black man who sits right behind the visitor's bench, in the front row. Leon rides the visiting teams unmercifully; to Maxwell one night: "Maxwell, you aren't a leg up on a warm six-pack of beer!" Another night he correctly appraised the dilemma of one of our most talented players, Carlos Clark. In my estimation, Carlos had as much talent as any guard in the league. But he wasn't aggressive enough, always seeming to hold himself back when his opportunity to play arrived, especially in the 1984-1985 season when he appeared to be in a great position to win the third-guard role on the team. Leon watched Carlos one night as we were huddling during a timeout; Carlos was standing on the periphery of the huddle. Leon barked out to Carlos, "Hey Clark! What you doin' out there, Man? Those guys are making over a million dollars a year. You better put your head in the huddle and make sure K. C. can find you when he goes looking for you. You can't be standing *outside*!" Leon would shout, but he could see, too.

Now, there are lots of Pistons fans besides Leon. Detroit set a league attendance record in 1986-1987, totalling over one million fans for the regular season. If and when the Pistons do win their first NBA championship, look for Lee Iacocca to give every Pistons fan in the city a rebate on their next Chrysler. Incidentally, I'm still somewhat of a Pistons fan because they gave me my first job in the NBA. I'm also an Iacocca fan because he knew how "not to be denied."

L. A. Clippers. They are the fans who can't get tickets to see the Lakers play. Clippers fans were disappointed by all the injuries to their players. Marques Johnson, Norm Nixon, Derek Smith and Bill Walton fell in the past five years. A reasonable ticket price and a decent record could have been an attractive selling approach for many of Los Angeles's NBA fans. My friend Don Chaney deserves apologies: they gave him a water pistol and sent him off to war. Having two teams in Los Angeles reminds me of my high school days; the Lakers are like the varsity team and the Clippers are like the junior varsity.

Phoenix Suns. Suns fans are a dedicated group. They have attended games at the Arizona Veterans Memorial Coliseum zealously for several years. But after nearly winning an NBA championship in 1976, they have witnessed a decline in the team's fortunes, including big problems there in 1987. If the team itself wasn't a diversion from common-day problems, at least the team's mascot, the Gorilla, continued to be. The Gorilla is the best cartoon-like figure in all sports, outdistancing even the San Diego Chicken. Phoenix's reputation as an NBA power arguably depends on the result of one game: the 1976 Game 5 triple-overtime defeat to the Boston Celtics and John Havlicek. It was perhaps the best basketball game ever played.

Chicago Bulls. Some of the loudest fans in the league. Coach Doug Collins, superstar Michael Jordan and the Bulls' fans form a perfect triangle because they are all fierce competitors. A few of their fans are some of the most obnoxious spectators in the league. But they help their team; they have as much influence as any fans in the league in helping their home team when they're on a roll.

Utah Jazz. Jazz fans are grateful to be in the league. The Utah Stars of the ABA enjoyed great success, but since the New Orleans Jazz moved to Salt Lake City in 1979, the city and the state haven't found the charismatic team to make the sport an artistic and financial success. Frank Layden's humor, downhill skiing and an opportunity to see visiting heroes from Utah perform helps, but excitement is sporadic for fans of the Jazz.

Seattle SuperSonics. There are some knowledgeable and animated fans in Seattle, although this receives miniscule recognition in the Northeast corridor. The fans in Seattle have watched very good and very bad teams; they participated in a sensational championship season in 1979 with great players like Dennis Johnson, Fred Brown and Gus Williams representing the city. But there have been lean years; that team was dispersed, management took a hard stance toward Johnson and Williams, and eventually the team landed in the cellar. But the franchise and the fans have returned primarily because Lenny Wilkens hired Bernie Bickerstaff in one of his last acts as general manager. Bickerstaff had been passed over several times before finally landing a coaching position. He had been an assistant in the league for eleven seasons. The area is fired up again because Bickerstaff has put together a team that hustles, period. Bernie paid his dues, kept his vision and would not be denied this golden opportunity to become a head coach in the NBA.

Sacramento Kings. Sacramento obtained the Kansas City franchise in 1985-1986, the season after I had left basketball. The Sacramento fans do seem to be a very appreciative group, grateful to have a major league franchise. The Kings hired Bill Russell to coach the team before the 1987-1988 season, and Russell hired Willis Reed as assistant coach. I firmly believe the Kings will have a winning system. If the Kings' fans are intelligent, they will pressure the organization to have the two coaches in uniform, because even at their retirement ages they are the two most talented players on the team.

Indiana Pacers. Always one of my most enjoyable places on the road. The fans are consistently warm and respectful toward athletes on visiting teams. They show a sense of pride in the Pacers, their sports and their city. They are attempting to build Indiana into the sports capital of America, having lured the Baltimore Colts to the Hoosierdome in 1984.

I think the fans there are classy, and I think they have an opportunity to succeed with their ambitious plans. I enjoyed playing in that city with all three teams that I played for.

Thank you Indiana. Don't be denied your dreams.

Chapter 16

The Final Season

After twenty seasons of organized basketball, my career came to an end after the 1984-1985 season. I had gone from the orange and tan floorboards of Wallace Rose Hill High, to an NAIA title with Guilford, to Israel, St. Louis and Detroit, until I had finally reached my place of destiny, the Boston Celtics. Not everything about that final year was good; I ended my career sitting on the bench, injured, watching as the Lakers adamantly closed the door on our team's bid to win back-to-back championships. We had come extremely close to our goal of becoming the first postmerger team to win consecutive championships, so the season ended on a frustrating note.

We were like an automobile that needed a tuneup that season. A high-priced model, mind you, but one that nevertheless had its fits. Henderson was traded. Maxwell held out that season and never attained his rhythm. He injured his knee and had to have an arthroscopy in February. This contributed to a complicated situation, because McHale was shedding his bench role naturally, with outstanding postup play and a visible, intimidating shot-blocking defense. When Max came back, he accepted his new role of coming in off the bench on the surface, but it is difficult for a player of Maxwell's stature to reconcile this reduced responsibility. Again, too much pride.

Not that there weren't good times. We all took pride in McHale's fifty-six-point team scoring record in March and Bird's sixty-point magic show in New Orleans several days later. We again had the best record in the league and seemed to be in the driver's seat to win back-to-back titles. But the giant had its shadow, too. We needed a third guard that season when neither Quinn Buckner nor Carlos Clark could get untracked and contribute solid minutes. We acquired Ray Williams in February, and Ray gave us some productive minutes as a penetrating, shooting guard, but it was tough for us to adjust to another style and another ego. Late in the playoffs, Ray's effectiveness decreased; at a team dinner after we had eliminated Cleveland in the first round of the playoffs, Ray was standing with a bunch of the guys in the private dining room the hotel had set up for us outside of Richfield, Ohio. Ray was a kind, sensitive person, but his animated court personality was driving the coaches to a degree of distraction. Red walked over to Ray, gave him sort of a hug, and then looked at him quizzically. He seemed to be saying, "You're a Celtic type person. I just wished you took better care of the ball!"

The jinx of winning back-to-back championships in the NBA is like one of the mystery stories Red loves reading. Only there isn't an ending. Teams have tried to ignore it, to work hard to play through it or to pace themselves for the playoffs and then regroup for a final push. But you can't pretend it isn't there, because teams are shooting for you every night. For a team in the bottom half of the league, defeating the defending champion can make its season. The Los Angeles Clippers could market that solitary win over the Celtics in February to sell tickets the following offseason.

Working yourself harder in training camp or pacing yourself has its problems, too. Teams burn out over the nine months of an NBA season; by the middle of the season you're walking around airports uncertain if you're in Chicago or Kansas City or Denver. Then you're back home to deal with family and personal business, but it's only March with six weeks to the playoffs. The playoffs require that you elevate yourself mentally and physically because the intensity of the games is that much greater. An NBA season is very demanding; you have to be vigilant. To win it all, you have to play through mid-June, and by the beginning of another equally demanding season you have slightly less capacity to deal with everything as effectively.

For an NBA team to win, it must be consistent. In professional sports, consistency equals victories; if you lose, the media and fans want to know why, regardless of how well you're playing. Get into a pyschological slump and opposing teams will jump all over you. Soon, any season-long game plan you might have constructed is revised, reworked and then junked. Losing further compounds any problems that might be under the surface. The most closely knit teams have their individual differences, which can become pressures when you're losing, detracting from the blend of physical talent and ego that is necessary to win the ring. With the common draft that has the best teams selecting low, the league is very talented top to bottom. Cliches like "going for it" and "on a roll" are fitting; winning the championship is usually a one-time ride, so you had better savor the taste.

So we had our work cut out for us that season, and matters became all the more difficult in the playoffs when we were hit hard with injuries. Parish's back hurt so much he was hardly able to run. DJ and Larry were also injured and tired. We defeated Detroit in six games and then got the jump on the 76ers to rout them four games to one. The Philadelphia series brought us into the finals against Los Angeles again. We threw the Boston Common at them in the first game in Boston, winning 148-114 and set all kinds of records, including a perfect eleven-for-eleven shooting performance by Scott Wedman. But because of television, Game 2 was held three days later, and the Lakers regrouped in the second game, spreading their half-court offense to allow Kareem Abdul-Jabbar more room to maneuver from the low post and providing better passing angles into the post. They led, 64-46, at halftime, won that game, and kept the upper hand throughout the remainder of the series.

Through a discouraging week in Los Angeles, the Lakers played one step ahead, even after DJ won Game 4 with a buzzer-beating jumper. We were wearing down. On the bench, Maxwell, Quinn and I talked about it, thinking that K. C. had to go to one of us. The Lakers were running seldom-used players like Mitch Kupchak in there for a momentary lift. We never got the call.

"I felt the way I felt when I was a kid growing up in Brooklyn," Abdul-Jabbar said after he had won the playoff MVP award. The Lakers had dethroned us, 111-100, in Game 6 to take the championship four games to two. It was a big moment for L.A.—the first time they had defeated Boston for the championship. But for me it was a tough way to end a career.

The most unusual team photograph I was ever in was the 1984-1985 picture. The team had changed personnel frequently that year, so Tod Rosensweig and Jeff Twiss of the Celtics' front office were forced to call the players and arrange it for the Monday after Game 6 of the finals. At the time, we didn't realize that it would be the day after we lost the championship. I put on my number 30 for the final time. The locker room was still tainted by the defeat the previous day. We lined up on the Garden floor, smiling wearily and posing for the photographers. Ray Melchiorre, our trainer, summed it up best. "I just never thought we'd lose yesterday." Celtic thinking. But defeat is real. Afterwards players packed their bags and cleared out for the year, like emptying the house after a divorce. There was some joking and some remorse. McHale sat there, still somber. Bird was tired and angry, yet relieved. DJ's attitude: once it's over, it's over, and do the very best you can to leave it behind.

But for me the day was a double ending. I was finishing a season and a career. After the photographs were taken, I walked around behind the chairs at center court. The parquet floor—ancient, legendary, hallowed— echoed faintly as I walked there for what could be the last time. I hadn't fully made up my mind yet. I wondered how I would fill the emptiness. I looked around the empty arena and cherished the moments, the good moments. As I looked around, I determined that I'd give the team and myself time to assess our respective situations. I knew that any time the Celtics lose, the season is not successful, and it was very tough to think of leaving on an unsuccessful note. I was deeply affected at that moment, and I knew I needed some time and some advice before I finally made up my mind. I told Michael Madden of *The Boston Globe,* "Any time is tough to assess a situation like this. But any time I have a difficult decision, I know where to begin. I'll go home to North Carolina and go do some fishing and talk with my dad."

I suspect my decision was predetermined in many ways. Dad told me that although he didn't really understand the particulars of my situation, I should do what was best for my family. I called David Wells, my old best friend and teammate at Wallace Rose Hill. Wells is an actor living out in Los Angeles, and I had been with him a few weeks earlier during the finals. Wells was shocked. "Leave the Boston Celtics? Are you experiencing delusions? Nobody leaves the Boston Celtics. You have to think long and hard about that one, M. L. I think you should stay with the Celtics until you're old and gray."

Yet off the court I was further along professionally and determined to advance in other professional areas. Sylvia pointed out a few important facts. During that last season I was beginning to complain about going to practice or a long road trip for the first time. I had adjusted to playing less, but there wasn't any more to accomplish in the support role. I wouldn't suddenly begin playing major minutes again. My financial adviser, Phil McLaughlin, and my lawyers, Dick Snyder and Norman Blass, all pointed out the financial opportunities and risks I'd be taking if I were to leave the Celtics. But there were challenges. I had a strong concept for a public relations firm. I wanted to become involved in youth programs. I was totally confident in by ability to establish a vibrant network to promote my ideas, which in turn would generate even more possibilities. It was time to step aside and let younger players have their due. I listened to my counsel, heard the words of my father again. That was it, boys, no more training camp. I was ready to make some new situations happen.

I called the general manager of the Celtics, Jan Volk, who besides being an astute, improving boss, is also a good friend. He talked to me about it for a while, listened and tested me. "Sure, M. L," Jan teased. "We know; when will you be coming down to sign a new contract?" "I'm serious, Jan." We circled around some more and he realized I was. Next was the call to Red Auerbach. We talked around even further. Red's maxim about retirement is that the player himself is always the one who knows it (that he's *really* ready to retire) first. Nobody has to tell him.

Thinking I might change my mind, Red told me not to tell anybody, to sleep on it. Suddenly he understood there wasn't any turning back. So we arranged for a press conference.

Mike Carey of *The Boston Herald* reported that day that Red Auerbach meant it when he told me in front of the press at the Celtics' rookie camp in Marshfield, "As proud as you were to be a Celtic, we were proud and happy to have you." And I began crying some.

K. C. Jones commented, "He's been such a competitor. In a way, this seems like the end of an era."

I said, "I've been wrestling with it for over a year, 'cause the money can be a consideration, too. I even made out a balance sheet and listed all the pros and cons, and it finally seemed like this was the thing to do."

Finally I was asked how I'd like to be remembered.

"As a guy who played with a lot of heart, who was always willing to do whatever he was asked. I'd like to think there'll always be room for a guy like that."

I present the championship trophy to the fans of Boston after our first title in 1981.

Courtesy of the White House

President Reagan congratulates us in the Rose Garden after our 1984 title.

After the 1984 title, I began thinking of my future as a veteran ballplayer and beyond.

Courtesy of WNEV Television, Boston

With Robert Kraft, head of the board of directors of WNEV Television in Boston.

With Ira Stepanian, president of the Bank of Boston (left), and Massachusetts governor Michael Dukakis. Together we have gone into the state's schools, telling kids that drugs are nowhere.

174

The team that swept Texas in 1982, keeping our winning streak alive without Larry Bird and Tiny Archibald.

Basketball consultant for the New Balance Giant Step program.

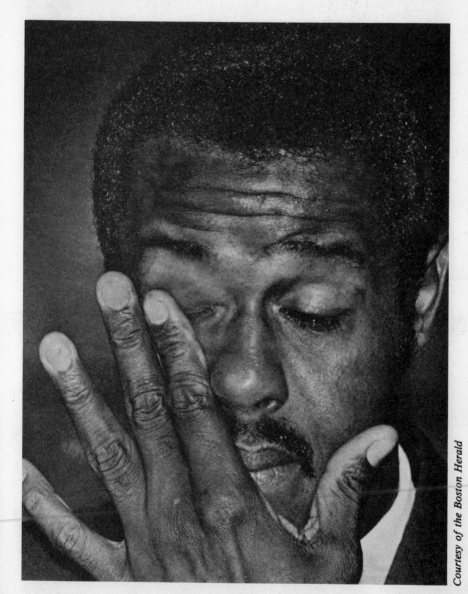

At the press conference announcing my retirement.

My family: M. L., Michael, Andrea, Janine and Sylvia Carr.

PART THREE
GAME PLAN

Chapter 17

The Storm

I've been in storms before, where the wind and cold rain blew hard in my face and the heavens weren't discernible. I battled an uncontrollable temper as a youth and became an impassioned ballplayer. Driven by emotion, I took charge of basketball games at every level. I was a part of three championship teams, an NAIA title and two NBA championships. In 1987 I was elected to the NAIA Hall of Fame. Yet before all that could happen, I was nearly swept away in a hurricane of a career crisis. At twenty-two years of age I was told I wasn't talented enough to play professional basketball. I was cut by two different teams. I had trained every day for years. I had nearly given up my marriage because of my commitment to basketball. I may have been only twenty-two years old, but being cast adrift by two teams in my profession was a blow.

My religious upbringing helped me. I remember in particular the story of Jonah, who was all right until his boat was submerged in a tidal wave. The idea that's always remained with me is that as long as he remained afloat, providing he didn't give up during the tempest, he had a possibility to come out all right. Of course he would end up inside the belly of the whale; he had his crises. But he found a way to survive.

My crises helped me when I made the transition from basketball to business. First, they prepared me for adversity. Second, they helped me see the parallels between different careers. If I could weather the highs and lows of basketball, I could do the same on the outside. Just as I would run extra miles to prepare myself mentally and physically to reach the level of play required in the NBA, a salesman travels an extra mile on the road to complete a working day feeling satisfied. That salesman *knows* he's tired, knows he physically cannot go any farther. But thinking about the kids and his wife back home, he completes that working day by making another call. If he lands the deal, he's had a successful trip.

I carry this knowledge with me wherever I go. I involve myself completely in every project I engage in. I send the same message to kids I address. I believe I have to. I tell these kids that there is nothing standing between them and their potential. They can succeed. With the discipline of the athlete, success will happen. With the total dedication of the career salesman or saleswoman, they won't be denied their dreams. I tell them to look at a photograph of a bum in New York City. If I were that bum sleeping on the street, you'd better believe I'd be the best bum there ever was. I'd drift into dreamland a pretty satisfied man. I wouldn't take that fate lying down; I'd be out hustling: "Give me five! Hey, buddy, can ya spare some change? Spare a dime?" All day! I'd be a rich bum, full and happy as I possibly could be. The message is twofold: I want for them to understand that even bums are human. I want them to know that whatever their lot or chosen course, they should be the very best they can be and fulfill their potential.

My pro career provided me with an excellent opportunity to work with young people. As a former player on the great Boston Celtics, I have the chance to be a role model. Kids will listen. They will believe. But you don't build credibility without commitment, and I think the kids I talk to know that I have something serious to say, something I believe in myself. It gives us something to build on.

In my waning days as a basketball player, I fully realized what was happening in my life. I had fought the battles earlier in my career as an established player. I understood the storm. I also understood that life doesn't end when you hand in your jersey. I knew I had to have a game plan.

My decision to play in Boston opened up some very real opportunities for an existence beyond basketball. I quickly moved to become involved in the community; within days after signing with the Celtics in 1979 I met with an ABCD group in Boston, an organization designed to upgrade sports programs in the city. But there were other moves, both endorsement ventures and work in the media. I did spots for example. I took on an interview program ("Ask M. L.") to give our Boston youth a voice on TV. I also wrote columns for *The Boston Herald* and local weeklies. As my career wound down, my minutes decreasing, my vision of the future began crystallizing more concretely. When I assumed the motivational role at the end of the Celtics' bench during my final two seasons there, I waved a towel to form a symbolic bridge between the fans and the players. But I utilized this with an eye fixed on my business career in the world of life after basketball. That towel brought visibility to the man who waved that cloth; I was the subject of a piece by Tom Callahan in *Time* magazine during the 1985 NBA finals. When I walk into a business meeting or even through the dining room of a hotel, people wave towels or napkins. Recently I spoke at a fund-raiser for the Concord, New Hampshire, Boys and Girls Club. When I walked to the dais to present my speech, the entire auditorium stood up and waved towels the organizers had passed out. The recognition is certainly rewarding, but the visibility has also been an important and useful tool.

I have made some important thrusts into the business community in Boston and in my home state of North Carolina. I have attributes that contribute to the success of organizations, and I believe I have strong instincts to ferret out promising investments in properties. Part of this game plan is associating myself with knowledgeable and competent counselors. Battles aren't meant to be fought alone; I realized this from the onset of my career in business.

I was always a positive thinker and a go-getter. My mother would come home from work and wonder where I was. I'd never wait around if I was out of work; I'd be out getting another job. If I was told there wasn't an opening to sell cars, I nevertheless became the second leading salesman—in the dealership that supposedly had no openings. And that experience has continued to be a useful vehicle because I see myself as a salesman, even in a corporate role. Enthusiasm, will and persistence are the salesman's tools, and I use them. I'm a people person. It's a logical first step to be personable with the receptionist and the secretary of the corporation. I'll want them to see me through the door and keep the message on the desk of the person in charge. I understand the rules of the game thoroughly and I'm not a man who denies reality. I was a ballplayer and I realize that that stature probably brought me through the door. So I'll talk the game to establish lines of communication. I hope we can do business.

A good salesperson remembers details. If the receptionist tells me her son, Michael, is a basketball player, I'll remember Michael and the game he plays. The next time we meet I'll ask how he's doing, all in the interest of establishing a win-win situation: be sure to build up a positive relationship with your potential client. If the first response is negative, I keep my eye on the door, totally focused. That door may open slightly. Then I return and renew my pitch. When I finally win, it's a result of that work ethic.

I'm that detail man, the one who went deep into his knee bends before the foul shot. When I'm approached to invest, I want to see plans concretely spelled out on paper, step by step; then we have something to work with. Similarly, when we are servicing a client, we make sure we maintain a high operations level. There's no other way, really, because

I believe my company is winning even as we are helping our client achieve a high level of productivity. I want to see us developing as a company, which takes place as we are fulfilling our contract. I'm keeping my sights on the future, too. And this applies to all of the areas I'm involved in: consulting, chemical servicing and representing corporations.

I know how important it is to keep your sights high after retirement. When I signed a secure contract in basketball I built my mother and father their dream home. That simple brick home is their castle. I've moved on to Boston, and my castle is different. We have a lovely home, but driven more by want than I'd like to admit sometimes, we aren't immune to problems. Material wealth is not a panacea for life's problems. It can *create* problems. One of my solutions is to work at building a strong, loving family, with my wife and children involved in my businesses. Sylvia was a co-chairman of the committee that held a dinner for the M. L. Carr Scholarship Fund for Guilford College in 1987, while the kids helped with mailing and detail work.

Another way I fight complacency is by continuing to strive. I'm always interested in winning a deal and doing it right. I take great satisfaction in making a sale. I become involved in humane causes and lend my name and time to situations I think are right for my family. This rewarding work brings recognition, but I don't regard recognition as my primary motive. It's personal development and in a way, it's survival. Still.

But I have no illusions. I know that the fall from the top is a long and painful one. You learn to appreciate what you *had* once it's gone. When your world begins crumbling down, the pain is long and complex. When you're at the top, you're like the ceiling of a building when the storm comes along. In a hurricane or a tornado, it's the ceiling that goes, not the foundation. I'm at a top, but I view it as a level. It's an opportunity. It's freedom.

The landscape of my life may change, but the values remain constant. I helped break through the practice of segregation in Carolina less as any master scheme than as an instinctive pursuit of what is right and just. I'm free now, but I won't forget the investment that I made to become free. The initiative that it cost must continue to be paid lest that freedom be taken away. To me, rights are the powers or privileges of free actions. At my present status of life, I'm fully intent on pushing forward, to learn more about my rights, powers and responsibilities. It is my right, for example, to become as versatile professionally as I can without injuring anyone. It is my responsibility to work to be the best I can be, with the measurement being my potential. I try hard to live up to the responsibility of freedom, continuing to accumulate wealth fairly and intelligently, and playing a part in loosening the shackles of illiteracy, substance abuse, teenage pregnancy, the tragedy of missing children, school dropouts and poverty.

I've never allowed myself to succumb to fear, never backed down from challenges, in integration, in basketball, in seeking a path to financial autonomy after my athletic career was over. It's been lonely sometimes, and there have been storms. But my past helps me as I look to the future—to fatherhood, business, helping young people. To a game plan for life.

As a student at Guilford I tried to become as active as possible in the community away from the campus. There was an older man who lived on the periphery of the college, Dr. Sam Bolden, who was trying to remain alive intellectually by exchanging ideas with students. I talked to the doctor frequently, trying to understand how he interpreted his life. I sensed there was something meaningful about him, and we would engage in long philosophical talks. He heard I was getting married after my senior year, and he insisted on painting a picture to give us as a gift. It wasn't very good really: it depicted the sea, the shore and a lighthouse. A storm threatened the men and women in a boat, and death appeared imminent. But the boat protected them.

The picture may not have been very good, but it has stayed with me. It reinforces the philosophy I discussed with Dr. Bolden. As long as you're in the boat, you're safe. The shore may be distant, but as long as you stay aboard you have an opportunity to live. If you stay moored by the lighthouse, you'll never know how far you'll be able to journey. You may need to battle the waves. You may even be thrown from the deck. But you'll just need to get back on.

You should never jump overboard, regardless of the heavy weather, because then you'd have no chance at all. But if you stay on the ship and maintain your course through the storm, you will find the other shore. And the sun will rise and the land there will be the most glorious you've ever known.

Chapter 18

Fatherhood

I have been known to deliver under pressure on the basketball court, but no sports experience can compare with the urgency I felt the night of the birth of Andrea, our third child. Andrea was born at home, in the middle of the night in the middle of the winter. When the time came, Sylvia understood instantly that she wouldn't have time to travel to the hospital for the birth. Fortunately, an obstetrician, Dr. Asterkoff, lives across the street from us. Calmly Sylvia told me what was happening, and I assured her she had plenty of time. I was composed.

No, she corrected, she was about to have the baby at home.

I jumped out of bed as if I had sat on a pin. I rushed down the stairs, out the door and over to the Asterkoffs. Sylvia's voice trailed me as I closed the door—without my house keys.

"M. L.," she called. "You have the phone number on the nightstand. Call him on the telephone."

But I was dashing madly through the early morning hours, a modern-day Paul Revere. "The baby is coming! The baby is coming!" I didn't want to deliver a baby in a house, even my own, although I had been born at home in Wallace. As I was running through the Massachusetts snow, I thought to myself how much easier it was to deliver in a ballgame.

I was able to get the doctor, but by the time I had returned to the house, with the doors locked, of course, the baby had already been born. Now, I like to have people over. But with the baby born and our friends from the neighborhood at our home, I was the reluctant host of a party at the foot of my bed, with my newly born daughter a co-host. After pausing for a quiet moment of joyful reflection, Dr. Asterkoff asked me to get a pair of scissors. Regular scissors? I was stunned. Yes, he assured me; he was going to cut the umbilical cord. What about a sterilizer? The doctor was laughing gently now; regular scissors would be fine.

"Should I boil some water?" I asked. He laughed; the reason the doctors in the movies did *that*, he said, was to keep the husband occupied.

He proceeded to cut the umbilical cord, and we all celebrated. Suddenly I slapped my forehead. I didn't know whether it was a boy or girl. I had forgotten to check!

Sylvia whispered: "It's a little girl, M. L.!"

Finally the ambulance arrived. I was pretty shaky; they told me to relax, to get some rest. There was nothing further I could do at that time, anyway. Sylvia didn't even really need a travel bag; all I needed for her, they told me, was a small bag. After rummaging around I located a shopping bag from an area supermarket. Their advertising slogan at the time was: "We'll Find a Way!" I remembered staring down at that slogan and laughing. Our family had found a way that night.

The baby is coming! The baby is coming!

The birth of a child is a big event in anyone's life, a major adjustment for any couple. Andrea may have been our third arrival, but her birth was as important and traumatic as the other two. Family, as I've said, is very important to me, and part of my own development has been the reconciliation of my career as a professional basketball player with my role as father. It wasn't always easy.

The birth of our first child, Michael, brought home to Sylvia and me the serious conflicts that can afflict families of people in the public eye. Michael was born in Detroit in 1977 after I returned from a road game against the Washington Bullets. After learning that Sylvia's labor had reached the final stages, I prepared anxiously to head to the hospital. The birth went well, and he was brought into the world at four-twenty-five that afternoon.

We celebrated the entire day—I had been awake all night—and then I headed to Cobo Arena to play a game that night. I was exhausted, but it is impossible to phone in and cancel when you're playing pro ball. I arrived at the arena minutes before tap-off, and after missing my first few shots of the game, I settled in and played extremely well. It was a matter of going to work as people do in any profession. But it was also a matter of the way I interpreted my presence in the public eye. I was a player, and I wanted to be out there. I felt the pressure of my public persona.

These pressures were reinforced by an incident after Andrea's birth. I was in the center of several promotions and activities related to my position in professional basketball at that time, and one of these, my "Ask M. L." series on a local television station, was interested in taping my segment from the hospital. The baby had been born only hours earlier, and without thinking, I immediately assented. I hadn't asked Sylvia, who had heroically delivered Andrea at home. Twelve hours after the birth, a camera crew went parading into the hospital. I was presenting Andrea to the viewers in Boston, but I hadn't considered whether the new mother had thought this best. I'm grateful that a potentially sensitive situation worked out (the show was popularly received and the family enjoyed it). But a celebrity in the public eye is constantly faced with the kind of demands that take someone light years away from a settled family existence.

For a professional basketball player's family, there are few family Thanksgivings, Christmases, New Years or Easters. I was either practicing or playing most of these holidays. The Celtics did their best to accommodate us; they had a traditional Christmas Party for the players' families, and at Thanksgiving the kids were invited to practice. It was thought that with all of the kids there together, the atmosphere would be festive. But it wasn't as it appeared: Michael viewed Thanksgiving at a Celtics practice as another occasion when he would have to share his daddy. He looked at it ambivalently. Janine, our second child, would have similar reactions when we went out to dinner. She regarded autograph seekers with a mixture of surprise and resentment. One night, when a woman approached the table to ask for a signature, Janine proclaimed, "My daddy's not signing any autographs." The kids wanted their father, and often they saw him belonging to an anonymous public. People would sidle up to my son and make remarks like: "You must be so fortunate to have M. L. as your father!" Or: "You have to be proud to be his son!" Maybe we had had a disagreement, and Michael would be forced to listen to the public acclaim. There was a constant battle to eliminate confusion; I'd explain that the public's constant solicitude was a compliment to the family. They saw the effort that I made on and off the court, and they appreciated it. I explained that it was best to see it as an honor from the outside. Oftentimes, however, this proved to be a point of departure for a long discussion. It wasn't an answer.

My children enjoyed seeing me out there on the court, but they lived with the pressure behind the scenes. I never had a schedule, for example. Sometimes I'd be home at 5 P.M., other times 2 A.M., sometimes not at all.

As a public figure you lose control of your time because so many of your activities are determined by the needs of the public. But if I lost control of my time, at least it was better than losing my name, as Sylvia did. Sylvia was known as "the wife of M. L. Carr." I would find that hard to deal with on a consistent basis. It's taxing and it's something the kids witness. In the family, circumstances at home didn't always fit with what was presented on the outside. All I had to do to feel good about myself was to go downtown. "Hey, M. L.!" I'd hear. "You're playing well. We're proud of you!" Regardless of what was going on behind the closed doors, I'd walk through town and be a hero. But for the kids it was a different situation at home. I may have been a legend in public, but that was because the kids had to tiptoe all afternoon so Daddy could get some rest for the game that night. If I had to reprimand them about something, they might second-guess their own opinions, their perceptions of their relationship with their father and, consequently, reality. I might tap Michael's backside for something he did wrong and then go out and sign autographs at a function in front of him. This wasn't hypocrisy—it was a result of the inevitable difference between public life and private life, and it could cause confusion for the kids. I wouldn't allow this to be too much of a problem, however; any time I punished the kids or corrected their bad behavior, I'd give love, too. I always included some message to communicate that there was an idea behind the action, a hug or a kiss.

One day I was headed off to the Garden for a game while my son Michael was preparing for a recital that night. He's tried to develop interests other than basketball. He is into acting, music and other sports. As I prepared to drive down to the game, he said, "Dad, you always choose the game instead of my activities." Perhaps you need to be at a particular stage of life to even *hear* this: some light was shed on my family situation and life after basketball, and I began thinking about retirement that night.

Sports can present additional problems for my son. He is immediately assumed to be a star player because I am his father. When he started school, all the kids wanted him on their team. But neither talent nor interest is necessarily inherited. How does he answer questions like: "Are you as good as your father?" Or: "You'll play basketball, won't you?" The son of a former Boston player was forced to transfer schools because of this type of pressure. The name, the expectations and the pressures were too burdensome, especially for some children.

How does a wife manage the conflicting images? When there is disagreement at home you travel off to the arena and again you're Mr. Perfect from the moment you walk through the doors. But Sylvia was always able to analyze the entire context; she was imperative that our marriage remain strong. She knew I felt bad about the pressures and she helped me out. The public places the athlete on a pedestal and interprets problems in the home as a result of the failure of his family to understand him. He'll come home from the arena and forget that, while he's on the pedestal, his wife has been running the house, paying bills, being nurse and doctor, playmate, father and mother. If the player desires a normal family life he has to work at it. It's complex, juggling public images that he knows are real with the seemingly pedestrian concerns of a happy family. I refuse to prescribe behavior for people, but it was always my feeling that a settled home life provided a stronger basis for knowing myself better.

A player's wife is not a passive observer. She is part of the team organization, too, and vulnerable to pressures from her own place in the public eye. Both spouses in this situation must be analytical to head off problems. Not crises—parents are greatest when there's a crisis. If I was going to a game or a social event and heard that Janine was in a threatening situation, I'd find my way to her. That was beyond debate. The tough call is discerning the trouble spots ahead of time, when all the child desires is the time parents could be spending with him or her. I was always ambitious. I'd book promotions, speaking engagements and business meetings late into the night. Sometimes I'd lose sight of what was an important commitment. I constantly reminded myself that nothing was as important as the family.

I won't prejudge. During a road trip I sat in the lobby of the Denver Hilton one night, reading the newspaper to pass some time. I began talking with a computer salesman, an older guy. It began as small talk but then—as strangers often do—we touched on deeper issues.

"How's everything for you, Carr?"

"Going well."

"Life on the road has to be tough on the wife and kids, right?"

He didn't wait for an answer. Life for him had begun changing late in his marriage. He found more gratification, he said, when he was out on the job trying to make sales. He was successful, but the beautiful mansion he had fashioned through twenty-five years of hard work had become like a prison. He had decided on a divorce. He could deal with it—the alimony, everything. Most of his life now was acceptable to him. What bothered him was that it had taken him so long to evaluate his priorities. Had he stayed in a marriage for years because of the comfort, sacrificing his well-being? He was living in an average old house now.

"But when I go home it's like a castle," he said.

After hearing that guy's story I thought of my family and counted my blessings.

My profession had its demands, and life on the road was one I had to live with. I enjoyed it to a point, but my weariness with that life, as my kids got more involved in school, was another signal pushing me to retire. It too caused adjustments for the family. For example, I'd want a home-cooked meal after being on one of those two-week swings through the Rocky Mountains. Sometimes you didn't know where you were when you woke in a hotel room after your afternoon beauty nap, and I'd resolve that by wanting to have a meal in my home. But on the other side of the door, my wife wanted nothing more than to get out and have dinner in a restaurant. We compromised; the first meal was at home the night I returned from a road trip. The following night we would go out.

Restaurants were another place where your notoriety was an issue. The Celtics had a strong relationship with Legal Seafood in Boston, easily one of the finest seafood restaurants in the country. In exchange for business and good will, the restaurant would hustle us through the lines that were always there on busy evenings. One night I went to the restaurant with another couple and didn't want to wait the hour it would normally have taken. The hostess was very nice and told us we would have to wait only a half-hour. We decided to do it—everybody waits for a good thing. As arranged, we were brought to the front of the line, ahead of several other patrons, including a woman who refused to take this favor quietly. She complained loudly, first to the young hostess and then to the manager. They finally brought her to a table, wishing to avoid an unpleasant scene. Unfortunately, she sat at a table near us, a stage from which to persist in her diatribe. I told her our table was an unwilling audience. "If you don't like this place and the service," I said to her, "there's a place down the road that will have you in and out in a blink of an eye. It's the place that has the Golden Arches in front of it. Please think about that and let everyone have a quiet, enjoyable dinner."

I regret saying that, because she represented something important to me. She made me wonder how those privileges are perceived by my children. How will they react when a maitre d' doesn't escort them to the front of a long line? Our children saw us being treated this way and they begin to look at us a little differently. You can get tripped up with false expectations. Life in the public eye is a constant balancing act. Just because you are a public figure, do you really deserve more? It's a matter of the public's priorities, and it can be misleading.

Spouses are sometimes convenient. I say that not in a demeaning way but as a matter of fact. I say it because, like any other wife, there are many times when Sylvia will use me to get out of an uncomfortable situation. I guess I'm guilty of the same behavior. When Andrea was three years old, I was standing in my bathroom taking a whiz when she popped in. I asked her to step out until Daddy was finished. She did, but when I came out, she said, "Daddy, that's not fair." Thinking she was talking about being sent out of the bathroom, I decided to find out if a hint of rebelliousness was appearing in my three-year-old.

"What's not fair?" I inquired.

"It's not fair," she said, "that boys can stand up and use the bathroom while girls have to sit down."

Then she asked me that one question that all youngsters ask.

"Why?"

Not wanting to use this as a teaching moment, I told her what any bright father would have told his daughter in a similar situation.

"Ask your mom."

I know her mother has the patience of Job. She would take the time to explain how God made boys different from little girls and how boys and girls each are special in their own little ways. I chalk another one up for Mom, who has bailed me out by keeping it simple. Keeping it simple in a family isn't always easy to do. In this day and age it has become much more difficult to set boundaries. But our youth have to have boundaries in the home so they are better prepared for outside interactions. They need guidelines. They complain about them, but deep within they want them because it shows them we care. It also gives them a framework or system to work within.

Nature will spank you when you go beyond its boundaries. I've only touched a hot stove once in my lifetime. I burned four fingers on my left hand, and you would be hard pressed to get me to touch another hot stove. But I was riding on the hood of a tractor on a hot summer day when I was 14 years old. I sat saddle-style with my back to the pipe. The tractor had been running most of the morning because we had been using it to transport the tobacco we'd been cropping in the fields. The driver made a quick jerk as he took off for the barn and as he swerved, my back touched the hot pipe. I learned, first of all, that I didn't have any business riding like that; but more importantly the man who owned the tractor had warned me about fooling around with it. I now wear a scar on my back. It reminds me never to ride with my back to a hot pipe.

Overcoming the difficulties of maintaining a public persona and having a fulfilling family life has been made easier for me by the example of my past. My life was different from the life of my children now. I lived by a known set of rules. The structure and hierarchy was clearly defined. I was always held accountable for my actions. At C. W. Dobbins Elementary School in Wallace, I harassed some of my schoolmates during a Halloween party, and the principal, Mr. Dafford, called my father at work. Daddy rushed right over from his job and gave me an old-fashioned whipping right at the school! Then he went back to work. When I got home from school that afternoon I received a full verbal spanking. It was painful and humiliating. But it was something I needed.

I now live in a very affluent community outside Boston, but in my view the commitment of parents has to remain the same as my father's. It is too easy to see schools as escapes for six hours rather than as an opportunity to grow through education, to advance, to interact and develop. I suspect that teachers struggle with this very tough problem. The majority reach their positions with admirable goals for educating our kids, but they spend a vast amount of their time disciplining. With more parental support, they could be free to teach. Teenage problems, for example, would be sharply decreased by increased parental involvement in reading programs, arts and crafts, contributions in specific educational areas. Parent participation makes an immeasurable difference because it reflects a visible presence of caring and concern. In many communities, parents work to provide material comfort, but this energy and interest isn't replicated in the educational setting. The school is a parking lot for the students' cars; there appears to be less enthusiasm for what's going on inside the walls. I hesitate to judge, but neither wealth nor the advances in technology of our age have made this a better life than the one I experienced in Wallace. Parents who are freed from material need must give time to produce a better life, commensurate with our progress in the eighties. And that time has to start at home. In order for us to maximize our potential as a community, state and nation, an enthusiasm for education must be fostered. If it means giving up time at the theater or at the Celtics game in Boston, then give it up, go to the school and watch your kids perform.

I'm more sensitive to these issues since retirement from basketball, especially as I visit schools throughout the state of Massachusetts. I sometimes had to pull away from my obligations to meet the needs of my children. Earlier in my career, Michael would say, "Let's do this," but I'd shrug and pursue my career, either at the game or with a potential business associate. Late at night, in his dark room, I'd walk in and he'd be sleeping the peaceful rest of the child. Then, I'd be all heart and ears and regret. If I had taken the time!

The difference between success and failure at home is the extra fifteen minutes we spend with our children, studying with them, practicing music or sports with them, listening.

Chapter 19

Business

I promised Sylvia that when I retired from basketball I would take a year off. But I was looking out too many windows, dreaming, as I did when I was a schoolboy in Wallace. The teacher kept telling me I wouldn't amount to anything if I kept on daydreaming. He should see some of the windows I'm looking out of now. I couldn't sit out a year in the business world. Impossible.

Plans for my career in business began early in my career with the Celtics. I made several appearances in conjunction with the team. I represented Tellos clothing in Boston and also ADAP Automotive on a more regional basis. I worked with New Balance Athletic Footwear in Boston. I was the first basketball player involved with the company, and I participated in research, design and promotion in their newly formed basketball division.

Always I kept an eye on the future. As my basketball career began winding down, I began to invest more time in promotions. It was like a kinetic bar graph: as circumstances in basketball required less, my promotions company, M. L. Enterprises, accelerated. Now the company is generating significant business, but I am also putting significant time into another venture, Carr Chemical Corporation.

But I have been careful as I move into business not to insulate myself from the community, not to retreat into an isolated executive world. I don't believe that would succeed anyway. Throughout Massachusetts I have been conducting an educational program for youths about the dangers of drugs. I have worked as a representative for the Bank of Boston since my retirement from professional basketball. This commitment hasn't a finish line. I have recently been appointed to the board of directors at Channel 7, one of the largest independently owned major-network stations in the United States. I remain an active force at New Balance and I hope to be part of their policy planning for several years to come.

I have made strides individually, but I try to maintain a sensitivity to the needs of our young. I have a commitment to reaching out to the community. I recognize my special position as a former professional athlete, and I try to use that position for the benefit of my family and the community.

I have some strong beliefs about the use of retired athletes by corporations. Though retired athletes are a reservoir of talent for the corporate community, I'm skeptical about how efficiently their abilities are used. In the business world, does a player's scoring or rebounding average determine his selling ability? Only partially; but many corporate decision-makers act as if ex-athletes have only their past achievements and visibility to offer. Now I'll be the first to admit that I have some real apprehensions about addressing the outside world after the sheltered existence of pro sports. But I went out into the business world determined to offer both my visibility *and* my corporate abilities to a company. Sure, I'm a former NBA star, and I want to use that stardom, but I'm also the guy who sold cars when I was told I couldn't, and I wanted that skill to be utilized along with my name. So I went out there aggressively, trying to associate myself with top-of-the line businesses and institutions. In 1985 I approached the Bank of Boston about the possibility of becoming affiliated with them. It was an unheard of proposition. There had never been an athlete affiliated with the bank. But the timing was right. The bank had at that time struggled through a period of decline, and the concept of an athlete lending his visibility to the institution was a nice idea to some, including bank officers Chad Gifford and Barry Allen, and President Ira Stepanian. We made a tentative agreement after a series of interviews and discussions; I would receive a look-see: ten appearances before a number of business groups to gauge my effectiveness. It was my first big challenge in the business world.

I delivered my first speech to about a hundred of their senior-level management team, including the president and chairman. But I wasn't intimidated. I researched the backgrounds of several of the bank's programs. The speech went so well that in the parking lot afterward, they approached me and told me to forget the other nine. They signed me on, and it's been a win-win association. We've made a significant thrust into schools with "The Bank of Boston-M. L. Challenge: Stand Tall Against Drugs" a program of motivational and educational speeches, appearances and educational materials. The program was awarded a presidential citation as one of the top hundred community outreach programs in the country.

In the course of our relationship, the Bank of Boston has utilized my abilities in distinct and creative ways. I've joined the bank's advisory board in the southern region. I have become a "Goodwill Ambassador," giving motivational speeches in-house. In a presentation before all the tellers, I urged them to take pride in their jobs, that they were representing the bank out front. I also gave a presentation to the credit card division to generate enthusiasm about the introduction of a new product, the Bank of Boston Mastercard.

The point here is that we have created a situation where my abilities and visibility have been constructively combined. Too often athletes are seen only as names, and their business potential is not fully realized. I know of many retired athletes with similar ability, but the business world has yet to take full advantage of them.

Of course athletes in advertising is nothing new. The benefits of using sports stars to sell goods has grown considerably in the last twenty years. The high visibility of athletes has tremendous appeal to corporations. Look at the sneaker industry. An athlete wearing a particular brand of sneaker is displaying the product as he plays. Where else could a corporation secure two hours of advertising without interruption? Chrysler Corporation doesn't get that. President Reagan doesn't get that. But New Balance, with James Worthy on the national network, has that advertising space. But it can go deeper than that. The nature of athletics is something corporate heads and corporations in their environment should be able to relate to. The high tech industry, for example, is a field that has had some peaks and valleys in the past several years, something athletes experience in their profession on a daily, weekly and monthly basis. So a corporation should have at least two methods of utilizing the athlete: using him or her for promotional reasons, and allowing the athlete to utilize that experience of the highs and lows to explain some of the ways to bring people out of sluggish periods in their industry. What the athlete needs is a familiarity with the structure of the industry.

A small company in Boston, Tellos clothing, put the Celtics' resurgence during the eighties to good use. Formerly Tellos was a small family business consisting of a few stores in town. But the son, young Kirt Vitello, had greater visions. He tied the Celtics' turnaround to his own ambitions for his store. He brought several Celtics into the store to help raise money for charities, and to make the attraction even more enticing he held giveaways and had sales. We were used in pictures for outside advertising all over Boston, and soon the business boomed. In the span of six years, he has developed sixteen stores and plans for expanding outside of New England.

A creative mind can fashion many opportunities for athletes and the company. TWA had a superb angle a few years ago. The airline showed Kareem Abdul-Jabbar and Wilt Chamberlain on an airplane, sitting comfortably in two of the seats. The idea, of course, was that if two seven-footers have comfort in the plane, a normal-sized person would be able to travel very comfortably. I've often thought this idea should be expanded. An airline could establish sponsorship of a team. Sports teams have rigorous schedules. They travel widely and cannot afford snafus. Why shouldn't a Delta Airlines identify itself with a team? This concept could be extended. Home as well as travel is part of every athlete's life. If an athlete is traded, he has to have a home. A major realtor could find such a player as a magnetic endorsement.

The athlete is the perfect person to introduce these advertising ideas. He's doubly perfect, if he's brought in and schooled in the workings of the business he's representing. What's the history of the company? Who are the main players of the business? What's the vision of the corporation, the size of the territory, the business's people and bottom line? The athlete should know all of these basic procedures. The athlete understands how to deal with victory and defeat on a visceral level; he understands the complex interaction of people in a team setting. Give him some background and substance and he can contribute meaningfully to a company.

Using this approach, I constructed M. L. Enterprises. We are business development consultants, and our promotional line is that our business will help a client fulfill its potential as a company, internally and externally. Our company utilizes an interrelated program of public relations, motivational speeches and seminars designed to improve interdepartmental communication. I've made the point previously, but it bears noting again: I'll use my experience as a ballplayer for maximum impact. So in addition to the central message of our business—that a company works better employing the practice of teamwork—I'll personally motivate a group with a speech to specified people in the company. I understood the need for sacrifice and veteran leadership when I sat on the end of the bench as twelfth man on the Celtics. I waved a towel in order to help the team do whatever was necessary for us to win. This is the message I carry.

An athlete is a potent symbol. The Boston-area Raytheon Corporation has used the images of Larry Bird and PGA star Tom Watson very effectively. Showing these great athletes in slow motion, with grace, sensitivity and charisma, they draw an analogy with their own company, a corporation as intent on perfection as Watson is on mastering the swing, or Bird is on sinking his shots.

I prefer tying in with top-of-the line companies and helping keep those companies at that high level. And again, the athletic analogy applies. If your corporation is at the top, everybody is trying to knock you off. You cannot live on yesterdays, and you cannot coast downhill. You must consistently rededicate yourselves to goals, you must continue to pay attention to detail. I tell corporations that there's a reason if I missed a defensive rebound playing against Doctor J. Sure, Doctor J is a better leaper than I am, but I still should have gotten the rebound nine times out of ten. If I had utilized my knowledge of fundamentals and boxed him out, I should have succeeded. If he beat me to it, I didn't do my job. Attention to minute particulars is an attitude associated with winners. The Celtics were successful because they didn't worry about what was going on down the corridor in the other team's locker room. We didn't care about the competition. We knew that if we shot correctly, rebounded and kept in shape, we wouldn't have to worry. Many companies are always looking over their shoulders. Winners don't. Edwin Moses, the champion hurdler who won over 135 races in a row, always has his eye on the target, the goal. He pays attention to his stride and his training program, and he runs in record time. Obviously we can't win every race. The real winner is one who wins in attitude. The measure of success is how well you have fulfilled your human potential. In basketball, according to my potential, I had a great career. But if I measure my achievements against Kareem Abdul-Jabbar's, I had a terrible record.

I tell corporations that to insure maximum success as a corporate entity, the corporation must honestly assess its own capabilities. What are your strengths? Weaknesses? I tell them that in my view, in order to realize maximum potential, one has to work on improving strengths *and* weaknesses. It's a matter of making demands on yourself, not being denied your opportunities. Prepare a scouting report, a corporate profile on yourself, on your opponent and on what you perceive as your opportunities. Knowing yourself, you can do your best.

I seek out the best in a bad situation. I broke the fifth metatarsal bone in my right foot in a game in 1980 and was out of the lineup for three months. It was my first major injury in the professional game. But something was wrong. I could accept the fact that I could be injured, it happens to a lot of players. What I couldn't deny was the feeling that the injury was caused by my sneaker. I felt the leather had stretched, causing my injury. The foot simply didn't have the necessary support to protect itself from the trauma of the fall. I began making inquiries about changing my affiliation from that sneaker company to a new one.

New Balance Athletic Shoe, Inc., is an athletic footwear company based in Cambridge, Massachusetts. The company had an exceptional track shoe for several years, and I approached them with a proposal for a basketball shoe. I thought New Balance was one of the best shoes I had tried because of the comfort and support. The ultimate test for a basketball player's shoe is how well it holds up to the constant running, jumping and sliding. The company's test product worked for me. I played four games and all ancillary practices with my previous shoe. With the New Balance shoe, I played eleven games and the practices. A player must discard sneakers when the sole of the shoe wears down, even if the upper structure of the sneaker remains in place. The New Balance shoes lasted longer because they, not my feet, were absorbing the stress. We entered into a contract. It was a nice way to begin doing some major business with a local company.

In my estimation, New Balance's concern was with quality. As in my other business relationships, I insisted on becoming well-versed with the product. I personally promoted the sneaker, and the company bgan advancing in the basketball shoe business.

My approach in product endorsement has been consistent. I select quality companies to represent because my name is on the line. I cannot afford to have my personal credibility damaged by being associated with poor products. I take the same approach with my own company; I believe people who work in my company should work hard, should work in an individualized style that best fits their skills, and should have fun doing it. They should have input. I need to be subject to the same rules and discipline as my employees. One morning, for example, I came to work at my leisure, without phoning the office. The company was left to account for my whereabouts, without being aware of where I actually was. Thanks to my vice president, Cyndi Gaucher, I heard about it when I came in later in the morning. No man or woman is bigger than the corporation, even the founder. I'm open to just criticism. It works for the betterment of the whole. I want quality.

M. L. Enterprises was a logical next step after playing and being active in the Boston business community as a player. The company works to assist companies in relating move effectively with their people. I pursue each consulting opportunity and speaking appearance with considerable effort. I need to be oriented to the specific needs and goals of the corporation I am brought in to work with. I'm intent upon entering into win-win consulting contracts. If the company I work with succeeds because of my interaction with them, then I've won. It may lead to further business, too. I thrive on networking in business and on cultivating contacts. All for positive purposes: these contacts motivate me.

What motivates me personally, past and present, is what I attempt to convey in the corporate environment. The concepts underlying teamwork apply equally to the corporation. After we won the 1984 championship, I made an appearance at Wang Laboratories as Wang was striving to reach its goals in the final quarter of that fiscal year. I appealed to their employees' pride and determination. As I continue in my consulting business in my life after basketball, I'll use my past as a point of continuity. If a potential client wishes to converse about basketball, I'll talk willingly. Is that an indication that the client refuses to respect my new role? Hard to say; but I realize that if I were someone else, I might not even get in to see this potential client. I'll trade that off any time. Besides, when I preach teamwork it comes from the heart. I accept a substantial fee to appear before corporate gatherings. But the thought of applying the theory of teamwork to the everyday work and research setting is important to me. At IBM, I delivered a speech to a management level group, stressing teamwork. At a conference of employees of the Commonwealth of Massachusetts, my aim was to support recognition of the productivity of state workers. The theme of the seminar was "Working for You: Lifestyle Opportunities for State Employees." I believe a major characteristic of corporate productivity is that corporation's investment in the whole person. If a worker's lifestyle is productive, that worker's output in the work setting will be too. If the person is fit physically and mentally, his work will be spiritually enlivened. In order for a worker to draw upon internal motivation, that worker must believe that the people in management believe in him. That person must have reserves of physical and mental strength.

My business approach attempts to integrate the practical with the philosophical. I have an aggressive approach; I won't sit back, and I'll work to put deals together, all with the idea that I am uniting quality groups in a win-win liaison.

My wife Sylvia continually works in the community, trying to lend her name and efforts to humane causes. One of her activities brought her to the Children's Hospital Festival, a function designed to raise funds for hospital services. At that function, she met Myra Kraft, a woman who is actively involved in hospital activities as well as several other human interest actions throughout Boston. Through Myra, I met her husband, Robert Kraft, president of New England Television Corporation, the group that purchased WNEV, the CBS affiliate in Boston. Under the guidance of Kraft and Chairman of the Board David Mugar, WNEV has revamped its philosophy and reconstructed itself along regional and community lines. Specifically, the station contracted with local news bureaus to report news events from specially constructed studios in those regional bureaus. In the city of Boston, there was a renewed effort to cover local community news. My work and visibility in the community was a selling point for Bobby Kraft. According to him, my interests in the community, drug programs, church, family and public service all contributed to my nomination to the station's board of directors. My association with a winner, the Celtics, was a boost. These are all images the station is attempting to project.

My approach to this position has been consistent with my approach to all of my commitments. I refuse to be regarded only as a symbol. I want to be involved, and if I am a symbol to young people in the community, I work at being present in the city. If I am unable to be everywhere to serve some of the community's needs, well, a strong voice on the board of a major television affiliate is a means toward fulfilling the responsibility of bringing about positive change and the development of a stronger sense of pride in our communities. I have researched issues the board has concerned itself with, asked questions about the station's proposed format change, become involved with sports reporting. The opportunity to sit on this board is a priceless one. The station is attempting to reach into every news, sports and cultural area in the city. I think by becoming involved in the decision-making process at this level, there is opportunity for meaningful social change as created by the station, and for laying the groundwork for further change down the road. As with all my business and community ventures, I am doing what I can to show that ex-athletes have the ability to contribute more than their images to the corporate world.

I am not the smartest guy in the world, but I'm far from the other end, too. An important asset I've brought to my business contacts is the knowledge of what I don't know. I know when to look for help. In difficult situations I always seek second, third and fourth opinions. When I was sued for $4.2 million by Tree Rollins of the Atlanta Hawks, I immediately sought out the best legal and financial advice I could obtain. There are some battles in life that you shouldn't fight alone. After the 1984-1985 season, when I was thinking of retiring from the game, I needed input from friends and professional people who knew me well. After listening to several viewpoints, I felt prepared to make an informed decision.

I have a trusted group of friends and advisors who assist me with difficult decisions. I'll call these men and women when I am fact-finding problems or propositions. When I was playing, I was constantly being approached for investments and endorsements. If there's an idea that can lead to a quick buck, any type of speculation whatsoever, an athlete will always hear about it. You build up a defense mechanism against a potential scam. I've been consistently cautious about these. I've had deals proposed to me that have appeared promising. One proposal had me investing ten thousand dollars in a production company. I had zero knowledge of the people or the business, so I quickly declined. Yet, after a friend of mine, Richard Balsbaugh, bought the Boston rock station WXKS, he began seeking out additional investors. He had been the general manager of the station, and in conversations we had, he insisted that his chance to buy the station was a "golden opportunity." He invested everything he had. He asked me if I wanted to get in at $250,000 as a limited partner. The overall plan included purchasing several more FM stations nationally, with all limited partners participating in the dividends as a result of getting in on the ground floor. But after thinking it over, I said, "No." The idea seemed feasible, but it meant borrowing the money, and if the deal fell flat, I would be paying off a note with nothing to show for it. What I didn't know at the time was that Richard is a go-getter and a man with a game plan. He had been in the business and he had an insider's knowledge of the trends in the industry. Now his corporation is paying back its investors three times the original outlay plus attendant tax benefits. He's bought seventy-eight stations. Now Richard says, "M. L., I wanted my friends in on the deal. I would love to be cutting you a check." I say it was a tremendous opportunity, but I've had some defeats in business, too, and for all the investments that go, there are a thousand that don't fly. If I had lost the money—investing with a friend—then I wouldn't like my response to that person if the deal didn't fly.

The point is that you need to check things out, and even when you do the checking out yourself, there's a lot you just don't know about. That's why I have what I call my mind group. It's nothing formal, just a series of phone calls that I make to advisors from diverse backgrounds who can give me important advice about my career. These people represent areas in business, medicine and family. They include Phil McLaughlin and Ted Samet, who are accountants; Dan Ciampa, a CEO of the consulting firm Rath and Strong in Lexington, MA; Dr. Harris Gibson, a close friend of the family; Jan Volk and Red Auerbach of the Boston Celtics; Dr. Gus White, an orthopedic surgeon at Beth Israel Hospital in Boston; and Sylvia, my wife.

But when I thought about retiring from the game, the first person I discussed the idea with was my father, John Henry Carr. Now, he's not

as active in my little group, for medical reasons. His wisdom is what
I miss most. Any time there was something going on, I could bounce
ideas off of him. He'd listen and then bounce them back. He'd listen
to the numbers and the details and then his answer would always be a
question: "What's the impact on the family?" His response was always
constructed around that core question. He always reasoned that any
venture that would cause stress on the family would probably be difficult.
With my father's illness, I've forced myself to pull away. He has enough
going on. Now I use his life as a guide. My father had strength, patience
and intelligence. The way he handled himself, as I see him in my personal
recollection, is guidance in itself.

The significance of the group in my life is that I can be open about
my vulnerabilities. With this group of people, I can tell them anything,
I can run thoughts and plans by them any time. What I am after is an
intelligent decision about a situation, a wise choice from competing
alternatives. So I'll ask these people to be honest. I do this so they won't
give me an answer that they think I'd want to hear. Ultimately, I think
I would resent them for appeasing me. I'll digest the information from
all of these people and regard it seriously. Then I'll sit down and weigh
the answers according to my career plan, my family and my personal
and financial goals. I've been open with them, and I get strong data to
go forward with. They can give me real input because they know my
personality. They know I'm pretty aggressive; they know when to advise
excessive caution. They'll compensate. They know I'll reach a little further
than they have advised.

In building my business in Boston, I draw on another level of advisers,
a group that has succeeded in business in Boston, a group that knows
the Boston community. This group includes Leo Kahn, the former owner
of Purity Supreme; Jack Satter, a part-owner of the New York Yankees
baseball team, Ron Homer, president of the Bank of Commerce in
Boston; Bobby Kraft, president of New England Television. Also Mal
Sherman and Ray Wysocki of Zayre Corporation. My mind group. There
are many different angles when you are approaching a problem. There
are many paths to success. I understand there are allies along the way,
and when I have an idea I know I have a sounding board—I'm grateful.

One of the best opportunities afforded me by my expanding network
of business contacts has been the chance to reach the community,
particularly young people, in different and effective ways. The Massachusetts Department of Public Health, Division of Drug Rehabilitation,
conducted a survey of drug and alcohol abuse among high school students
in the fall of 1984. It found that 55 percent of the students surveyed had

used alcohol ten or more times in their lifetimes; 29 percent used marijuana ten or more times; and 5 percent used cocaine ten or more times. To me statistics like these reflect and area of need, which is why I have become as involved as I can in the prevention of the problem.

I began a series of appearances in schools throughout Massachusetts beginning in the spring of 1986. These were designed to urge students to direct their energies into constructive activities, to make their own decisions. I worked closely with the Bank of Boston. At a press conference to kick off the program we tried to rally students against drug abuse and to make sure they understand that true friends, like good teammates, don't push each other into experimenting with drugs.

The following year I helped New Balance kick off its Giant Step program. In conjunction with the Massachusetts Department of Youth Services, I gave motivational talks and conducted clinics at six DYS secure treatment facilities statewide. New Balance also attempted an innovative project as part of the program. They gave youths basketball shoes for wear-testing and asked them to give their responses about the attributes of the sneaker. Also, New Balance examined the possibility of placing youths in jobs within the company when some of the youths might be ready to reintegrate themselves back into the community.

If athletes are highly valued as symbols of inspiration in our culture, then I'm pleased to be respected because of my experience as an athlete. If my experience as a Boston Celtic has opened doors for me in business, then it is something I value and am grateful for. I prefer to believe that the reason athlete's images are emblazoned in bronze, in places that have sacred meaning in the Hall of Fame, is because athletes symbolize what is best in all of our endeavors. At their best, they exert themselves to the maximum of their potential, they have self respect, discipline and a healthy love for their line of work. Sports may have become commercialized over the last twenty years, but it is up to athletes to use those commercial possibilities constructively as they pursue life after sports.

I have pride in my country, pride in the opportunities it provides. When I was playing ball I used to remind myself to give a word of thanks during the playing of the national anthem before the game. In the business world, in corporate America, anyone who is persistent and creative generally has the chance to be successful. There isn't any doubt that we live in a competitive business environment, but anybody can win.

Like the Celtics and the Lakers, America and Japan are always worrying about one another. After World War II, Japan saw how America had built itself up, and they went to work. They invested more

time, paid strict attention to detail and revolutionized the way they worked
in their factories. The Japanese gave education a high priority. Evolving
through the sixties and seventies, Japan sustained strict discipline
nationwide while America underwent an era of social and political
upheaval. Japan concerned itself with issues in the business environment.
America's work on social issues had to be done. Somewhere along the
line Americans became complacent, and in certain fields the Japanese
surged ahead, marketing their advantage expertly. They proclaimed that
"Japanese-made is technically advanced." American-made wasn't junk,
but the Japanese ad campaign created an inferiority complex about
American goods. But the Japanese advantage was a *perceived* advantage.
Lee Iacocca, president of Chrysler Corporation, has been important to
the country because his leadership and marketing skills have caused people
to think and buy American. "The Pride Is Back!" is a message of
awakening for Americans—that the available technology is here, too.
Perhaps in an interdependent economy, this message is oversimplified,
but I drive an American car and I try to buy American to help keep jobs
here. If there are more people working in factories, and the technology
is in reality advanced, then beneath the abstraction created by the image-
making of marketing, the economy is healthier, with more people working
and more people returning their business to you, whatever your field.

During the 1987 NBA finals, another clash between the league's
glamour organizations, L.A. and Boston, Lakers coach Pat Riley was
asked about the mystique of the Boston Garden. Boston had won 100
of 103 games in that building constructed in 1920, where championship
banners adorned the ceiling.

"Mystique?" he replied sarcastically. "The Celtics market mystique.
We do the same thing in Los Angeles. We call it *showtime.* The Celtics
have tradition and history. We have Hollywood and the ocean. Seems
all the same to me." The Lakers and the Celtics are always jockeying
for position. The Lakers went to school on Boston, as Japan went to
school on America. The Celtics always have had Celtics Pride, and the
team publishes a tabloid with that very name. But in 1987 the Lakers
displayed pride in their team, too. Kareem Abdul-Jabbar made a phone
call to Magic Johnson during the previous summer. He told him that
Magic had to become the central focus of the team now that Kareem
was getting older. So in 1987, Magic led the team down the stretch. The
roles were better defined. Sixth Man of the Year, an honor that seemed
to be created by Celtics players—Frank Ramsey, John Havlicek, Paul
Silas, Kevin McHale, Bill Walton—went to Michael Cooper.

The point is, in a peaceful competition, the level of play had improved dramatically. One of the reasons the 1984 championship was so gratifying to me personally, was that we, as a team, defeated that exceptionally talented Lakers team. K. C. Jones, in interview after interview, would reiterate the same theme. "The Lakers are better players." By 1987 these great players had integrated Celtic team principles within their scheme. They defeated a great Celtics team, a veteran team who, despite injury, was great enough to win that year. The Celtics' own cohesion was as collectively focused as any champion in any year. The Lakers were even better, and the quality of play was the best it's ever been. So I'd have to disagree with Pat Riley. I'd have to say that he learned a little of that mystique himself.

In this country, history is a very important motivator. Back to the beginnings of our country, individual initiative has been key. We created towns out of wilderness. Whatever the elements or terrain, we put transportation and communication systems into place. As a people, we have never been content; our forefathers were not denied the opportunity to explore and establish the structure of the nation. We are free to explore personal and professional boundaries. My own business philosophy refuses to let me become complacent, knowing this history and its opportunities.

Our country has a great deal to offer—not only to the public figure, but to the public in general. The educational standards, medical and technological areas make you proud. Traveling through the country as a ballplayer left me proud. The history and the democratic ethic provide an accessible climate, telling us to press forward. Any time you feel as if you're tied down, you must push ahead. In America, in a healthy competitive environment, you have the freedom to do that.

Chapter 20

College Recruiting:
Some Questions

The higher I climb the ladder of the business world, the more occasion I have to utilize my talents outside of basketball, the more upset I get with the dangerous and flagrant exploitation of college athletes that has become so common over the years. And the worst thing about this situation is that with the right advice, the right guidance, choosing a college can be the most rewarding experience in an athlete's life.

Several years ago, a major press conference convened at Satch's, the Boston restaurant owned by former Celtic Tom "Satch" Sanders. The occasion was the announcement by Cambridge Rindge and Latin High School's star center, Patrick Ewing, that he would attend Georgetown University. The Jamaican-born Ewing's decision had been the subject of speculation for years. Patrick had been the target of every major college in the country. He had been under the spotlight for all four years of high school.

The importance assigned to Ewing's choice of schools reflects one of the priorities of our culture. The revenues generated by the NCAA tournament are astronomical; the athletes starring in the tournament are household names; and the stakes are extremely high for the schools, coaches and players who participate in the games. But for all of the hoopla surrounding Patrick's signing, much about the young man was overlooked. He selected Georgetown, it turned out, because of the emphasis the school placed on academics. Its coach, John Thompson, works extremely closely with the basketball program's academic coordinator, Mary Fenlon. Patrick needed that attention. As a foreign-born student, he lacked some of the language skills necessary for immediate entry into an advanced collegiate environment. Throughout his college career, Patrick Ewing was a highly reluctant interview, partly because of Coach Thompson's restrictions, partly because Patrick was understandably self-conscious of his language barrier.

Patrick Ewing was an exceptional case, and not only on the basketball court. He received the kind of guidance that many young athletes do not receive. Through the co-operation of Rindge and Latin's coach, Mike Jarvis, and John Thompson some of the problems that might have destroyed the young man's talent were averted. Patrick did well at Georgetown and went on to win an NCAA championship. But many young men are not so fortunate. Reforms have been pushed through NCAA conventions during the past few years regarding eligibility requirements, recruiting violations and alumni abuses. Yet with the pressure on coaches to win, the margin of error remains a problem. As a student-athlete, I gave as much time to my game as I did to the books or other areas my talents might have taken me. I suspect the same is true for youngsters now. The bottom line is that recruiters will push as hard as they can for a talented player. They lack the concern that a player might be completely ill-equipped to handle a dramatic change in environment. The player is a youngster; there's no evading that reality. The player doesn't really comprehend the pressures of a collegiate environment until he's been there. When the youngster is meeting with college recruiters, or fending them off, he has huge gaps in his knowledge about the school he's attending, and he might be wise to ponder some questions he or his parents could ask of a college program. Asking these questions could avert some of the tragedies of today's recruitment policies:

1. *What is the coaching staff's background?* A student should know about the experience of a college coach: the people that coach has worked under; the size of programs he's worked for; how long he's been at the school; and most vitally, what guarantees there are that the coach will remain at the school after recruiting the athlete. Basketball at the collegiate level is not all business, as the NBA is. Students form attachments to people who recruit them. But the coaches are all different, with different ambitions. For every John Thompson or Dean Smith, men who are secure in their posts, there are several younger men who are climbing the career ladder. A student should know a coach's history before he agrees to play for him.

2. *How involved will the staff be in monitoring the student-athlete's academic achievement? Does the athletic program have a tutor program for its student-athletes? What is the percentage of athletes who graduate from that particular program?* In recent years there has been a concerted effort to eliminate the academic abuses of certain programs. For example, the eligibility requirements for freshmen players has been monitored more carefully. Bylaw 5-1-(J) requires minimum standardized test scores and grade point averages for freshman athletes. I am a little uncomfort-

able with this rule—I think there's a built-in bias to the test scores, probably discriminating against the kind of intelligence that isn't well-versed in the type of questions they ask—but the attention paid to the student is welcome. The battle is better fought when the rules are in place. Athletic-academic coordinators make phone calls to professors and teachers in the university, but the interaction between the academic and the athletic areas is often full of abuse. The money is too great, the stakes are too high, and the athletic program is largely self-policing. The student entering the university has to have assistance in finding his way around the maze academically. Individualized tutorial programs are a must. Finally, the student must have an idea about his chances of graduating. Last year Bobby Knight was openly critical of a cable network scheduling a game late in the evening. The game started late and went into triple overtime, which, as Knight pointed out correctly, had the kids returning to Indiana at three o'clock in the morning. "How can they possibly study?" Knight asked. No one could answer because everyone knew the kids couldn't work. It's an unreasonable tradeoff. The kids receive the immediate gratification from playing ball, but they miss classes, fall hopelessly behind and many times do not graduate. The academic system must be responsive to the player's needs. The coaching staff and the athletic program must make sure it happens.

3. *Will there be added pressure placed on the athlete by overzealous alumni?* One of my Celtics teammates told a writer that he had received money from alumni while in college. The recent probation of SMU tells as that alumni violations can be extensive. There are well-meaning alumni who identify with the team's fortunes, support the program by buying season tickets and contribute tax-deductible monies for scholarships. Yet the abuses have outweighed the benefits. The booster clubs have perpetrated injustices from offering cars to student-athletes to creating a climate of insecurity for coaches by demanding a coach be fired. It's unfortunate, but again the youngster is the one who suffers, learing early in his career that the sport is a business, and that the first rule is that of survival. Protect yourself, because the coach may be fired. Down the line the student may decide to transfer—in effect, playing out his option at the amateur level. It's the student perspective of a system that stresses victory and material gain. But the purpose of athletics in school should also be to establish stability, peaceful competition and fun. Scouting at the professional level is so extensive that if a player is good enough, he will be drafted. The student doesn't have to become a wanderer in search of an opportunity. He can improve right where he is.

4. *Has the school the student is considering ever been placed on probation for any illegal recruiting or other wrongdoing?* Media coverage has become considerably more vigilant in this area. Satellite communication, employed for newspaper, radio and television coverage, has helped students and their families become better informed about program abuses. Yet some kids just don't know about the history of schools, nor, in some cases, are they concerned. The NCAA should be as vigilant as they can be. A young athlete should be provided with a school's history, and it should be provided openly.

5. *What would your staff do if it learned that one of your players was receiving payments for playing?* Agents are permitted to contact college coaching staffs about players but aren't allowed to deal directly with the player himself. If an agent contacts the player, it's a direct violation of the player's collegiate standing. But it has happened repeatedly since the league began expanding, and since a court order allowed for the hardship rule. Youngsters can enter the professional draft at any time, not just when their college class has graduated. When an athlete expresses interest in going hardship, he becomes a target for agents. Heisman Trophy winner Mike Rozier of Nebraska signed with an agent while still in school. A young athlete needs to be aware of the stance of the school regarding this process, because situations can vary drastically. One player who signed in school might be under extreme pressure to do so. Does the school summarily dismiss that student, thereby grouping him with another who is commercially minded and exclusively out for his own gain? These details need clarifying.

6. *What is the school's policy regarding substance abuse? What is the athletic program's policy?* The death of the Boston Celtics' 1986 first-round draft choice, Len Bias, may be the most tragic story in the history of sports. I don't want to open up old wounds, but drug usage is a theft. It steals happiness, talent and power from young athletes. Unfortunately, Len Bias's death serves to illustrate how the collegiate system fails the athlete. I only knew him for a short period, but I was thoroughly impressed with this young man. You only need to meet his mother to realize what a loss we had—not for his superb basketball skills but for the person himself.

The shortcomings of the system have been flung into all of our faces. Should there have been four years of sustained counseling to assure that he wouldn't be unreasonably pressured in his final semester of college? He was trying hard to impress professional scouts because his career was obviously about to be in the NBA.

Action and legislation against drug use is one of the most debated issues in sports and society. Yet I feel ambiguous about drug testing in sports. Something instinctual in me worries about the implications of Big Brother and the infringement of the right of privacy. But I am 100 percent for the notion of supporting people who want people to be the best they possibly can be. The NCAA tests athletes selectively before major events. Perhaps we should expand this and have athletes consent to testing, as an example for people in society and, in particular, for the fans who support us most passionately and could benefit from our example. But if collegiate and professional athletes consent to testing, then I think that people throughout the athletic industry should be tested as well. Include administrators, athletic directors and coaching staffs on the collegiate level. Include owners, managers or coaches, the commissioner and front offices of major leagues. After all, that *is* the professional sport. The professional sport is more than what takes place between the lines of the playing areas. I think there's an element of fairness there. (At the amateur level, I would also include other kids who represent the school, too. It's unfair to test only the athletes. The president of the student body is an authorized delegate of the school and would have to test, too.)

The point is that society as a whole is combating an evil. That's why I favor testing, though in a nondiscriminatory manner. Drugs permeate society, with a tremendous impact on people of every age and status. Drug usage has crossed all barriers of wealth, age and gender. To combat it, I think the educational process is the most viable tool.

Why are young athletes apparently more vulnerable to drugs? I think they are in a high profile position. They have extra time. If they aren't able to be productive with it, doing things to cultivate the mind, intervals between practices and games can become extremely boring. But I'm not one who subscribes to the idea that just young athletes suddenly arriving into money and fame from impoverished backgrounds are vulnerable to drug usage. As I say, I think the problem has become all-encompassing.

It's critically important for the prospective student to know the program of the school he's entering. Is there guidance? Are seminars offered, counseling the young athlete on scheduling, off-campus activities, and four-year planning? Does the athlete understand that the problems begin when he or she leaves the athletic field and finds his or her place in everyday life?

7. *What is the social life on and around campus?* The problems of adjusting to college life can be monumental for a student if the setting isn't researched carefully. I considered going to Oregon State or one of

the bigger ACC schools when I was in my senior year at Wallace Rose Hill. But plainly, the fit at Guilford College was best for me. The transition from high school to college is a major one, and the student needs to understand the entire surroundings. I think a positive example of a student finding a place suitable for his needs was Ron Harper, the outstanding rookie for the Cleveland Cavs in 1986. Harper was a great player from Dayton, but he had a speech impairment that required intensive off-campus remedial measures. He realized that with this momentary shortcoming, he might be hopelessly lost if he went to a larger school. He went instead to Miami of Ohio, a fine school in a rural setting. Allowed to mature at his own pace, he has performed exceptionally well.

The core issue is that the athlete is a special talent. In order for the talent to develop properly, that player must be able to step back and correctly guage both short-term goals and long-term objectives. Every individual's pace of development is different, and finding the right school with the right social and academic surroundings is essential.

8. *How does the school's academic program rate with similar schools? What are some of the honors received by the school and athletic program?* I suspect that the recruiters who are intent on landing a prospect often talk too much about the virtues of the athletic program. I'd want to know not only how the athletic programs stack up against competing schools, but also how the academic programs compare.

I think the student needs to be aware of all of the honors student-athletes have been considered for. Have there been academic All-Americans? Does the school take extra measures to encourage athletes to excel in programs? Is there a way that the athlete can achieve a maximum benefit from representing the school in athletics, while still receiving a quality education? Will the student be able to have an intellectual appreciation of competing in athletics, in addition to achieving peak physical conditioning? Will the best of the athletes have an understanding of how to become role models in a society that treasures its sports?

9. *Recruiters visit the homes of athletes they are trying to land every day. Does the coaching staff and/or the athletic department maintain communication once the athlete is in the program?* Recruiters called my house virtually every day from the end of my junior year in school through the time I finally made my decision in the spring of my senior year. I was an important recruit. But the stories about other players, including Moses Malone, for example, relegate my tale to insignificance. Moses lived in Petersburg, Virginia. Recruiters would go to Petersburg and "sleep on the porch." When recruiters came to see him, it is said he would jump out the window and run away. The pressure can be that bother-

some. Yet when the player is at the school, I've found that a communication gap sometimes exists. Coaches and people in the athletic program are either too busy or insensitive to the needs of families, especially those families whose sons or daughters are the first offspring at college. That vital family connection is easily damaged by the time and distance. Will professionals in the college or university assist in making the transition smooth?

10. *What do the college's former athletes do after their eligibility has concluded?* The transition from the boards to the boardroom, from years of glory to years of a more sedate, less glamorous life, is stressful. For basketball players who want to play in the NBA, the effect of not making it can be damaging. An athlete entering school should be aware that the odds of reaching the professional ranks are extremely slim. General managers and scouts honestly don't think highly of the prospects of players drafted below the second round. The student needs to be acutely aware of the necessities of education while in college. If he sees former players in constructive, happy positions, he is more inclined to believe that the school has the whole of the athlete's future at heart—not just his basketball potential.

Chapter 21

A Message to a Hero

In the homes of many black people, if there are any pictures at all, there are at least three: one is of Jesus Christ, our Savior; another is of John F. Kennedy, who provided a deep sense of inspiration for our people in the early sixties; finally, there is probably a picture of the Reverend Doctor Martin Luther King. Of all the influences in my life, the gospel preached by Dr. King was perhaps the most meaningful. Dr. King established a system of nonviolent action as an effective tool for peaceful change. He delivered speeches with an almost Godlike resonance. In the sixties, when blacks were finally making significant progress into the mainstream of American life, it was Dr. King who provided the moral, spiritual and philosophical leadership. He initiated the drive for civil rights and equal citizenship under the law.

While I was participating in the end of segregation in Wallace, Dr. King was leading peace marches in the South. In Washington he delivered his electrifying "I Have a Dream" speech. He had climbed a personal mountain from humble beginnings as a minister in Alabama. Throughout his life he fought discrimination and dedicated himself totally to his nonviolent beliefs. "I have a dream," he said that day in Washington, "that one day this nation will rise up and live out the true meaning of its creed: 'We hold these truths to be self-evident—that all men are created equal.' I have a dream that one day on the red hills of Georgia the sons of former slaves and the sons of former slaveowners will be able to sit down together at the table of brotherhood." This was a revelatory moment for us. Dr. King was at once humane, historical and international. He won the Nobel Peace Prize and brought worldwide recognition and international brotherhood to us, as blacks and as Americans. When it was convenient and safe and even necessary to back down from his beliefs in nonviolent social change, Dr. King never would. He saw the threats to his life and his family as obstacles to transcend. His assassination in 1968 united black people everywhere. His death formed a bridge between generations of blacks. If young blacks took to the streets and rioted in empty disbelief, their acts were finally understood by their elders. Likewise, if older generations retreated to the church in silent vigil, the young understood their action. That day, riven through the clouds of mourning, was a rededication among blacks, a sense of renewal. Whatever Dr. King lived for, we would carry on with all of our being. Dr. King would never be replaced, but in his death the system he lived for crystallized. In our feeling of hopelessness and despair, we truly would not be denied our opportunities for a happy, loving and productive life. We needed to carry on. For Dr. King, for ourselves, for America.

I've spent much of this book talking about my own success, on the basketball court and in the business world, and I credit myself with rising to the occasion and taking advantage of my opportunities. But in a very real sense, I could not have done what I did without the efforts of Dr. King, the help of others and blessings from the Almighty. He more than anyone created those opportunities, and his example continually gives me the hope needed to carry on when times get bad. So in a spirit of pride and thanks, I write this open letter to Dr. King:

Dr. King,

So many people in their lives have the thought: If I could only start over! But I know in your life, Dr. King, as in my own and in so many people's lives, there are struggles. As you advised us, I have tried to keep the dream alive. The way you lived your life and courageously held onto your dream is an inspiration to us.

A lot of people struggle to put their past behind them. They need to know that if they have erred, it's not the end of the world. You had a dream, Dr. King, and you were gunned down. But the seed was planted. The dream has been passed on, heard, interpreted. The dream is alive; it is a vibrant force and a clear message.

You said these words to an audience in the mid-fifties, urging them to resist discrimination, but your words still apply now: "I want to say that in all our actions we must stick together. Unity is the great need of the hour, and if we are united we can get many of the things that we not only desire, but which we justly deserve." People who feel deserted should not yield to the feeling that they are alone or can't find improvement and happiness among their fellows. They should find inspiration in unity, in nonviolence, in listening to your approach and your well-established game plan. Deterred in so many of your thrusts, you still saw opportunities where so many could only see defeat. You wouldn't be deterred. You saw beatings, death, bombings of your family, and you continued to preach against those evils. There hasn't been another man so profound and determined in his commitment, so understanding of the tremendous cost that had to be paid.

In your "I Have a Dream" speech in Washington, you prayed that we would not be denied. You planted seeds in people's minds, so that they would see it come true, with or without you. I believe, Dr. King, that if you had a chance to live your life over, you would do the same thing. You lived for justice for all of God's people. Your family is beautiful, committed to caring and helping. I see them continuing the work you were so dedicated to. I have to believe that your family's commitment had such strength that you would pay the price again.

I want to give you an update on your dream of racial equality and justice because I believe positive steps have been made. There are occasional aberrations: Howard Beach in New York in 1986; Fulton County in Georgia in the early eighties. These incidents take place, but the dream has been so well-planted in the minds of God's people that they will not stand by and allow these injustices to overshadow the progress that's been made. There still is a concern about continued economic dependency and the widespread use of illicit drugs by so many of our young people, potentially our brightest minds. I have a concern for the floaters and the dropouts. I fear the casual attitude so many take toward achieving a comprehensive higher education. Like you, I believe that issues that divide the culture will only be cured through the educational process.

But your dream of fellowship and brotherhood is slowly becoming a reality, evident by the association and tremendous accomplishments of such a cross section of people throughout this country. We are forever reminded of your dream of all men having the right to liberty and the pursuit of happiness.

Dr. King, I suspect you'd be interested to know that since 1968 we've had Shirley Chisholm, a black woman, run for President; that a black man, the Reverend Jesse Jackson, has run and will run again in 1988; that on a legislative level, the Equal Rights Amendment will insure progress to counter discrimination against women, an injutice this country should not stand for. Your dream is becoming a reality in many ways. And by the way: you might be interested to know that the nation has made your birthday a national holiday. I don't think you wanted personal accolades, but it is fitting nevertheless as you dedicated your life to helping others.

We have our own commitment. Your actions taught us that we're entitled to every right afforded every other citizen. But with those rights come responsibilities. It was great to obtain the right to vote, but black people have to exercise that right. It's great to have the opportunity to better education and better schools, but we have to cultivate an ambition and enthusiasm to attend these schools and stay in them. We can't take the high price paid for these rights lightly.

In my own experience, I've seen sports have a powerful impact on society, helping bridge the gap between separate peoples. But the struggle continues. There has recently been concern about the lack of minorities in the ownership and managerial positions of professional sports teams. Until recently, the media has failed to present minorities as capable outside the realm of play. Ironically, the emergence of minorities into positions of leadership in athletics has preceded their visibility by several years. Men like Gale Sayers in football, Hank Aaron in baseball and Wayne Embry in basketball have been strong influences in athletic administration and team development.

In sports, as in life, the costs are high. The price that was paid has brought dividends. Black players grace the arenas and fields with glory, acknowledged as champions in every respect. Bill Russell, Oscar Robertson, Wilt Chamberlain and Kareem Abdul-Jabbar in basketball; Hank Aaron, Willie Mays, Frank Robinson and Bob Gibson in baseball; Jim Brown, O. J. Simpson, Willie Lanier and Mean Joe Greene in football; Arthur Ashe in tennis. All were brilliant performers; all raised the standard of excellence that you, Dr. King, helped make possible.

Sports provide an example of the possibilities and stresses of life in the late twentieth century, as men and women of every background, people of high morals and good will, attempt to build and live in a world you helped lay the foundation for. There are imaginative enterprises in our culture designed to build a world of hope, and I believe minority viewpoints are being heard. Still the price is high: stress exacts a cost from all of us, black and white. For many of us, there is the balancing act of reconciling their heritage as victims of discrimination with their exciting present endeavors in all areas of life. It can be overwhelming at times. Yet we are more equipped than ever to see your dream become a reality.

For you, Dr. King, the cost was terribly tragic. But you counted on that cost. You told the world that you had been to the mountaintop. That you had seen the other side. You found the cause-that's-bigger-than. We've listened.

M. L. Carr

Chapter 22

Game Plan

When I retired from basketball, I suddenly became aware that the roar of the crowd had become deafeningly silent. The awareness touched me deeply. Athletics digs a hole so deep into your emotional being, that when the games are gone there is a gap in your being. As the days, weeks and months went by in my first year of retirement, an understanding arrived: with all the personal milestones I had etched out in sports, including my financial rewards, the only thing that closes that gap is team victory. If I hadn't won the championship rings in 1981 and 1984, there would be a hole in my heart.

After we won the 1981 championship, emotions tore through our celebrating locker room like fire. It was an experience I will cherish forever. We had beaten the odds. I recall riding through the city in the championship parade and realizing how proud Boston was of its champions. Hundreds of thousands of people lined the streets to tell us that they felt part of it too. That day we were, in a sense, transformed into symbols. People saw the result of hours of individual and team practice, of the anguish involved in hiring the right people, of working together to make it happen. We could be proud; Boston could be proud. The hour of that ride through the city, with the confetti streaming out of office buildings, was unlike any other I have experienced. I presented that trophy in the festive air that day to the people of Boston. I held it aloft from the balcony at City Hall. I wanted it known: the championship was something we could all build on.

Today I drive in and around the greater metropolitan Boston area, sometimes as much as fourteen hours a day. I'm trying to establish a successful business career. I have built two businesses, and in a sense, I am in another game. It's like beginning another life, and I'm finding again that I need a game plan, as I did when I picked up the pieces of my basketball career after Mike Storen cut me that day in 1973. I reconstructed my career—I was a successful player in the NBA. When the opportunity to play professional basketball presented itself, I was not going to be denied my chance. And when the time came to cut back my role, I waved the towel with spirit. I was the best twelfth man in the game. I scored a victory over my own ego, sacrificing my personal needs for the welfare of the team. That time of my life was thrilling.

Since I invested wisely and cautiously, as a retired player I have the best of both worlds. I'm involved in interesting and challenging businesses, but I am free to pick and choose how I delegate my time. I draw constantly on my career in basketball—its discipline, its focus, its inspirational value—for my business methods. Like many a young professional, I follow the Celtics. Like others who care about the game, I followed the adventures of the 1987 season. As I watched the team last spring, I reflected again on the part it played in my life. I began rediscovering facets of myself, and the part I have in the winding trail of Celtics history. And as I thought back, I thought more and more of Red Auerbach...

In 1985 we held a Red Auerbach Weekend. All of the Celtics' championship teams were honored that weekend, thirty years of triumph. Red has always said that of the sixteen championships in the franchise's history, there isn't one that means more than another. They are all special in their own way. He's telling a simple truth. He's also telling why he's won so many times. He has won with many different people and at many different stages in his life. Time may change all of us and demand certain shifts in our views, but Red has always retained his fierce competitiveness. As a younger man, he coached the team in 1958 and fought with Ben Kerner, owner of the old St. Louis Hawks, when the Celtics' dynasty was only one championship old; in 1983 Red came charging out when the Celtics and 76ers fought in a preseason game. His fire! Red has cut back on his time in the Celtics' offices now, but he's still able to transmit his competitiveness to his players, coaches, general manager and fans. Red is a fan in his heart. He'll be out of his chair applauding when Dennis Johnson makes a great pass or when Larry Bird scores the decisive basket. Red Auerbach is the personification of the competitive spirit. If Boston ever constructs a new Boston Garden, it should be named Auerbach Arena.

Now, as a young businessman, I watch Red with a different eye. I admire his negotiating skills and the loyalty he builds within his system. Red says this about loyalty: "I'll give it, but I expect it. If you withdraw it, it's war, and I'll do whatever I can to show you you've betrayed that loyalty." Within the Celtic family, few do.

On Red Auerbach Weekend generations of players came together, from fifties stars Ed Macauley, Bob Cousy, Bob Brannum, Jim Loscutoff, Frank Ramsey and Tom Heinsohn, to the sixties greats John Havlicek, Bailey Howell and Tom Sanders, to the seventies stars Jo Jo White, Don Chaney, Dave Cowens and Paul Silas, and the men of the eighties: Cedric Maxwell, Kevin McHale, Robert Parish, Dennis Johnson. One of the most touching moments came when Red singled out Bill Russell for a special ovation from the crowd. Bill has always shied away from formal situations. He had turned down an opportunity to have his number 6 retired in a public ceremony. Instead, Red and a few friends did it privately. That night the crowd cheered long and emphatically for Russ. It was a profound moment that became more poignant when the band played "Night and Day," a Cole Porter favorite of Red and his wife, Dorothy. Red walked around to the small groups of Celtic teams. Within the boundaries of the parquet floor at the Garden, he was transcending the barriers of time. With watery eyes I was honored to be part of that select few. We were all there to try and understand the impact the Celtics have had on our lives. Red taught us how to win in basketball, but more importantly, he taught us how to be winners.

His principles apply to business. Red Auerbach isn't a man who stands over his people as a domineering boss. He creates an environment where you drive yourself, where you expect to win. The creative winning spirit engulfed us that weekend. It flew through the air, it flaunted the barriers of time. That inspiration dwells within me every day, driving away the clouds of pessimism.

Basketball was a means to an end, and I always tried to keep the end in perspective. I know I received plenty of rewards, but I always tried to give something back. I came up in an Age of Cool. Many players back in the seventies considered themselves above the fans and wouldn't sign autographs, but they still played their hardest, they still competed fiercely to win. On the floor I held nothing back. I wanted to achieve my fullest potential as a player. But I continually reminded myself of the meaning of my success. I wasn't born into royalty, and I remembered that. It was a blessing and an honor to perform. I was thankful to put on a uniform. I knew millions would have traded places with me. Playing in the NBA was a one-in-a-million shot, a dream come true. I worked hard, but my fortune was directly dependent on the fans. To take all of this for granted would be disastrous.

So if I was in the presence of the legends at the Auerbach Weekend, I was grateful to be able to walk in that company.

No matter what was said or written about me, I never compromised my effort or my style. I remember playing basketball and seeing military trucks escorting the team off the flight in the heart of war in the Middle East. I recall playing in the Eastern League and having to work in the penitentiary to support the family. I can hear the words of coaches telling me I wasn't good enough, telling me to forget about playing basketball. I can remember John Henry Carr and Lula Mae Carr going off to work before dawn, day after day after day, barely making ends meet, but retaining a sense of pride in who they were.

If I could do it over again, I'd do things the same way. When I was criticized for rough play, I'd remind myself that no one seemed to care what I was doing, or who I was, when I traveled the countryside in Pennsylvania, played in the minor leagues, or sat in an airport in Zurich, Switzerland, for twelve hours. I didn't play for good press. I played for passion and pride, and with the encouragement of good friends and family I made the grade. Who was I to tell kids, who were there to pay honor to me, that I didn't have time to sign an autograph?

It would have been easy to yield to temptation, to weakness, and go the wrong way as a youth. Davis Lee helped me out considerably, demonstrating that a disciplined approach to life would point me the right way. And basketball was my tool.

I have been speaking to troubled youths in secure-treatment facilities in the state of Massachusetts. The odds are already stacked against them. I spoke to a group in the Roslindale Security Prison last summer and told them that I, like them, went through some heavy things. But I asked myself at an early age: Where do I want to go? What do I want to do? I drew a mental picture from Wallace, North Carolina, to Boston. I'd envision myself being a Tiny Archibald or a Jerry West. At the end of the daily working session, I'd run three extra laps. I knew I would have to because others were out there working every bit as hard. I worked on achieving a focus for my goals. I told them that it was up to them to put the past behind them. To make a comeback. Everybody makes mistakes, but don't compound the mistakes.

Life can be lonely. When I walked out to practice by myself, I sometimes thought I was the only one in the world playing. And when I walked into the arena and I was the villain of the Celtics, I sometimes felt I was the only one in the arena.

People like you are like great athletes, I said. People. Athletes make the grade by concentrating on details and practicing for endless hours. They give themselves every opportunity to succeed. They combine an unceasing work ethic with a fearless capacity to dream. Ultimately you kids have to ask yourselves questions, much as I did when I was younger.

You have to ask: Do I care about me? Ultimately you have to get yourselves out of here. You have to be your best.

The competitiveness of NBA basketball demanded you be at your best at all times. The difference between winning and losing was nearly always slight: a save of a loose ball, following through on an open jump shot when time was running out, executing an offensive play flawlessly. We needed supreme concentration on the part of five professional players. Friends of mine, great players, had some difficult times with the pressures of the game and couldn't cope with it all. They are good people who couldn't overcome dependency problems as younger players. But they still have a chance to salvage productivity out of their lives. I'm often jolted by reports of young athletes who dissipate their potential as players because of drug, alcohol or gambling problems. My memory swiftly returns to the images of my contemporaries: who went wrong and why; who went right and why. I nearly fell by the wayside. I considered using drugs, if only for a fleeting moment. I was twenty-two years old. But I would not, I could not make that choice. I *was* momentarily defeated the day I was cut, but I would not succumb to drugs. I had had the joyful experience internally of seeing myself dominate a basketball game when the NAIA championship was on the line. I had the ability as a player to size up a situation, see what was needed to be done and make it happen. That was *my* talent. That was *me*. I wouldn't allow drugs to steal my abilities away.

As a father and a businessman, I am involved with youth and I care deeply about the athlete, his difficult social environment, and how he can best utilize his potential. It's important to all of us. Most of all, it's important for the life of the young athlete. I have tried to express these feelings in this poem:

An Athlete's Prayer

I once knew a player
Who could shoot and run
Who seemed to be having
So much fun.

As days and weeks and months went by
I heard through the grapevine
That this player
Was getting high.

For practices and games
He began to come late,

The great shot he once had
Was no longer straight.

His attitude changed
From day to day
One day he was sad
The next he was gay.

This once great player
Whom we all adore
Just couldn't get
The job done anymore.

But let's not forget
He's still a great kid
He just had a problem
That he kept hid.

So wake up great fans
In this, our U.S. of A
Let us be as concerned about the *player*
As we are about his play.

Recently I drove home. While on Highway 41, I thought about what I've attained in life. Why was it me, I thought, the familiar rural setting of Wallace passing by, who was the one plucked from all of my friends? Why was I able to go through the major knocks and come out shining? I continue driving on my way to my parents new house. Thinking. Through the town. Past the Dairi-O, past Back Street.

We would run through the night as kids, risking our reputation for the sake of having fun. We never thought too much about social issues, but we lived in a place where integration was just a crazy idea. In the midsixties, the times demanded change. We were young, and we wanted to have our share of fun, but when our youthful energies were confronted with injustice, we took a stand.

Looking out from my car, heading home. Past the Holiness Church and on through, past the Rockfish Country Club where I caddied for Davis Lee.

I recall the spirituals and the gospel of my church, my father John Carr a deacon, my uncle a minister. I look at the church and I *feel* the eternity of the Lord, from the memory of the church community swaying under the influence of the power of prayer to the present moment, when I bow my head and give thanks. My third child, Andrea is sleeping peacefully in the back seat of my car. The sun's beams illuminate my mind. I remember the days on the golf course, when Davis impressed his idea of my future upon me. Keep working! Later it became: play well, ignore the racial remarks and I'll take care of them.

When we won the first championship in 1981 and were counting down the seconds, I looked behind the bench. Davis was standing there, looking at the scoreboard clock, watching the time when his—our—dreams had reached fruition.

Each time I return to Wallace, experiences, battles and triumphs are evoked again in the theater of my mind. An absolute stillness frames the hot summer day in North Carolina. I can almost hear the sounds of the past. I drive past the house in which I grew up. I hear John Henry Carr's porchside chats with people in the community...my father and mother praying for me through the cracks in the walls...a baby crying...

The images descend as I drive to my parents' new brick house in Wallace. They're older now and experiencing some of the unavoidable problems of aging. But somehow they retain their dignity! I drive up the road and approach the land my father purchased when land was inexpensive. There is a blissful continuity to life here. We built their new home on the land he bought for us kids. My father and mother are at home here, living a simple, peaceful life. On the land where tobacco, corn, beans and strawberries once grew, Daddy works around the house in the morning and then sleeps some in the shade of the holly tree in the front yard. When I drive up to the house, he's resting. The sun's burning down.

It's a usual morning for my parents. They're retired but they haven't ever retired their sense of purpose. Mother does her chores in the morning, and then at midday, she attends prayer service at church. She visits frequently with family and attends to my father's needs if he falters. My father's health problems force him to rest. So when I drive up to the house that morning, I playfully try to sneak up on him and surprise him. But as I cut through the front yard, he lifts his head up and sees me.

He immediately makes me feel good. "Somebody asked me, 'Where's your son, M. L.? Is he up in New York' " he says. "I answered that he wasn't in New York. For all he's done for me, I think M. L.'s closer to heaven." I sit down next to him, stretch my legs and lie back in the sun. I take some lemonade. Daddy starts talking about his days as a working man.

"No surprise J.P. Stevens became the largest textile plant in the state here. Drew from a history of the cotton plantations in the state. I worked in the fields as a younger man; later I worked in the factory. I didn't really take any issue about working. I just wanted the work, was grateful for the money it brought and the opportunity for a future the money would create. I'd work and then I'd wait for extra time. Then the boss would praise me. If you didn't like the conditions, you had one of two choices. You either quit, or you carried on. But if you bust loose from your job, you'd better have something else.

"Sometimes in the early years, I'd know of situations in my family where we'd get twenty-five cents a day. In those years, a black family could survive. But how were you to get any sort of freedom? There wasn't any way to have your financial freedom."

Mother walks out to join us. She asks Daddy how he's doing. She picks up the conversation, saying, "Oh, things were never that bad. You just became used to it, that's all. We had nine children in our family and we lived in a two-bedroom house. When we woke up in the morning we used to tiptoe on the floor. Wasn't too much space on the floor. Just got used to it, that was all."

Mother had some hard times. When her father died she was nine years old. She had to work every day to contribute some money for the family. She picked cotton every day under that burning sky. "Then we'd get a half-hour for some lunch and then went back out there and picked some more." She fell pretty far behind in school, but she was lucky. A teacher in her school found out about what she was going through and invested enough time to enable her to catch up in her studies. She was able to make it through high school and still work the fields. "But we learned the value of conserving," she says proudly now. "On Sunday, we'd have a family dinner, and each person would get one biscuit. We'd look forward to that biscuit! There wasn't too much for Sunday dinner. Maybe we'd get a slice of ham sometimes." My mom was shy and withdrawn. Grandmother Kenan was a taskmaster, and since conditions were so demanding, she may never have been able to leave the confinements of that early life if not for Daddy. She says now, "I could begin to rest some inside because once your father won my mother's approval, I finally had someone who stood up for me."

The images fly by me now. He's working, and after work he's waiting for more work. She's weaving her way among nine sleeping children to get to work. But she waits after class to obtain the necessary schooling so that she can keep up.

My heart is pounding with satisfaction when she says, "I'm going off to Church, now." She's driving the white Cadillac I bought for Daddy and her a couple of years ago. This woman, driving the Cadillac, is the same woman who drove herself under the sun, who kept pursuing a happier life when it would have been so easy to weaken. We wave goodbye to her as she diligently keeps her eye on the road.

Daddy continues talking now. "My twin brother was a different man than I was. He was more adventurous, and he'd challenge the limits and rules more than I did. I'd work hard and save for the future. I always looked at the land around me and decided that I wanted it for some real hope for the future.

"When we built the new home, I wanted to have a simple home built of solid red brick. I wanted a place where I could work comfortably. I lived on this land most of my life. That's history. I take a tremendous amount of pride in knowing that we were able to deal with our problems and still have a loving family.

"As I say, that's a story of history. My daddy was a sharecropper. He knew about the land—why, he'd take the tobacco leaves, then he'd flatten them, dry them, hang them out on a pole. He'd get crops ready for market. I learned from him how to make your time and your money count for everything. So I saved my money so I could own the land we had been slaving on."

Until the mideighties, my heritage of slavery had never been known to me.

"No. Your Great-Granddaddy Louis Carr never said too much. He'd look at me, when I was a little boy, and his look would tell me what it was he wanted me to do. I respected that look of his. Some people you just didn't say much to. You just went about your business." How do you interpret that silent stare of Great-grandfather Carr? I'm a Carr, and I have to believe that his silence was a refusal to acknowledge that he was ever a slave. In his own mind he was never in servitude.

A few years ago, my parents called us and told us they were planning a visit to our home. I had been to Wallace earlier that year, and while looking at my father's immaculately preserved tools, I wondered out loud to him, "Daddy, if you've taken so much pride in keeping the tools, why don't I keep them, now. That way, they'll continue to be passed through the family." When I grow older, my son Michael will take them and keep them. Michael is the oldest in our family. So in the months leading up to their visit, I made a plan. I had a wall redesigned in the hallway leading from the front door of my home. We had the wall recessed and installed spotlights to highlight the tools that my father, grandfather and great-grandfather resourcefully employed to build a business. In the center we placed photographs of daddy and his twin brother and other tributes to our origins. I won't forget my father's reaction when he walked through the hallway. He stood there. After a moment, he retraced his steps and took a seat on the stairs opposite the little informal Carr Museum. He sat there, looking at the tools and the photographs for a long time.

When I left my parents' home in Wallace that day, having spent it in reminiscence, I drove through the neighborhood of one of my former teachers. On the front step of his home was a small statue, a statue of a black slave. Some ideas remain backward. That statue made me recall my spirit to fight for an opportunity when it would have been safer to back down. I can walk in any circle because I remember my father's lesson of giving respect if I want it back. I had the right to my share. I didn't have to read my father's mind that evening when he sat back and took in the artifacts of our family history. I had participated in it. I worked the land and worked with tools. I see myself as a man who has been able to project my family heritage of patient, enduring strength and, in a sense, reshape it, form a new destiny. In Wallace it was helping to create an integreated school system, thus helping to improve education. There is nothing I could believe in more.

In basketball I learned early that I had to see my strengths and weaknesses personally and be the final judge of just how talented a player I was. With faith and discipline, I tenaciously stayed with my goals and worked my way into a solid position with probably the best sports franchise in history, the Boston Celtics. At the time of my retirement in 1985, the Boston Garden had been a sellout for five straight seasons. I respected that, and I reveled in winning two championships as a player. But the autographs always were easy to me. Perspective was never a problem. When I left the game, I looked forward to my opportunities in business, much as John Henry Carr had done when he bought land with meager earnings in the forties..

If I am fortunate enough to live in a culture where athletes are regarded as symbols, then I should say that symbols of inspiration for me are people like my father and mother, my wife Sylvia and my children Michael, Janine and Andrea, and Sylvia's family. And friends and guides in a personal and historical sense, like Red Auerbach and Dr. Martin Luther King, Jr. They help me drive to accomplish my goals.

Every day I have internal conversations with myself. Somewhere inside, I'm speaking with the generations before me and the grandchildren of my children. I promise something daily to these future generations because we are struggling with real problems. I tell myself I will stand up for the things I believe in. I will face life's challenges as they come and rise to the occasion, no matter what the adversity. I will not be deterred by what others say or think of me. When negative barriers are put before me, I will find a way to get over, under, through or around them. I will continue to dream, but I will never stop working to make my dreams become a reality. If my world starts to crumble I will focus on the positives and will not give up. With God's blessing and the help of others, I can and will fulfull my purpose. I will not be denied.